The Clinical Paradigms of
MELANIE KLEIN
and
DONALD WINNICOTT

The Clinical Paradigms of Melanie Klein and Donald Winnicott: Comparisons and Dialogues seeks to introduce the distinctive psychoanalytic basic principles of both Klein and Winnicott, to compare and contrast the way in which their concepts evolved, and to show how their different approaches contribute to distinctive psychoanalytic paradigms. The aim is twofold – to introduce and to prompt research.

The book consists of five main parts each with two chapters, one each by Abram and Hinshelwood, that describe the views of Klein and of Winnicott on five chosen issues:

- Basic principles
- Early psychic development
- The role of the external object
- The psychoanalytic concept of psychic pain
- Practice and theory

Each of the five parts concludes with a dialogue between the authors on the topic of the part.

The Clinical Paradigms of Melanie Klein and Donald Winnicott: Comparisons and Dialogues will appeal to those who are being introduced to psychoanalytic ideas and especially to British Object Relations. It will also appeal to those experienced psychoanalysts who wish to develop an understanding of how the conceptualisations of these two schools might be compared and contrasted.

Jan Abram is a Training and Supervising Analyst of the British Psychoanalytical Society. She is the author of many publications, including: *The Language of Winnicott* (1st edition 1996, awarded Outstanding Academic Book of the Year 1997 and a Classic Book P.E.P.) and editor of *Donald Winnicott Today* (Routledge, 2013). She was a Visiting Professor of the Centre for Psychoanalytic Studies, University of Essex (2011–2013) and University of Kyoto, Japan (2016). Currently she is Visiting Professor for the Psychoanalysis Unit, University College London, and a Visiting Lecturer for the Tavistock Clinic, London.

R. D. Hinshelwood is a Fellow of the British Psychoanalytical Society; previously Director of the Cassel Hospital, and Professor at the University of Essex (now Emeritus). He has written extensively on Kleinian psychoanalysis, including *A Dictionary of Kleinian Thought* (1989) and *Clinical Klein* (1993). He has taken an interest in and published on the problems of making evidenced comparisons between different psychoanalytic schools.

ROUTLEDGE CLINICAL PARADIGMS DIALOGUE SERIES

Jan Abram and Robert D. Hinshelwood

Series Editors

Under the joint editorship of Jan Abram and Robert D. Hinshelwood, the *Routledge Clinical Paradigms Dialogue* book series will develop studies of conceptual research by promoting dialogue between different psychoanalytic theories. Following the success of their co-authored book, *The Clinical Paradigms of Melanie Klein & Donald Winnicott: Comparisons and Dialogues*, which introduced the distinctive psychoanalytic principles of both Klein and Winnicott together, the editors proposed this series in order to show, through the unique format of a dialogue, how the distinct schools of psychoanalytic thought have evolved and how certain misunderstandings have arisen.

Books in the series follow the same format as the original book, with each being written about two prominent psychoanalytic authors by two internationally recognized scholars. Through these unique pairings, each book will engage in systematic, extended examinations of the similarities and differences between psychoanalytic orientations, setting them apart from existing literature in psychoanalysis.

The volumes in this series will appeal to clinical practitioners in practice and in training, who have different levels of knowledge and experience of psychoanalysis, and for any with an interest in comparing and dialoguing between the psychoanalytic schools of thought.

For more information about this series, please visit: https://www.routledge.com/Routledge-Clinical-Paradigms-Dialogue-Series/book-series/RCPD

The Clinical Paradigms of Melanie Klein and Donald Winnicott
Comparisons and Dialogues
Jan Abram and R.D. Hinshelwood

The Clinical Paradigms of Donald Winnicott and Wilfred Bion
Comparisons and Dialogues
Jan Abram and R.D. Hinshelwood

The Clinical Paradigms of MELANIE KLEIN and DONALD WINNICOTT

Comparisons and Dialogues

Jan Abram & R. D. Hinshelwood

LONDON AND NEW YORK

First published 2018
by Routledge
2 Park Square, Milton Park, Abingdon, Oxon OX14 4RN

and by Routledge
711 Third Avenue, New York, NY 10017

Routledge is an imprint of the Taylor & Francis Group, an informa business

© 2018 Jan Abram and R. D. Hinshelwood

The right of Jan Abram and R. D. Hinshelwood to be identified as authors of this work has been asserted by them in accordance with sections 77 and 78 of the Copyright, Designs and Patents Act 1988.

All rights reserved. No part of this book may be reprinted or reproduced or utilised in any form or by any electronic, mechanical, or other means, now known or hereafter invented, including photocopying and recording, or in any information storage or retrieval system, without permission in writing from the publishers.

Trademark notice: Product or corporate names may be trademarks or registered trademarks, and are used only for identification and explanation without intent to infringe.

British Library Cataloguing-in-Publication Data
A catalogue record for this book is available from the British Library

Library of Congress Cataloging-in-Publication Data
A catalog record has been requested for this book

ISBN: 978–1–78220–310–0 (pbk)

*To those who have taught us and to those we have taught
and
for all those who have engaged in this project
on dialogues and comparisons, at home and abroad*

*Jan Abram & R. D. Hinshelwood
in dialogue at the 2nd Klein/Winnicott Conference
on 21 November 2015, Warsaw, Poland*

CONTENTS

ACKNOWLEDGEMENTS	xi
ABOUT THE AUTHORS	xiii
PREFACE	xvii
BIOGRAPHICAL NOTES AND CHRONOLOGIES	xxi

Introduction	1
PART I **Basic principles**	9
1 Melanie Klein R. D. Hinshelwood	11
2 Donald Winnicott Jan Abram	19
Summary	26
Dialogue	29

PART II
Early psychic development — 39

3 The Kleinian baby
   R. D. Hinshelwood — 41

4 The Winnicottian babies
   Jan Abram — 46

Summary — 51

Dialogue — 54

PART III
The role of the external object — 67

5 Anxiety and phantasy
   R. D. Hinshelwood — 69

6 The environment–individual set-up
   Jan Abram — 76

Summary — 83

Dialogue — 84

PART IV
The psychoanalytic concept of psychic pain — 95

7 Melanie Klein and internal anxiety
   R. D. Hinshelwood — 97

8 Donald Winnicott's concept of aggression
   Jan Abram — 104

Summary — 108

Dialogue — 109

PART V
Practice and theory 133

9   Whose reality? Whose experience?
    R. D. Hinshelwood 135

10 Holding
    and the mutative interpretation
    Jan Abram 141

Summary 148

Dialogue 149

APPENDIX 177

GLOSSARY 182

Afterword 207

REFERENCES 209

INDEX 219

ACKNOWLEDGEMENTS

We wish first to acknowledge David Bell and Karl Figlio for initiating the idea of creating links between the Institute of Psychoanalysis and the Centre for Psychoanalytic Studies, University of Essex, through the joint funding of the post of a Visiting Professor. The brief for the appointed Visiting Professor was to forge links between clinical psychoanalysis and academic psychoanalysis. Jan Abram wishes to acknowledge her thanks to David Bell, who when President of the British Psychoanalytical Society (2011–2013), invited her to apply for this post; and to Bob Hinshelwood, who responded openly and enthusiastically to the idea of a workshop on comparing and contrasting these different psychoanalytic theories.

Our thanks also go to all those involved in organising and speaking at the original workshop at Essex University: Roderick Main, who was then Director of the Centre for Psychoanalytic Studies, Karl Figlio, the Founder of the Centre, Nick Temple, who was President of the British Psychoanalytical Society in 2013, and Rachel Chaplin, Member of the British Psychoanalytical Society.

We also want to thank the Polish Psychoanalytical Society, which invited us to conduct a subsequent workshop in Warsaw later in 2015. We are especially grateful to Anna Czownicka, who chaired the programme, and to several other Polish analysts who played a key role in making the conference such a success—Elzbieta Bohomolec, Ewa Modzelewska-Kossowska, Ewa Sacilowska-Gasior, Marzena Kaim and Beata Maciejewska-Sobczak—as well as the translation team: Magdalena Kaczorowska-Karzniakow, Katarzyna-Skrzupek, and Marta Gil-Gilewska.

We are also grateful to Oliver Rathbone who responded with enthusiasm to our original synopsis and then patiently waited for the manuscript; Rod Tweedie and the team at Karnac also deserve our thanks, as well as the new Routledge team in the late stages of the book's preparation.

Special gratitude goes to Klara and Eric King of Communication Crafts for their meticulous copy editing and helpful advice.

Not least, we would like to thank our forgiving spouses and family who tolerated our obsessive emailing during certain intensive stages of the dialogues.

Jan Abram (London)
Bob Hinshelwood (Norfolk)

ABOUT THE AUTHORS

R. D. Hinshelwood trained in medicine at University College Hospital in London, graduating with both a BSc (in anatomy) as well as an MBBS. His training as a psychiatrist took him to Shenley Hospital (1967–1969), when he published his first papers (one in *Nature*, and one in the *British Journal of Psychiatry*), and then to the Marlborough Day Hospital (1969–1976) and the experience of developing a cooperative-style therapeutic community with colleagues there. During that time he gained his Diploma in Psychological Medicine; he also entered his own personal analysis, with a view to training as a psychoanalyst at the British Psychoanalytical Society, from where he qualified in 1976.

He was then appointed Consultant Psychotherapist to St Bernard's Hospital in 1976 where he developed psychoanalytically informed courses and support for mental health staff. This has become a life-long interest in the psychodynamics of psychiatric and other organisations and the practical consequences of this stressful work; he wrote a number of publications in this area including *Observing Organisations* (Hinshelwood & Skogstad, 2001). During the 1970s and 1980s, he was active in the developing world of psychoanalytic psychotherapy, teaching on the training course of a number of organizations, in the course of which he mastered the intricacies of Melanie Klein's thought and wrote *A Dictionary of Kleinian Thought* (1989; 2nd edition, 1991), now translated into a dozen languages. In 1984 he founded the *British Journal of Psychotherapy*, editing it for ten years, and in 1996 founded *Psychoanalysis and History*, publishing both journals until 2006. He became a Member of the Royal College of Psychiatrists in 1990 and a Fellow in 1993. One outcome of this period was his book *Suffering Insanity* (2004)

In 1993, he moved from his consultant role at St Bernard's (which had become Ealing Hospital) to become Director of the Cassel Hospital (the long-standing therapeutic community founded by Tom Main). He retired from the NHS in 1997 and was then appointed as Professor at the Centre for Psychoanalytic Studies at the University of Essex. In 2002 he was Visiting Professor at the Committee on Social Thought, University of Chicago. The academic world offered an opportunity to consider the study of clinical psychoanalysis and the problem of comparative studies between rival psychoanalytic schools; this led to "Repression and Splitting: Towards a Method of Conceptual Comparison" (Hinshelwood, 2008) and *Research on the Couch: Singe Case Studies, Subjectivity and Psychoanalytic Knowledge* (2003). His interests include, of course, the events and publications connected with this present book with Jan Abram.

Jan Abram is a Training and Supervising Analyst of the British Psychoanalytical Society and is in full-time private practice in London. She is Visiting Professor, Psychoanalysis Unit, University College London, where she is convener for the Winnicott Unit and Contemporary Clinical Theory for the MSc in Theoretical Psychoanalytic Studies. She is Visiting Lecturer for the Adult Department of the Tavistock Clinic, where she teaches "The Evolution of Psychoanalytic Paradigms of the British Psychoanalytical Society (1919–1971)" for the second year of the M1 Course in Psychoanalytic Psychotherapy.

Her present administrative posts include Chair of the Archives Committee for the British Psychoanalytical Society, and Progress Advisor for candidates following the psychoanalytic training at the Institute of Psychoanalysis. She was formerly Chair of the Scientific Committee of the British Psychoanalytical Society.

She is currently Chair of the "Paris Group", which is a research group on the "Specificity of Psychoanalytic Treatment through

Inter-analytic Group Work" – a Working Party of the International Psychoanalytical Association and the European Psychoanalytical Federation.

Her book *The Language of Winnicott* was published in 1996 and awarded Outstanding Scholarly Book in 1997. A second edition was published in 2007. *Donald Winnicott Today* was published in 2013. Her next book will be a collection of her clinical papers, *The Surviving Object: Psychoanalytic Essays on Psychic Survival*.

Between 2011 and 2013 she took up the post of Visiting Professor for the Centre for Psychoanalytic Studies, University of Essex, a jointly funded post between the University of Essex and the British Psychoanalytical Society. Subsequently, she was Visiting Professor at the University of Kyoto, Japan, in 2016, where she taught, lectured, and supervised. During this three-month sabbatical she started work on the present book with R. D. Hinshelwood via email and Skype meetings.

PREFACE

This book arose out of an idea for a workshop that Jan Abram suggested to R. D. [Bob] Hinshelwood in 2011, when she was Visiting Professor at the University of Essex (a post funded by both the Institute of Psychoanalysis and Essex University). The idea of a dialogue to compare and contrast theories had been instigated through Jan Abram's teaching experience, in which she found that students were frequently puzzled about the different schools of psychoanalysis that had emerged since the Controversial Discussions (1942–1945). The first workshop was held in March 2013 at the Centre for Psychoanalytic Studies at the University of Essex.

Having left the NHS in 1997 in order to take on the academic appointment at the University of Essex, Bob Hinshelwood had become much more involved in the varieties of psychoanalytic thinking, as well as in highlighting the importance of clinical work as a vital input into comparing different schools of thought. This culminated in the investigation of the comparable (or not comparable) concepts of repression and splitting (Hinshelwood, 2008).

As a consequence of this workshop, we were invited by the Polish Psychoanalytical Society to hold a similar workshop in Warsaw, which took place in November 2015. By this time, we had evolved a way of discussing the principal elements of both Melanie Klein's and Donald Winnicott's work. For both workshops we had invited a psychoanalyst to present verbatim sessions of an ongoing intensive treatment. The purpose was to show, in the second half of the day, how we applied each theory to clinical work. This focus appears at various points throughout the chapters and dialogues in this book.

Both workshops met with significant success and were well attended. We believe this is not only because comparative work in our field is unusual, but also because Klein and Winnicott are, after Freud, among the greatest psychoanalytic thinkers of the twentieth century. Moreover, because of the political divisions that had emerged after 1945 in the British Psychoanalytical Society, for two British-trained psychoanalysts known internationally for their work on Klein and Winnicott, respectively, this kind of dialogue is unprecedented. The workshops were run with a maximum amount of time for discussion, and we found that analysts and students alike were stimulated and hungry for further opportunity to explore and examine the differences between Klein and Winnicott. For us, the experience of the two workshops was so stimulating that writing a book about it seemed the most natural thing to do. The research undertaken for our reference works – R. D. Hinshelwood's 1989 *A Dictionary of Kleinian Thought* (with subsequent editions: a second edition in 1991, and *The New Dictionary of Kleinian Thought*, edited by Elizabeth Spillius and colleagues, in 2011) and Jan Abram's 1996 *The Language of Winnicott: A Dictionary of Winnicott's Use of Words* (with a second edition in 2007) – meant that we felt well placed and motivated to attempt this collegial exploration of similarities and differences in book form. But it is also true to say that the workshops had energized us to understand more about each other's perspective.

Our main aim with the structure of this book was to retain a sense of the lively and spontaneous interchanges we had achieved in both workshops. To that end, the book steps out of the mould of psychoanalytic publications, as it is an attempt to create a dialogue between, arguably, the two major thinkers – Klein and Winnicott – who had originated significantly different clinical paradigms that emanated from the Freudian classical paradigm of the 1930s. If we look back to Plato, we are reminded that the aims of the

Socratic method were to facilitate a "cooperative argumentative between individuals based on questioning and answering questions in order to stimulate critical thinking and to draw out ideas and underlying presumptions" (Wikepedia: Socratic method). Following these aims, we found that there was a considerable need to get some of the differences much clearer, as the adherents of each framework of ideas had not only a deficient understanding of the other, but also active misunderstandings in some respects.

The book is divided into five parts. Since Winnicott's ideas were mostly – at least to begin with – stimulated in discourse with Klein, it made sense that Bob start each part with a chapter on the given theme, with a subsequent chapter by Jan on Winnicott's concepts. There is, then, a Summary and table of comparison of the main points that have emerged from the two chapters, followed by a Dialogue. Thus the core of this book is made up of ten chapters and five Dialogues.

We wrote the Dialogues by email to each other in response to the chapters that had already been written. This method allowed a degree of thoughtfulness in preparing each step, although we tried to maintain the original spontaneity of the emails, which we believe is crucial. To that end, we decided to edit very little and retain the misunderstandings as they arose rather than editing them out. We wanted to show how, coming from our different areas of expertise, we had thought we knew what the other meant and then discovered that we had often misperceived and/or misunderstood something.

The result for both of us has been extraordinarily interesting. Our responses occurred in the fluidity of discussion as we attempted what we consider to be a rare engagement between these two quite different, though related, psychoanalytic schools.

Our overall aim has been to make the book both short and accessible for the beginner and of interest to the experienced clinician and/or learned scholar of psychoanalysis. This inevitably means that there are limitations to the scope of the book, as our effort has been to home in on the main convergences and divergences between our protagonists – Melanie Klein and Donald Winnicott.

The Dialogue form is an experiment, and we hope the reader will find it as interesting and stimulating as we have found writing it. It was in the Dialogues that we found we were really able to try to get to grips with each other's views. Those who persevere with reading our interchanges will notice a degree of mythologising by one side or the other. We hope it will be apparent that we have indeed learnt from each other throughout this process by being as frank as we could be in the Dialogues. This does not mean that all of the misperceptions were resolved. Sometimes a perception from outside a particular frame of reference can be genuinely revelatory, requiring further reflection, but resistance to listening to each other can be very tenacious and was something on which we concentrated a lot of attention. As Roger Money-Kyrle commented about political groups (which psychoanalytic groups certainly are):

> . . . it is easy enough to use psychoanalysis polemically, to uncover flaws only in one's political opponents. But if we find ourselves doing this, without first applying it pretty rigorously to our own opinions, we should suspect a "mote and beam" principle operating in us, and a "scapegoat" motive. [Money-Kyrle, 1964, pp. 374–375]

We hope the dialogue form will be a felicitous style of engagement for readers who come inevitably with the long tradition of myths about one or other of our protagonists, but we hope also that it gives an account of how issues have emerged, evolved, and been clarified for both of us. We hope that the road we have taken together can be freshly and fruitfully trodden by all readers, so as to give insight into the rich details and nuances that can be discovered through this compare-and-contrast approach.

BIOGRAPHICAL NOTES AND CHRONOLOGIES

Melanie Klein qualified as a member of the Hungarian Psychoanalytical Society in 1919; Winnicott qualified as a member of the British Psychoanalytical Society in 1934, and was fourteen years Klein's junior. So they entered the world of psychoanalysis in different eras, when there were different preoccupations in psychoanalysis, and different conditions for psychoanalysis in the wider culture.

Klein's entry was at a time when, after the First World War, there was general optimism for a new world order; a special regard for psychoanalysis had developed because psychoanalysis was the only psychology to have a practical grasp of the war neuroses that had become endemic at the time. Winnicott, in contrast, had entered psychoanalysis at a time of despair over the persisting economic depression, the gathering cloud of Nazism, and the emergence of seemingly insoluble differences within the world of psychoanalytic ideas.

Nevertheless, Klein and Winnicott were colleagues during an intensely creative time in the evolution of psychoanalysis in London. To this extent they were important to each other, although after 1945, at the conclusion of the Controversial

Discussions, Klein did not refer to Winnicott's work, and his work was largely ignored by the Kleinian development. Winnicott, on the other hand, consistently found himself in dialogue with both Freud and Klein in almost all of his writings, and, as pointed out in chapter 2, his scientific innovations can be seen to emanate from his discourse with Klein and her followers.

Initially Klein's work with children in psychoanalysis was of deep interest to the paediatrician Winnicott, and his medical experience with children's development was an important backdrop for the new theories of Klein and her colleagues about the very early weeks and months of human development. In fact, for some ten years after Winnicott's qualification, he was regarded as a fairly central member of the Klein group. However, his emphasis on the contribution of the environment to the formation of the intrapsychic world (Winnicott, 1945a) was perceived by Klein to distract from her exploration of the internal world (Klein, 1935, 1946). This perceived difference began a progressive divergence as Winnicott sought his own constructions of the infant's experience, problems, and solutions. During the Controversial Discussions, it became clear to Melanie Klein that Winnicott could not be trusted to show complete allegiance to her ideas, and so he was "dropped" as one of her group (see chapter 2). By 1945, at the conclusion of the Controversial Discussions, Winnicott initiated his "independent" path, as did many of Klein's previous supporters, leaving her somewhat isolated and despairing. Winnicott applied himself to "settling down to clinical work", as he said, and started to forge his own language and ideas, which were in contrast to the Kleinian development during that epoch.

We certainly acknowledge that there were many others working in the areas we are covering – notably, W. R. D. Fairbairn, Michael Balint, and John Bowlby in Britain, Harold Searles and Frieda Fromm-Reichmann in the United States, and many others – and at the time Winnicott and Klein were thinking through the clinical advances of these analysts. For this book we have restricted our focus simply to the clinical paradigms of Melanie Klein and Donald Winnicott, with brief attention to the developments made by their adherents and followers. Thus, we have limited the scope of this introductory book, with the hope that others may subsequently be inspired to expand on the topic.

Chronologies

Melanie Klein [1882–1960]	Donald Winnicott [1896–1971]
1882 Born Melanie Reizes, in Vienna	
	1896 Born in Plymouth, Devon
1903 Married Arthur Klein, and moved to Hungary	
1904 First child, Melitta, born	
1907 Second child, Hans, born	
1914 Third and last child, Erich, born	**1914** Pre-medical course, Jesus College, Cambridge
1914–17 In intermittent analysis with Sandor Ferenczi	
	1917 Surgeon probationer in the Royal Navy
	Foundations (1919–34)
1919 Qualified as a psychoanalyst in the Hungarian Psychoanalytical Society	**1919** Read Freud's *Interpretation of Dreams*
Moved to Berlin, a refugee from the anti-Semitism in Hungary (while Arthur Klein moved to a job in Sweden)	
	1920–22 Qualified in medicine – specialised in paediatrics
1921–24 With Karl Abraham's encouragement, developed play analysis for children	
1923 **Key Publication 1:** "The Role of the School in the Libidinal Development of the Child"	**1923** Two hospital appointments: Queen's Hospital for Children, Hackney; Paddington Green Children's Hospital
	Began analysis with James Strachey

Melanie Klein [1882–1960]	Donald Winnicott [1896–1971]
1924–25 Second analysis, with Abraham	**1924** Set up in private practice
1925 Karl Abraham died, 25 December	
1925 Moved to London at the invitation of the British Psychoanalytical Society and immediately became the most acclaimed researcher in Britain	
1926 Anna Freud's critique of Klein's child analysis method	
Symposium in the *International Journal of Psychoanalysis* in defence of Melanie Klein	
	1927 Registered as a candidate at the Institute of Psychoanalysis
	1929 Began to attend Scientific Meetings of the British Psychoanalytical Society
	1931 First publication, "Clinical Notes on Disorders of Childhood"
1932 Key Publication 2: *The Psycho-Analysis of Children*	
	1933 Terminated analysis with James Strachey
	1934 Qualified as a psychoanalyst for adults
	Phase One: The environment–individual set-up, 1935–44
1935 Introduced the depressive position	**1935** Qualified as a child analyst (the first male to do so)
1935 Key Publication 3: "A Contribution to the Psychogenesis of Manic-Depressive States"	Became a full member of the British Psychoanalytical Society; reading-in paper, "The Manic Defence"
1938 Sigmund and Anna Freud became refugees in London, and a part of the British Psychoanalytical Society	**1935–41** Consultation with Melanie Klein, and second analysis with Joan Riviere
	Named by Klein as one of the five Kleinian analysts
1941 Evacuated to Scotland during the Blitz	

Melanie Klein [1882–1960]	Donald Winnicott [1896–1971]
1943–44 Scientific meetings of the British Psychoanalytical Society devoted to Klein's developments in theory and technique	
1944 Lost her pre-eminent position in the British Psychoanalytical Society	
	Phase Two: Transitional phenomena (1945–59)
	1945 Presented "Primitive Emotional Development" to the British Psychoanalytical Society
1946 Introduced the notions of psychotic anxiety, the schizoid mechanisms (splitting and projective identification), and the paranoid-schizoid position	
1946 Key Publication 4: "Notes on Some Schizoid Mechanisms"	
	1947 Presented "Hate in the Countertransference" to the British Psychoanalytical Society
	1948 Presented "Reparation in Respect of Mother's Organised Defence against Depression" to the British Psychoanalytical Society
	1951 Presented "Transitional Objects and Transitional Phenomena" to the British Psychoanalytical Society
	1954 Presented "Metapsychological and Clinical Aspects of Regression within the Psychoanalytical Set-up" to the British Psychoanalytical Society
1955 Introduced primary envy	
	1956 Became President of the British Psychoanalytical Society
1957 Key Publication 5: "Envy and Gratitude"	**1957** Two new publications: *The Child and the Family: First Relationships* and *The Child and the Outside World: Studies in Developing Relationships*
	Presented "The Capacity to Be Alone" to the British Psychoanalytical Society
	1958 Publication of *Collected Papers: Through Paediatrics To Psychoanalysis*

Melanie Klein [1882–1960]	Donald Winnicott [1896–1971]
	Phase Three: The use of an object (1960–71)
1960 Died on 22 September, in London	**1960** Presented "The Theory of the Parent–Infant Relationship" and wrote "Ego Distortion in Terms of True and False Self"
	1962 Presented "The Development of the Capacity for Concern" and "Morals and Education" to the British Psychoanalytical Society
	1963 Retired from Paddington Green Children's Hospital
	Presented "Communicating and Not Communicating Leading to a Study of Certain Opposites"
	1964 Published *The Child, the Family and the Outside World*
	1965 Became President of the British Psychoanalytical Society for the second time
	Published *The Family and Individual Development* and prepared an introduction for a book, *The Piggle* (published posthumously in 1977), on sixteen sessions with a small child
	1967 Published "Mirror-Role of Mother and Family in Child Development"
	1968 Awarded the James Spence Medal for Paediatrics; presented "The Use of an Object" to the New York Psychoanalytic Society
	1969 Wrote on and around "The Use of an Object" and prepared two books: *Playing and Reality* and *Therapeutic Consultations in Child Psychiatry* (both published posthumously in 1971)
	1970 Wrote on the themes of creativity
	1971 Prepared a paper for the 27th IPA Congress to be held in Vienna, on "The Psychoanalytical Concept of Aggression: Theoretical, Clinical and Applied Aspects"
	Died on 25 January, in London

Introduction

This book has been structured to allow two main functions – to compare and to dialogue. There are five parts, each with two chapters on the proposed theme, followed by an attempt to summarise more systematically the main issues that emerge, and then by a Dialogue between the two authors, which had been conducted by email. We have tried to retain the spontaneous, and sometimes possibly wandering, nature of the Dialogues.

This short introduction highlights the themes and discussions that grew spontaneously out of the chapters and throughout the course of each Dialogue.

Part I sets out the basic principles espoused by Klein and Winnicott and illustrates the very different ways in which their innovations in psychoanalysis constitute Kuhnian scientific revolutions founded on Freudian classical psychoanalysis. Throughout the book, each chapter and each Dialogue demonstrates how a different clinical paradigm evolves from Freud's original and foundational clinical paradigm. The one pre-eminent thing both Klein and Winnicott had in common was that their psychoanalytic advances emerged from clinical work – that is, high-frequency child and adult analysis. However, it is perhaps not such a remarkable fact that their interpretations of Freud's work are so different, and the legacy of these differences continues to reverberate in psychoanalysis today, as this book clarifies.

In chapter 1, Bob Hinshelwood shows how Melanie Klein's advances in psychoanalysis were deeply influenced by her analyst and mentor in Berlin, Karl Abraham, and Hinshelwood lays stress on this influence. In chapter 2, Jan Abram outlines the evolution of Winnicott's formulations and shows how deeply influenced he was by Melanie Klein. While Klein's writings can be seen to be the outcome of her personal dialogue with Abraham, Winnicott's writings show a continuous dialogue with Klein and the Kleinian development of the epoch. But it has to be remembered that while Klein was formulating her new theories in Berlin and London, Freud and the Viennese were consolidating classical psychoanalytic theory in Vienna and were already in disagreement with some of her new ideas during the 1930s. Winnicott, on the other hand, qualified as an analyst in 1934, when Klein was already a senior analyst of the British Psychoanalytical Society and making her major psychoanalytic advances. This was only five years before Freud died in 1939, a year after escaping to London from Nazi Austria.

The Summary at the end of the first two chapters particularly illustrates Klein's influence on Winnicott in child analysis. However, it ends by highlighting the two major and interrelated divergences: the environment and the death instinct. These two clinical and theoretical issues permeate, in different forms, the ensuing sections.

The Part I Dialogue, initiated by Hinshelwood, following his reading of Abram's chapter 2, homes in on the Freudian concepts of primary narcissism and instinct theory. The Dialogue elaborates on these themes, with some surprising results for both authors. For example, Hinshelwood emphasises that Klein was not really a drive theorist, and when she referred to "instinct" in her work it was not the same "instinct" that Freud had referred to. Meanwhile, Abram suggests that Winnicott was also not a "drive theorist"; he privileged relating and the meaning of the parent–infant relationship over instincts. Interestingly, both Hinshelwood and Abram conclude that perhaps Klein's and Winnicott's "apparent" allegiance to instinct theory was more about paying "lip service" to the prevailing Freudian theory than true agreement with it.

Melanie Klein and Donald Winnicott are arguably two of the most significant pioneers of early psychic development as a concept in psychoanalysis. In Part II, chapters 3 and 4 highlight how they each theorised the baby's state of mind from the start of life. In these chapters, the elaboration on their concepts comes to the fore. While Klein emphasised that innate factors ("death instinct") caused the newborn anxiety, Winnicott emphasised that the absolute dependency of the infant on the environment (the parent–infant relationship) either facilitated or impeded development. These two different theories of early psychic development expand the arguments introduced in Part I. The Part I Summary underscores the differences on the concepts of "ego" and "self" in relation to internal and external and the meaning of subjectivity and objectivity. Hinshelwood emphasises Klein's concept of the ego boundary at birth, while Abram emphasises Winnicott's theory of "merger" between object and subject in the newborn.

The Part II Dialogue starts with Hinshelwood's challenge to Abram on the notion she introduces, in chapter 4, of Winnicott's concept of hate as a developmental achievement. This Dialogue really highlights fundamental differences between Klein and Winnicott (and between Hinshelwood and Abram!), on the issues of biology, frustration, and the meaning of hate, sadism, and envy. While Hinshelwood focuses on Klein's view of the infant's tremendous struggle with innate aggressive forces, Abram focuses on Winnicott's meaning of the holding and facilitating environment. This Dialogue shows the difficulties that both authors face in conveying to each other the different perspectives both clearly feel aligned with. Ultimately, Hinshelwood is clear that the Kleinian baby has a huge amount of anxiety to deal with related to the paranoid-schizoid position, whereas Abram defines two Winnicottian babies: one who is held from the beginning in the arms of a good-enough mother and so does not experience "unthinkable anxieties", and a second whose mother is not good enough. The second Winnicottian baby is, therefore, terrified and in a state of mind Winnicott describes as "primitive agony" – like "falling forever", rather like the Kleinian baby.

The chapters in Part III, "The Role of the External Object", follow logically from the themes on early psychic development in Part II. Once again, two different symbolic matrices are illuminated. In chapter 5, Hinshelwood selects the Kleinian concepts of anxiety and unconscious phantasy in relation to deeper layers of the unconscious and Klein's formulations of the paranoid-schizoid position and the depressive position. Abram, in chapter 6, selects Winnicott's "environment–individual set-up" to illustrate that "there's no such thing as a baby" – rather, always a baby in relation to an environment. The Part III Summary again highlights the different approaches. For Klein, the baby is object-related from the start, in contrast to Winnicott's view that the baby is "merged" with the object from the start and "unintegrated". The Part III Dialogue grapples with the way in which Winnicott agreed with Klein about her description of the depressive position but could not accept that the paranoid-schizoid position was an innate state of mind in the newborn. The question of the different ways of understanding Freud's Oedipus complex concept are also addressed, Klein placing the Oedipus complex earlier in life, whereas Winnicott argues that the Oedipus complex was a developmental achievement that may never be reached by some individuals. Both perspectives depart from the classical Freudian theory, with its emphasis on psychosexuality.

While clinical work has been at the foundations of all the chapters, in Part IV there is more direct focus on the concept of psychic pain. Predictably, by now, Hinshelwood shows how "internal anxiety" constitutes psychic pain for Klein, while Abram stresses that Winnicott's theory of dependency accounts for the degree of psychic pain. The Summary elaborates on the themes of the previous chapters and starts to crystallise the main differences.

The Part IV Dialogue begins with Hinshelwood's question concerning the infant's sense of responsibility alongside the issue of what is innate. Abram's response is based on her sense that Hinshelwood has not understood what she had wished to convey in chapter 8, and the Dialogue intensifies around the issue of infantile responsibility, ambivalence, and the notion of normality and pathology. Abram's effort is to illuminate Winnicott's use of language, especially related to the term "omnipotence". She identifies a difference between Winnicott's notion of "illusion" (of omnipotence) at the core of the sense of self and a pathological omnipotence arising from a failing environment. Hinshelwood emphasises that

Klein's consistent focus on the internal world of the infant is more helpful than Winnicott's oscillation between the infant's perspective and the observer's. This Dialogue contains some contentious issues related to technique in the clinical setting. There is a to and fro as both authors attempt to clarify complex concepts, and it becomes evident that they are not quite managing to convey to each other what is being explained. One of the interesting outcomes of this tussle is how, gradually, the issue of "illusion" in relation to a concept of "primary creativity" emerges. Abram claims that Klein has no theory of primary creativity, and Hinshelwood, based on a discussion with Hannah Segal, develops his rejoinder.

In the final part, Part V, both authors attempt to clarify the real differences in technique. Hinshelwood cites Klein's intuition about anxiety and illustrates why her technique focused on deep interpretations because of the patient's "response to interpretations" (see Glossary). James Strachey's 1934 paper on the therapeutic action of psychoanalysis is cited once more as the classical paper that highlights Klein's technique. Hinshelwood emphasises, in chapter 9, Klein's stress on "the point of maximum anxiety" in the session and cites her case of Ruth. In chapter 10, Abram reclaims the Strachey paper, as it were, to highlight how she thinks Winnicott worked in the session. She stakes a claim – one perhaps not all British-trained analysts would agree on – that Strachey's paper exemplifies how the majority of British-trained analysts work across the three different schools. However, she makes the point that for Winnicott – especially in his late work, as seen in *Playing and Reality* (1971b) – the crucial nature of providing a holding environment was privileged in technique because, without it, mutative interpretation could not occur. The controversial concept of regression as perceived by Klein and by Winnicott is raised, and the Part V Summary illuminates fundamental clinical problems as perceived by them.

The Part V Dialogue brings into sharp relief the different epochs in which Klein and Winnicott evolved their theories. Hinshelwood shows how Klein may have been "left behind" by new developments emerging in the 1950s, particularly in relation to the concept of countertransference. Abram's response, however, is to question whether Klein was really left behind and illustrates her (Abram's) agreement concerning Klein's caution about the use of the countertransference, comparing it with Winnicott's definition of three different types of countertransference. Perhaps this is one of the most difficult Dialogues in the book – it is certainly the longest – although it compares with the Part II Dialogue in terms of the struggle each author engages in. But, perhaps it is not surprising, since what becomes apparent is how the "theoretical" conflicts are related to the "personal" painful history in the context of the British Psychoanalytical Society, as referred to in several of the chapters.

Following the discussion of countertransference, the concept of "corrective emotional experience" comes to the fore in Hinshelwood's comments on Winnicott's technique. Abram vigorously attempts to demonstrate that this is not an aim in Winnicott's technique, and she turns to the well-known clinical example already cited in chapter 6 to illustrate her point. Hinshelwood, however, not convinced, turns to the clinical example from one of Klein's followers, Roger Money-Kyrle, already cited in chapter 8. Hinshelwood illustrates that the two examples show a clear difference in technique, while Abram argues that both, despite differences in metapsychology, can be seen to be interpreting to the patient from their profound countertransference experience. Abram does not claim that they are precisely the same, but that both analysts can be seen to be working within the transference–countertransference frame. But, in this final Dialogue, Hinshelwood does not agree with Abram's point. Finally, she returns with a further explanation of the terms "illusion" "omnipotence", and "creativity", as discussed in Part IV. Abram attempts to illuminate Winnicott's particular use of words and the extent to which they can lead to misunderstanding – especially his use of the terms "omnipotence" and "illusion". Then, in Hinshelwood's final comment, he clarifies the way in which Klein conceptualises "perception". What becomes clearer is how specific kinds terminology can so easily confuse. While Winnicott appropriates non-analytic words like "playing" and "illusion" that, for him, were intended to extend Freudian notions of "free association" and transference, Klein refers to "unconscious phantasy" with perhaps the same intention – that is, to advance psychoanalysis. Thus, as both authors set out to do from the beginning, further clarification comes to light about the different ways in which Klein and Winnicott evolved their concepts of the "transference". These differences inevitably affect their specific approaches to technique. The question is whether or not the differences are irreconcilable. And the challenge of the whole project is whether each can appreciate the other's point of view. Both authors clearly recognise that each Dialogue constitutes specific beginnings to further Dialogues, and – similarly to the analytic treatment – resolution of these differences is not the ultimate aim.

PART I

BASIC PRINCIPLES

Chapters 1 and 2 present brief introductions to the origins of both Klein's and Winnicott's theories: Klein independently from Winnicott, and Winnicott in discourse with both Freud and Klein. The chapters outline individually our protagonists' main conceptual advances and illustrate how they differed from each other in their interpretations of Freud.

CHAPTER ONE

Melanie Klein

R. D. Hinshelwood

Key concepts   Child analysis; unconscious phantasy; anxiety; object relations; deeper layers; depressive position; paranoid-schizoid position

---

Melanie Klein's first analyst, Sandor Ferenczi, in Budapest, probably encouraged her to make observations of children – specifically her own. This was a relatively common occurrence after Freud published his case of Little Hans in 1909 (Freud, 1909b). Klein became a member of the Hungarian Psychoanalytical Society in 1919 on the basis of a paper in which she reported observations of school-age children, their curiosity, and their problems with enquiring (this paper formed part of her 1921 publication, "The Development of a Child"). In 1921, she moved to Berlin, where she began to develop a specific therapeutic technique with children.

Klein's terminology

The period after the First World War was one concerned with establishing classical psychoanalysis and, at the same time, contending with the dissent of Carl Jung, Wilhelm Stekel, and Alfred Adler (see Jones, 1955). It was therefore important for Klein constantly to clear her name, as it were, and to establish her completely orthodox credentials. This she did by using the language of psychoanalysts of the time, often giving her own slant on the meaning, which contributes to making Klein's writing difficult to read. It obscures much of the originality of the ideas she developed (about the dating of the Oedipus complex, the origins of the superego, the existence of transference in children, and the use of analytic technique with children). This is to be noted that in her understanding of "instinct"; without an education in medical science – or in any science – Klein did not use the term "instinct" in the precise sense that Freud and most psychoanalysts used it. She did not see it as comprised of a biological energy that is the stuff of motivation. Nowhere in her writings does she discuss anything like the economic model. So, although she repudiated the economics of psychic energy, she never explicitly stated that, and this leaves it difficult for us, as readers, to recognise how her focus on anxiety disregards the economics of psychic energy.

Developing a form of child analysis

Supported in Berlin by Karl Abraham (who, in 1924, became her second analyst), Klein worked out a method of analysis for children that was strictly based on adult psychoanalysis. She argued that if the adult method required the patient to freely associate thoughts in his or her mind, then the equivalent in children is free play. She then proceeded to ask: what happens next in an adult analysis? And she replied to herself that the patient at times resists the invitation to freely associate; so, she thought, the equivalent in children is an inhibition in their play. At the time, in the early 1920s, the technique of adult analysis was evolving into what was called resistance analysis, the resistance demonstrating when the ego activates some defensive manoeuvre. What does the adult analyst then do when resistance intrudes? The analyst makes an interpretation of the now unconscious content that has been repressed. So, therefore, Klein thought it was obvious that the child analyst should do the same: interpret (see Klein, 1932).

Her work therefore commenced with the enquiry into the effects of interpreting the problems of the inhibition of play. What she found was absolutely clear-cut to her: again and again she reported how, in the aftermath of an interpretation of unconscious content, inhibitions in play were reduced and more spontaneous play emerged.

What was the unconscious content she interpreted? Her approach seems to have been that play is not necessarily light-hearted and fun, but that it contains the core conflicts that lead to repression. She therefore observed the narrative of the play as if it were the kind of thing that Freud had called unconscious phantasy: "There exist unconscious phantasies (or day-dreams) just as there exist conscious creations of the same kind which everybody knows from his own experience" (Freud, 1901b, p. 266). Such unconscious phantasies are narratives influential in the developing minds of children, as well as adults. The phantasy of the Oedipus complex is about the relationships with the two primary objects, mother and father, involving murder and incest. Freud rightly noted that most children had not actually witnessed or been involved in murder and incest, and if the oedipal configuration and complex is, in general, valid, it occurs in the child's mind and not in the real family (not usually, of course, in real families). Thus, Freud thought that the child, with its endowment of this huge brain, engaged in various story-telling activities to make sense of what happens to it, thereby making sense of peculiar sensations and states of arousal that the older child, or adolescent, can only much later recognise as sexual. Such imagined stories are not necessarily conscious, and the unconscious ones are, of course, more compelling as they cannot be assessed for their real value or be told to others for reassurance.

Klein's interest focused on how the children actually played out their narratives in front of her very eyes with the toys she provided in the playroom. Though she did not say so, it is quite possible that she thought this very visible narrative with toys might even be more transparent than the free-association method with adults. Even if she did not think so, she did believe she had a good method of accessing these unconscious phantasies at the formative periods when the child was developing them.

So, in 1921, she began to develop a play technique for children with, she felt, the encouragement of Karl Abraham. Though Melanie Klein was not a research scientist, it seems likely that she did think she had developed a very serviceable method for investigating the earlier phases of childhood – one that, she thought, was better than the traditional psychoanalytic method of extrapolating back from adult analyses. Freud's Wolf Man case published in 1918, when Klein was just beginning to think of a career as a psychoanalyst, must have been an important case in point. The patient, in his twenties, brought a dream from the age of 4. Freud claimed a "genetic continuity" between the meaning of the dream when analysed twenty years later, and the meaning the dream must have had when it was dreamt in childhood (Freud, 1918b). Klein surely thought that a method that analysed at the age of 4 years was at least as good as Freud's "post-hoc" method, twenty years later.

Instincts or relationships

Like many aspects of research, a new method of investigation throws up new kinds of data. Play often expressed much anxiety, and Klein felt that many of the children she saw were quite tortured by their anxieties. In fact, in her unpublished autobiography (available online: see Klein, 1959), she says that she found herself constantly focusing on anxiety – she never discussed the drives and instincts. It was the children's immediate, perhaps heart-wrenching pain she felt asked to see and connect with that drew her attention. Their play conveyed awful scenes and outcomes, as if the child were pointing the adult's attention to these desperate narratives. Indeed, she thought the children were trying to indicate these anxieties to their adults. And so she formulated the view that – unconsciously at least – the child was intentionally communicating through play. It was Freud's peculiar unconscious-to-unconscious communication, as he expressed it (1912e), and the adult's responsibility was to pick it up. The child, she thought, was as ready as any adult to try to comprehend the contents of the unconscious, the conflicts within it, and the anxieties arising from the conflicts. This constantly pointed Klein towards the point of maximum anxiety; the concept of instinct in the classical view as the motivating force was replaced by the motivating urge to reduce anxiety.

The child's play with toys presented to Klein the relationships with and between important persons and issues in his or her life. It is not surprising that Klein tended to formulate her understanding in terms of the object relations – the relations between persons – as she watched the children manipulate objects (toys) representing the important persons. This new emphasis on the state and fate of the object contrasted with the conventional focus at the time on the distribution and flow of instinctual energy.

Klein did, therefore, put forward theoretical changes, and more adventurous ones as time went on. Most important for understanding the contrasts with Freud and Winnicott is that she thought the ego from the beginning distinguished itself from the world around (from the environment).

The deeper layers

Klein investigated what she called the deeper (or "psychotic") layers of the mind and the unconscious, involving specific anxieties and defences. From 1929, at least, Klein was working with a few schizoid and schizophrenic patients, both children and adults. And this set her research in the direction Abraham had been investigating prior to his death in 1925. By analysing the pregenital phases of early development in adult manic-depressives, Abraham was led to emphasise the importance of object relations, and in particular the incorporation and evacuation of the objects that are emotionally important. To the end of her life, Klein continued to pursue Abraham's work, so that early development prior to the genital phase became Klein's speciality.

She made many specific discoveries, but one overarching general one: following Abraham, she asserted that there were specific mental processes that were "different from" the mechanisms described by

Freud and the Viennese and classical psychoanalysts. She had to distinguish the deeper mechanisms from those classical defences such as repression, undoing, and reaction formation as described by Anna Freud (1936). Klein's contribution was identifying two subcategories: the classical ones, just listed, and the more primitive ones from the pregenital phases – projection and introjection, and, eventually, splitting and forms of identification (Klein, 1946). These are two separate classes of mental process; she was not just adding to the classical list. She called these processes the primitive mechanisms and assigned them to the "deeper layers" of mental functioning, by which she meant that they were characteristic of the earliest moments of psychic development and remained active deep in the unconscious.

Klein argued that the primitive mechanisms, in the deeper layers, were the very earliest methods of dealing with anxiety. Early anxiety is different from that in classical psychoanalysis, where the problem is the oedipal conflict. Beneath that, and underlying it, are other anxieties; they are about survival or annihilation, about the formation or disintegration of the ego and of its objects. In this deep layer, there appeared to be two fundamental anxieties: an anxiety about the fate of the object, and an anxiety about the survival of the self. These she called the "depressive position" and the "paranoid-schizoid position", respectively (see chapter 5), with each anxiety being dealt with by a specific selection of the primitive defence mechanisms.

Clinical approach

Klein evolved her approach at a time when psychoanalysis in general attempted to interpret the unconscious distortions that a patient made in his or her interpretation of others – that is, the apperception. Freud (1911b) realised the importance of the reality principle and named it, and he evolved the practice of working through the unreality of the distortions (apperception) in relation to the analyst's take on the reality of the others in the patient's world. Klein's appropriation of this was, first of all, to accept the validity of this method and, second, gradually to emphasise that the work is in the here-and-now. The reality that is most in play at the time that the analyst can challenge the patient's distortions is the reality in the session and the distortions the patient makes of the analyst – the transference neurosis, as Freud called it. An often forgotten British psychoanalyst expressed this here-and-now approach as: "only such forces as exist at a certain time can have effects at that time" (Ezriel, 1956. p. 35). But perhaps the clearest and most eloquent expression of this approach adopted by Klein was the paper by James Strachey (Winnicott's analyst) in 1934, which was republished in 1969.

Klein's emphasis on the therapeutic benefit of reality-testing has, of course, been highly adapted by development after she died and by Bion's work in developing the idea of container-contained as a basic principle of clinical work. This evolved from the here-and-now emphasis of the 1930s, by emphasising the analyst as the actual external object for the patient, who performs a particular internal function for the patient – the function of giving meaning to the patient's experiences. External objects are not the important thing – it is their meaning. So Bion gave a Kantian formulation of the external world.

Strictly speaking, the later development is not part of the comparison between Klein and Winnicott that we are focusing on, but containment needs to be acknowledged here as it runs so parallel to Winnicott's own development of his clinical approach.

* * *

In this chapter I have briefly covered the major basic principles of Klein's approach:

» the invention of child analysis in conformity with adult practice;
» unconscious phantasies;
» the logic of genetic continuity;
» focusing on the experience of anxiety rather than the economics of psychic energy;
» playing with toys as a significant pointer to the emphasis on object-relations;

- » the ego boundary is from birth;
- » the deeper ("psychotic") layers of the unconscious;
- » the greater importance of pregenital over genital layers;
- » the Oedipus complex in part-object terms;
- » the two fundamental positions (paranoid-schizoid and depressive) of anxiety, defence, and object-relations.

CHAPTER TWO

Donald Winnicott

Jan Abram

Key concepts: Paediatrics; emotional development; human nature; ordinary devotion; maturational processes; facilitating environment; squiggle game; transitional phenomena; use of an object

---

Winnicott's theoretical matrix

Donald Winnicott's work evolved across three chronological phases, as he advanced major psychoanalytic theories that have radically affected the practice of psychoanalysis (see Abram, 2008, 2013; see also Chronology, this volume). The core of his investigations centred on the subject's experience of the environment and how that shaped the growing mind and sense of self.

After the First World War, in 1919, Winnicott discovered Freud's publications, which initiated his desire to become a psychoanalyst. In 1929 he started the analytic training at the Institute of Psychoanalysis, and in 1931 he published his first book: *Clinical Notes on Disorders of Childhood*. The following are the proposed chronological phases:

Phase One: The environment–individual set-up (1935–1944)

During this period Winnicott was working in private practice with both adults and children alongside his paediatric work. His concept of the "environment–individual set-up" (parent–infant relationship), alongside the appreciation that the baby was emotionally developing from the start of life, contributed to an advance in psychoanalysis.

Phase Two: Transitional phenomena (1945–1959)

The concept of transitional phenomena evolved from the theory of the environment–individual set-up and elaborated on the concept of imagination and psychic transitionality. Winnicott started to forge a theory of how the infant moved from apperception to perception.

Phase Three: The use of an object (1960–1971)

The fate of the self-preservative instinct related to a primary benign aggression was crystallised during this final phase of Winnicott's work (Abram, 2012a).

The above phases of Winnicott's work can be used as markers to locate his psychoanalytic contributions throughout this book.

Donald Winnicott's introduction to Melanie Klein

Towards the end of Winnicott's ten-year analysis with his first analyst, James Strachey, the latter positively encouraged Winnicott to approach Melanie Klein about applying psychoanalytic theory to child analysis. Since the 1920s, Winnicott had been applying psychoanalytic concepts in his work as a paediatrician, and, while he was able to confirm that the roots of psycho-neurotic conflict were located in the Oedipus complex, he also came to see that troubles started much earlier than those attributed to the classical Freudian Oedipus complex (dated from between 4 and 5 years of age). While valuing Freudian theory, he also, like Klein, saw that babies could be emotionally ill from the very beginning of life. Winnicott wrote that it was an important moment in his life when Strachey recommended he seek consultations with Klein, and he explains that this is how he came to the "learning area" of Klein, which changed him "from being a pioneer into being a student with a pioneer teacher" (Winnicott, 1962b, p. 173). This would have been a year or so before 1934, when Winnicott qualified as a psychoanalyst with the British Psychoanalytical Society. A year later, in 1935, he qualified as the first male child analyst and was in regular supervision with Klein for his child cases.

Winnicott wrote about not knowing much about the politics of psychoanalysis when he started his training in 1929. By that time Klein had been living in London for three years, and she was in the process of becoming one of the most influential analysts of the British Psychoanalytical Society. Initially, her ideas were well received by most of the indigenous members of the Society, however, as Hinshelwood has indicated in chapter 1, her different interpretation of instinct theory was tantamount to a "repudiation of the economic theory" (as well as her revision of concepts like the Oedipus complex, dated from the earliest stages of development). This meant that for some Freudians her ideas were considered to threaten the classical Freudian template. In the mid-1930s, there had been an attempt to discuss some of these differences between Vienna and London, known as the "Exchange Lectures", but the talks had not progressed (King & Steiner, 1991, pp. 22–24).

At the time of qualifying as an analyst, Winnicott was not fully aware of some of the criticisms from Vienna about Klein's contributions and was probably not interested. What inspired him was Freud's development of psychoanalysis as an understanding of human nature. Through his paediatric work, and in tandem with his personal analysis, he increasingly found the application of Freud's theories invaluable for an understanding of children's "clinical disorders" (Winnicott, 1931). When, around 1933, he did start consultations for his child cases with Klein, he very much appreciated her clinical acumen, saying how she would remember his cases and clinical material better than he did himself (Winnicott, 1962b, p. 173).

To begin with, there was a great deal about Klein's way of working with children that, for Winnicott, "made sense" and "joined up" with his case-history details and psychoanalytic theory. Her approach to child analysis as equivalent to adult analysis was also no trouble from his point of view as he also agreed with that approach. Winnicott found Klein's set of small toys "truly valuable" and "an advance on talking and drawing"; he wrote:

> Melanie Klein had a way of making inner psychic reality very real. For her a specific play with the toys was a projection from the child's psychic reality, which is localized by the child, localized inside the self and the body. [Winnicott, 1962b, p. 174]

So although Winnicott continued to make use of drawings in his therapeutic consultations with children and adolescents (a game that famously became known as the "squiggle game"), when he treated children in analysis he would have followed Klein's methodology and technique as a way of gaining "glimpses into the child's inner world". Later, his ideas about playing and interpretation, although different from Klein's, clearly built on some of her conceptual and technical foundations. Winnicott did not repudiate Freudian instinct theory, but, similarly to Klein's focus on early psychic development, he agreed that something was happening in the baby's mind right from the beginning of life. His well-known phrase "there's no such thing as a baby" emphasises his different perspective from Klein (Winnicott, 1952a). Thus, for Winnicott, from at least 1945 onwards, the mother (as environment and object) was primary, and instincts were secondary. This changed Freud's concept of primary narcissism and shifted the chronology of economic theory. Winnicott's specific extension of primary narcissism meant that it became a "clinical" concept (Roussillon, 2010), because Winnicott showed that the baby's self was inscribed with the parent–infant relationship (see Glossary). In other words, the "self" incorporated, de facto, a combination of the infant's "inherited tendencies" alongside the original object/environment. This fact about the individual self would inevitably be revivified in the transference relationship, which is why it is designated as a clinical concept.

Winnicott valued Klein's ability to identify mental mechanisms of her patients and then apply them to the growing baby. While, like many analysts, he could not deny the importance in clinical work in identifying the two mechanisms of "talion dread" and "the splitting of the object into good and bad" (paranoid-schizoid position), at the same time he saw it as an error to locate these mechanisms in the earliest moments of the infant's life. For Winnicott, "deeper in psychology does not mean earlier" (1962b, p.177), and therefore Klein's formulation of the "paranoid-schizoid position" as universal in the newborn

> . . . ignore[d] the fact that with good-enough mothering the two mechanisms may be relatively unimportant until the ego-organization made the baby capable of using projection and introjection mechanisms in gaining control over objects. [Winnicott, 1962b, p. 177]

In other words, the infant had to "develop a capacity to project" – a mental mechanism that was already a sign of development.

Winnicott largely agreed that Klein's observations about the stage of development she referred to as the "depressive position" was clinically useful, and he considered that her most important contribution to psychoanalysis was the "depressive position", which, he said, "ranks with Freud's concept of the Oedipus complex" (Winnicott, 1962b, p. 176). Later, he revised and developed his own way of seeing this crucial stage of the infant's development and named it the "stage of concern", which emphasises a healthy quality to depressed feelings. In other words, the ability to feel sad illustrated emotional maturity. These notions stem from Freud's work on mourning and melancholia (1917e).

So far we can see that Winnicott valued Klein's contribution to psychoanalysis on a theoretical level and, in his clinical work with children, benefitted from and admired her clinical sensibility and insights. He summarised some of the points with which he agreed:

1. Applying psychoanalytic technique for adults to work with children, assisted by the use of small toys.
2. The localisation of fantasy by the child related to bodily functions.
3. An emphasis on the importance of benign aggressive elements (not from the death instinct) in object relationships from the beginning.
4. Development of a theory that illustrates how the individual reaches a capacity to repair through an awareness of a sense of guilt (the depressive position).
5. An understanding of the result of denial (manic defence).

However, there were also aspects of Klein's theory that Winnicott gradually came to disagree with. These differences can be divided into two overarching concepts: the death instinct and the environment. Both are inextricably linked. While the death instinct in Kleinian development is different from that in the Freudian development, Winnicott could not agree with either formulation. For him, destructive tendencies were related to what Freud had named as the self-preservative instinct and the infant's need to survive. Self-development, for Winnicott, depended on what occurred between the infant's inherited tendencies and the environment. The infant's (unthinkable) anxiety was caused by the environment's failure rather than being initiated by an innate destructive tendency of the baby.

Clinical approach

We have seen in this chapter that Winnicott largely agreed with Klein's technique of working with children and that it is likely that, at the beginning of his analytic work with children, he followed her techniques as he was gradually finding a personal way of working with children. One of the most famous texts that demonstrates his way of working with children can be seen in the book written in 1968 and published posthumously in 1977: *The Piggle*.

In the aftermath of the Controversial Discussions, Winnicott wanted to "settle down to clinical work" in order to get away from the tensions of the Controversies. His aim was to clear a mental space in which to work out what he thought about the best way of working with patients. It was primarily his clinical experience that led him to develop different formulations, some of which were expansions of Freud's – for example, he created a theory of playing that emanates from Freud's "fundamental rule" of free association at the heart of the analytic process. And his conceptualising of the "stage of concern" is a good example of how he elaborated and revised Klein's concept of the "depressive position".

So it is important for the reader to bear in mind that for both Klein and Winnicott, theory should always be clinically led. In other words, theoretical formulations must be based on psychoanalytic clinical evidence stemming from the analytic setting/situation.

James Strachey's 1934 paper, as cited by Hinshelwood in chapter 1, is pivotal for all British analysts, and it is probably true to say that all analysts have been profoundly influenced by this paper on technique in relation to the "mutative interpretation". Countless examples of clinical papers from British analysts demonstrate the way in which Strachey's methodology is followed even today. In chapter 6, I quote from one of Winnicott's well-known clinical examples to illustrate how he worked in the transference; in Part V, Bob and I examine further the issues and differences related to practice and theory.

Summary

This summary outlines the points where Klein and Winnicott were in agreement, or disagreement, regarding their basic principles.

In chapter 1, Hinshelwood started by establishing a view of Klein's basic principles:

1. The invention of child analysis in conformity with adult practice.
2. Unconscious phantasies.
3. The logic of genetic continuity.
4. Focusing on the experience of anxiety rather than the economics of psychic energy.
5. Playing with toys as a significant pointer to the emphasis on object-relations.
6. The ego boundary is from birth.
7. The deeper ("psychotic") layers of the unconscious.
8. The greater importance of pregenital over genital layers.
9. The two fundamental positions (paranoid-schizoid and depressive) of anxiety, defence, and object relations.

In chapter 2, Abram finished with a summary of what Winnicott agreed on in Klein's work

1. Applying psychoanalytic technique for adults to work with children, assisted by the use of small toys.
2. The localisation of fantasy by the child related to bodily functions.
3. An emphasis on the importance of destructive elements in object relationships from the beginning, but not the death instinct.
4. Development of a theory that illustrates how the individual reaches a capacity to repair through an awareness of a sense of guilt (the depressive position).
5. An understanding of the result of denial (manic defence).

Table 1 presents a comparison between the two lists. From this comparison, the main disagreement concerns the ego boundary as a feature from birth for Klein, which Winnicott disagrees with. However, Abram suggested two more overarching concepts: (1) the death instinct; (2) the environment.

Both of these are the main issues between Klein and Winnicott, and we return to disagreements between them on these matters in other chapters – the "death instinct" in Part II, and the "environment" (as well as the "ego boundary") in Part III. We may find that one source of disagreement is that they had different views on what Klein thought – and indeed on what Winnicott thought. That is to say, Klein might have disagreed with what Winnicott thought she thought! And, indeed, it may be that Winnicott would have disagreed with what Klein thought his position was on each. These disagreements resonate through the rest of the book.

TABLE 1   Points of agreement and disagreement between Klein and Winnicott

Klein	Winnicott
1. The invention of child analysis in conformity with adult practice	1. Applying adult psychoanalytic technique to work with children assisted by the use of small toys.
2. Unconscious phantasies	2. The localisation of fantasy by the child related to bodily functions.
3. The logic of genetic continuity	3. Inherited tendencies and the (psychic) environment
4. Focusing on the experience of anxiety rather than the economics of psychic energy	4. Parent–infant relationship primary; instincts secondary in structuring the self. Life drive in the newborn constitutes benign aggression.
5. Playing with toys as a significant pointer to the emphasis on object-relations	5. The assessment of an ability to play signifies health. Playing is a developmental achievement
6. The ego boundary is from birth	6. Absolute dependency = merger between mother and baby phase before object relations
7. The deeper ("psychotic") layers of the unconscious	7. Unconscious processes relate to early psychic development but are not de facto psychotic unless the mother is psychotic

Klein	Winnicott
8. The greater importance of pregenital over genital layers	8. Me has to be distinguished from Not-me before the infant can recognise the third. Thus the Oedipus complex is a developmental achievement founded on maturational processes facilitated by the environment.
9. The two fundamental positions (paranoid-schizoid and depressive) of anxiety, defence, and object-relations	9. Development of a theory that illustrates the individual reaches a capacity for concern through an awareness of a sense of guilt. An understanding of the result of denial (manic defence).
Early work on sexuality focused on the impact of the parents and the primal scene. Oedipus complex starts much earlier than the Freudian Oedipus complex.	10. Oedipal anxieties are secondary to primal anxieties related to dependency on the environment. The classical Freudian Oedipus complex and its complications are incorporated into Winnicott's theoretical matrix as seen in his clinical work.

Dialogue

R. D. HINSHELWOOD: I want first to take up your point about primary narcissism. This might be important to clarify discrepancies between Klein and Winnicott. You say, Winnicott thought that mother was primary, not instincts. That seems absolutely crucial, and both of them would agree, I think: Winnicott coming from his paediatric background, and Klein from her child analysis background. They must have met on this ground. And you say this shifted the chronology of the economic theory, but this may need more expansion in detail. For Klein, it didn't shift the economic theory – she just didn't use such theory. And it didn't shift the chronology of the early months; as she saw it, most phases of the libido concertinaed into an early mixture. There is, in fact, no primary narcissism: it was not a phase in development for Klein. And in consequence she could say that there is an ego from birth. Winnicott nevertheless did think of a chronology to some extent – a primary omnipotence that takes the place of Freud's primary narcissism. Instead, Klein described two states – or positions, as she called them – centred around two different anxieties, which within a few months begin to oscillate from one to the other.

What we mean by primary narcissism is a state in which there is no separation at the beginning of life between the baby and others. In fact, there is not an ego. Alternatively, there is the view that Klein adopted that an independent and separate object does exist (in fact, object-relating, in Freud's terms). Perhaps Klein and Winnicott diverged on this. And whereas you say Winnicott thought that projection and introjection came along later after a degree of organisation of an ego, Klein would say that the existence of an ego boundary – self separate from other – is sufficient ego-organisation for projection and introjection, and, being there from the beginning, these mechanisms are deeply implicated and powerfully influential in supporting the separation of one from the other, self from its objects. And, moreover, they are especially important in defining what is inside and what is outside – that is to say, they have a powerful influence over the sense of what the self feels itself to be. I expect we will come back to this later.

It is, of course, one of the really interesting things that Winnicott concentrated a lot of thought on – how does the complex of the baby's ego plus the object it thinks of as part of itself gradually become disentangled? If Kleinians did not think there was an ego boundary at birth, then it would be necessary to have just such a process as Winnicott inventively observed – his process involving the transitional object. That Klein thought babies do merge with mother was, of course, a process Klein did agree with, but it came secondary as the ego boundary became fractured by the baby with a loss of sense of self, when for some reason the baby could not handle the separation.

One important thing to say also is that these discussions about what happens at the start, straight after birth, are of course entirely speculative, and although some evidence can be acquired from clinical sources, and from the experimental psychology of the infant like that of Margaret Mahler (Mahler, Pine, & Bergman, 1975) and Daniel Stern (1985), it is essentially pretty much unknown – even unknowable. However, it remains debated even though it seems like mediaeval theology, and we could all profitably abandon such an abstruse and remote question about the newborn baby's psychological capacities. And yet there is a very good reason why we need to get clear what each of our protagonists thought: it is because their models of the earliest days and months strongly influenced the way each of them thought about the unconscious of their patients, about the nature of the transference that unfolds, and about the principles for clinical practice.

There is one more thing to say about the point you raise about the changed chronology of the economic theory versus the absence of a true instinct theory. Because Klein did not use the concept of instinct as it exists in biology, in medicine, and in classical psychoanalysis, she was less at risk of developing a mechanistic theory of the human mind as some other schools of psychoanalysis have (not, I think, Winnicott, probably). Moreover, in my own view, I think that Klein's reactions to the children she observed and had as patients, and the evident suffering of some of them, led her directly to a different basic position of observation and intervention. She did not consider what they said in terms of the energy they had difficulty in dealing with. Instead, she considered her patients' experience of themselves in their world of others. For instance, she could say in her Autobiographical Notes:

> I still cannot answer what made me feel that it was anxiety that I should touch and why I proceed in this way, but experience confirmed that I was right. [Klein, 1959]

This is a different approach to that in adult analysis. This is an awareness of the child's anxiety, perhaps more difficult to avoid for anyone working with a child. It is the child's experience that is in one's field of vision, not a mental "apparatus". I suspect it was much the same for Winnicott, though he was a biologist and a doctor. Klein says she could not give an answer why she observed from this altered perspective, but it seems to me it may be possible to give this answer now, looking back: I think it simply did not make sense to her to consider psychic energy in a child, and squeeze their heart-rending anxieties into that mould. I suggest it brought out a maternal response directly from seeing the child's own experiencing of its anxiety, as it might do in anyone.

This focus on experience rather than energy seems a significant basic principle, which I think Winnicott with all his humanity probably shared. Touching, as Klein said, the experience of anxiety, and of course being touched by it, as I suggest, diverges quite sharply from an approach to something as mechanical as energy and defences. Possibly psychoanalysis should attempt to find a mediated, dialectical approach to bind these two divergent trends together (I'm not sure). But in the time period we are interested in, there was a progressive movement to diverge, and our two protagonists were very probably much on the same side. If so, it is therefore the case that their debate about the first months of life is about the baby's experience in the first months of life, and not so much about energy and structure. Of course, perhaps infants don't actually experience their sensations and emotions, don't have a self (or ego), but there are very few mothers who would agree, and who will actually operate from that position; for family and intimates, their babies do experience things, for good or bad.

It is good at the outset at least to get clear what our two protagonists had in common when they started, and in what they differed. I guess that is what should be the outcome of the discussion of this first part.

JAN ABRAM: I agree that it is important to explore the differences between Klein and Winnicott related to Freud's concepts of primary narcissism and instinct theory. You are clear that Klein simply did not find a use for instinct/drive theory, and this is why her work, overall, repudiates that part of Freud's work. This is one of the concepts that exercised the Freudians in Vienna about Klein's "new theories". So, as you say, there is no economic theory in her work since she just didn't see the use for such a theory.

It seems to me slightly contradictory to say this, however, since her conceptualising on early anxieties very much focuses on the innate death instinct that, she said, caused the earliest anxieties. While I do appreciate your point about this not being, strictly speaking, a biological instinct that she was referring to, is it not true that neither was Freud – the innovator of instinct theory and of the death instinct – simply referring to biology?

Freud's instinct theory originally developed as he was in the process of formulating a theory of human sexuality. Towards the end of his life he wrote:

> The theory of instincts is so to say our mythology. Instincts are mythical entities, magnificent in their indefiniteness. [Freud, 1933a, quoted in Laplanche & Pontalis, 1973, p. 215]

Both Klein and Winnicott would, I think, have agreed that a somatic pressure does have an impact on the emotional development of the human infant. But their emphasis, it seems to me, is different, and we see this in more detail in Part II in our focus on the newborn infant in their theories.

So, might it be true to say that Klein's repudiation of instinct theory is inextricably linked with her repudiation of Freud's notions of psychosexuality? Very often the criticism from (classical and contemporary) Freudians about both Klein and Winnicott is that sexuality is either subsumed or deleted in their theories. It seems to me we have to address this if we are to recognise the specifics of what both Klein and Winnicott evolved and to acknowledge that in the process there were important Freudian concepts that were sidelined or negated. Were they "repudiating" Freud's work on psychosexuality or were they "extending" it?

Let me now turn to "primary narcissism". Winnicott did not refer to a "primary omnipotence" but, rather, the "illusion of omnipotence". But this illusion only occurred if, and only if, the mother was able to adapt to the infant's needs. It was her capacity to tune in to the baby's needs that made the baby feel he was God (Abram, 2007a, pp. 200–216). In my view, Winnicott extends and elaborates Freud's concept of primary narcissism. René Roussillon (from French psychoanalysis) clarified how Winnicott made Freud's concept of narcissism clinically useful by emphasising how it could not be thought about in a solipsistic way because it developed in the "context of the primary psychic relationship" (Roussillon, 2010, p. 270). So the state of "merger" between infant and mother refers specifically to the infantile subjective state of mind. The infant is not yet, at the very beginning of life, able to differentiate Me from Not-me. Meanwhile, from the observer's point of view the infant is wholly dependent on the m/other who adapts to his needs (whatever the needs may be at any given moment).

When you refer to the "gradual disentangling" between object and infant, I agree that this is precisely what Winnicott was most interested in defining, as I pointed out in chapter 2 and as we will see as the chapters move on. This is where the transitional object comes into play, and it is that concept that culminates in "the use of an object", as I have previously argued, in his final work on aggression (Abram, 2012a).

I don't think I agree with you about the "speculative" when we examine early – that is, infantile – states of mind. I have the impression that neither Klein nor Winnicott would agree with you either! Why? Because I think for both of them – and this is where they do come together – they were firm believers in the power of the transference. Therefore, it was possible to reach very early infantile states of mind through the course of analysis. When Winnicott said, "there's no such thing as a baby", he showed how this was related to his personal analysis, admitting that he could not see a baby as a human being before the first five years of his analysis. In other words, it was only through analysis that the "clinical infant" can be appreciated. It was another reason why he found it more valuable to work with the adult patient on the couch rather than "observing" infant's in the way both Mahler and Stern did. This raises the controversy between André Green and Stern about the difference between the "observed" infant and the "clinical" infant (Sandler, Sandler, & Davies, 2000). This is why I tend to agree with Green that it is on the couch that the patient is able to reach infantile states of mind and the analyst is able to explore and observe through the dynamics of the transference–countertransference matrix (Green, 1991).

RDH: Thank you for the clarifications. There are several points that grab me from these discussion comments of yours. First, sticking in my role to Klein, I want to say something about "repudiating" Freud. I think Klein really did not realise that she was as divergent as she was. She constantly used the word "instinct", but it was never quite in the sense of Freud's biological myth. I think she used the word because others did. I think she used the word because it was important in the early 1920s to demonstrate one's absolute allegiance to Freud and to dissociate completely from Adler, Stekel, Jung, and Rank, who were all going their own way. I often wonder how, if Karl Abraham had not died early, in December 1925, his originality could have avoided him being seen as dissident. And Klein, I think, was too young an analyst to have an overview to recognise how original Abraham was at the time. So my point is that Klein forged ahead with her exciting project to develop her play technique, without much attention to the bigger picture beyond. And that entailed simply using the words others did. There was no deliberate repudiation, I think. My sense is that Winnicott did not either.

I think you touch on another point that has always interested me about Winnicott. He was on to something profound (that there is no such thing as a baby) when he referred to Freud's footnote (1911b, p. 220fn.). It highlights, but without being sufficiently explicit (in my view), the discrepancy most analysts overlook – that is, one of perspective. When Winnicott says there is no such thing as a baby, he is taking a perspective that looks on mother-and-baby from outside. At the same time, he is talking about the omnipotence of the baby's experience, which is from the baby's perspective. It always seems to me to be better to take one perspective consistently. And I would claim that Klein unrelentingly observed from the baby's point of view. And yet, of course, Winnicott has a point, since he is saying: wait a minute – you cannot separate the perspectives so easily. The nature of experience is ambiguous; there is always a paradox of "Me" and "Not-me", and of omnipotence and of granting the object separateness. It may be that in an interchange between these two divergent schools, it is important to hold in mind that there are different standpoints on this ambiguity about which perspective to speak from.

Now, finally, a point on transference. You disagree with my scepticism about knowing the actual experiences a baby has at these earliest stages we talk about. You argue that transference is a transparent window onto the past. What is created in the relationship in a session is what was experienced in the very same relationship in infancy. It does seem a big claim, and one would have to question how that could be checked, and with what sort of evidence. I do believe it is what Freud found he had bequeathed to psychoanalysis. And we tend to accept it as a truism of psychoanalytic theory and practice. It seems to me that it is the one most important thing that Susan Isaacs contributed in her 1948 paper on unconscious phantasy. Following on from the play technique, the mind is constituted by a world of objects/others that are interrelated with each other and the self. And, moreover, transference, even in adult analysis, can be reinterpreted as the playing-out of stories with two objects – just like play therapy. Except that, in adult analysis, the two "toys" to be played with are the analyst and analysand.

However, the implication of this is that the transference is this story-telling of relations with objects that are currently active, and anxiety-provoking in the present. Or, we could say that transference is not so much a transferring of anxious relations from the past into the present, but, rather, the transferring of anxious relations in the phantasies of the unconscious into the present setting. This amounts to an equation, which is implicit in Klein, that what is deepest in the unconscious represents what is earliest in development. But representing what is earliest does not necessarily mean it is a point-by-point replication of the past, in the way that Freud saw the transference repetition. The deepest layers of the unconscious throw up unconscious phantasies, but as mediated by the layers through which they emerge, mediated by the defensiveness in terms of modifying phantasies that have been tried and adopted in the many months/years since infancy.

Freud (1895d) thought that Anna O's paralysed arm was an exact replica of the transient palsy she got from hanging her arm over the back of the chair when she was sitting up all night with her dying father. It is not, in any case, a replication of infancy. Rather, it is like Isaacs' example of the child that screamed at the age of 18 months when mother's broken shoe flapped like a devouring mouth, while nine months later the child could represent her terror at being eaten up using words rather than screams. There is a genetic continuity between the original experience of terror, but the continuity is in the evolving mediations in the personal history. We don't remember history, only our current constructions of it. Not least is the alternation between a paranoid-schizoid mode of remembering something and a depressive mode.

JA: I had not meant to convey that what we experience in the transference in analysis is an "exact replica" of what happened in the past. But a belief that there is a historical process that is ongoing through the analytic relationship is really what I wanted to get at. Let me cite André Green again when he defined the historical process thus:

> For the psyche, the historical could be defined as a combination of:
> What has happened
> What has not happened
> What could have happened
> What has happened to somebody else but not to me
> What could not have happened
> And finally – to summarize all these alternatives about what has happened – a statement that one would not have even dreamed of as a representation of what really happened.
>
> [Green, in Abram, 2016a, pp. 2–3]

This is really what I was wishing to convey about the transference. I take this point up again in chapter 6 when I discuss Winnicott's transference interpretation to his patient. The clinical example I quote, from a chapter in *Playing and Reality*, shows clearly how

Winnicott was able to experience something that emerged in the analytic work which related to and belonged to the early mother of the patient. This is not such an unusual experience for analysts working in high-intensive treatment.

You have clarified what you think about Melanie Klein's reference to the death instinct, and that is important, but you did not address the point I made that instinct theory emerged out of Freud's work on psychosexuality. This seems to me to be such an important and controversial area in both Klein's and Winnicott's work. So, it is important for us to address this. As I said above, I think it is another major concept that many Freudians consider is neglected by both Klein and Winnicott.

RDH: Just a quick point about Klein and sexuality. From early on, Klein wrote very extensively on the early stages of the Oedipus complex, and its relation to the primal scene as Freud described it in the Wolf Man case in 1918 (about the time when Klein was probably starting to think about becoming a psychoanalyst). Her membership paper in 1919 was about the interference of oedipal anxieties that cause the inhibition of learning. She was certainly still interested in this at the time of her paper in 1935 on the depressive position and the anxiety about damaging the parents due to the feeling of exclusion by the parental couple. And her final work on this was in 1945.

You are right that she then moved on to the importance of splitting of the ego in 1946. These schizoid mechanisms, she seemed to feel, were not just pregenital, but lay beneath the neurotic level of repression and the Oedipus complex. It was a level concerned with the formation of the ego itself, not with the oedipal and sexual conflicts. It is necessary to have an ego, or self, before sexual problems and satisfactions can become predominant in the self. I am pretty sure that Winnicott followed this existential level when he later established his framework of true self and false self. But, just before Klein's published work on schizoid mechanisms (in 1946), Winnicott (1945a) did describe the ego's state of unintegration. And you remember Klein debated in 1946 whether to accept his idea of primary unintegration, or whether loss of integration was due to a secondary self-splitting of the ego/self. She aligned with the latter. But the point is that both Winnicott and Klein were interested at this time in the existential problems of the self, which must come before the preoccupations with sexuality, the early stages of the Oedipus complex, and gender differentiation.

JA: Before completing this dialogue for Part I, I would like to add a word about "unintegration" and psychosexuality in Winnicott's final formulations.

He used the term "unintegration" for the early "merger" between the infant and his environment–m/other. Unintegration is at the centre of "being" and the precursor of the ability to relax and enjoy deriving from the experience of the holding environment (Abram, 2007a, pp. 59, 67, 70, 93, 162–63, 299, 303, 311, 348; see also Glossary, this volume). Thus the term "unintegration" in Winnicott's work is associated with his concept of health, which refers to the infant's early good-enough environment – that is, a mother who is able to surrender to the state of mind Winnicott named "primary maternal preoccupation" and to gradually recover from it (see chapter 6). Thus, Winnicott postulates a "primary unintegration" from which a "primary integration" develops (1945a, p. 149; see also Glossary, this volume). In contrast, disintegration infers that a certain amount of integration has already occurred.

Although Winnicott's "revision" of psychoanalysis focused on relationship – that is, the parent–infant relationship, which is at the roots of the (sense of) self – his view of the Oedipus complex is not so different from Freud's. This is what he means when he says of Klein's theories that "early is not deep" (Winnicott, 1967c, pp. 570, 581). It is clear in his clinical work (as we read in several publications) that he does not ignore sexual development and oedipal difficulties. However, for Winnicott, the issue that causes mental illness for each individual was whether or not she or he had been held from the beginning of life during the phase of absolute dependence. This focus shifts the emphasis away from innate internal anxiety (Klein) or instincts and psychosexuality (Freud). However, this does not mean that Winnicott ignored or wished to repudiate both theories (Klein's and Freud's). Through his clinical work he came to see that there was a more fundamental core issue for each and every baby. This question led Winnicott to different and more nuanced formulations on human nature compared to those of Klein and of Freud.

PART II

EARLY PSYCHIC DEVELOPMENT

Chapters 3 and 4 present the different infants according to each theorist. Each chapter illustrates how the "internal world" was shaped. Klein's focus was on the effect of internal anxiety in the baby, while Winnicott observed how the infant's absolute dependency on the environment either facilitated or impeded growth.

CHAPTER THREE

The Kleinian baby

R. D. Hinshelwood

KEY CONCEPTS   Active self; ego-boundary; binary narratives; life and death instincts; narcissism; reality principle

---

Kleinians are divided on the question of the baby's experiences before speech supervenes. Some regard it as a practical metaphor for thinking about the deepest layer of all relationships from birth to adulthood; and others consider that it is really possible to know what the experiences are through analytic work via the method of genetic continuity (see Isaacs, 1948). Melanie Klein herself was probably of the second group, believing that intuition could access the reality of the newborn baby's experiences. Indeed, she would have argued that the unconscious phantasies, at whatever age, in the deepest layers, are the experiences the baby was having as a newborn. Whether that assumption is valid or not, the constructions made by the infant have importance for theory and practical work.

How do we know babies?

Babies are "known" from clinical work by inferences derived from the psychoanalysis of children. The Kleinian analyst Esther Bick also developed, with the encouragement of John Bowlby, the systematic direct observation of babies with their mothers/carers from birth (Bick 1964). Of course, mothers themselves have from times immemorial used observation, but the Bick method was developed as a training exercise, from the 1940s, for child psychotherapists and psychoanalysts. In a limited way, it is also claimed to provide some research data. There are also laboratory methods for scientific investigation of babies, developed by Margaret Mahler, Daniel Stern, Colin Trevarthen, and many others; as you have said, Jan, these yield what Stern (1985) has called the "experimental infant", as opposed to Green's "clinical infant" (see Sandler, Sandler, & Davies, 2000). However, clinical listening to conscious and unconscious expression of experience is the primary source for understanding the issues and puzzles arising in infancy.

The Kleinian baby is construed as active. It has its urges, connected especially with its bodily sensations. In line with its roots in Freud's theory of unconscious phantasy (see chapter 1), these sensations are represented in the mind from the beginning, and they take the form of narratives. A phantasy narrative about bodily sensations gives emotional and psychological meaning. Gaining this store of meanings is the bedrock activity of the mind. At the outset, the narratives take the form of an active relationship with some object, and that object is also active in inter-relating.

Narratives of experience in unconscious phantasy

I shall attempt a description, insofar as possible, from the infant's point of view (as Klein came to see it). She referred to the newborn, suckling infant as being in a psychological position she called paranoid-schizoid. Here I describe that paranoid-schizoid position.

There seem to be two basic narratives at the beginning. On the one hand, the narrative is a "good" one: there is a satisfying object (or other person). While the baby is in intimate relation with the external world (or environment), it is obviously not at first adept at recognising what the objects in the external world really are, and it responds in active ways based, more or less, on innate expectations. When satisfied, it is actively "sucking" satisfaction from an object, which is generously "giving" the satisfaction, with a wish to satisfy. The baby may have little conception at first of what milk is, or of what satisfaction is – in fact it probably equates the two – material and immaterial, body and emotion. It is likely that Winnicott would agree.

On the other hand, there is the "bad" narrative, in which there is a dissatisfying object that causes frustration. Here things differ, perhaps, between Klein and Winnicott. For Klein the dissatisfaction is symmetrically opposite to the satisfying one. The narrative would be that the baby has to protect itself from an object, another person, who aims to cause the dissatisfaction, because the object actively wants to hurt, harm, and even "kill" the baby – whatever that may mean to the baby – giving rise to an innate feeling state of distress. It is felt bodily (as, say, hunger pains in the tummy), and, moreover, there is this evil object right there, where the pain is, aiming to cause such distress.

For Klein, the symmetrical binary form of these innate object relations correlates well enough with Freud's life and death instincts: love and life-giving bodily urges, or terror and then a blind self-protective rage against something that destroys for the sake of it. That there is a binary division among the narratives – satisfying ones or dissatisfying – may have been acceptable to both Winnicott and Klein. However, the causes would not have been symmetrical for Winnicott, I assume. For Winnicott, the narrative of frustration is not regarded as innate; for Klein, it is. For Winnicott, there is no death instinct, and this must lead him to repudiate any innateness about terror and rage.

The relating infant

Thus, for Klein, the baby has, from the beginning, an experience of being in a relationship with an "other". And, moreover, and in contrast with Freud's descriptions, the object (as the baby sees it) has its own intentions – good or bad – towards the baby. The elements of these unconscious phantasies are, in fact, extremely elementary. However, to recognise that there is an object implies that, from the outset, the baby has an experience that it has a boundary, that there is some outer space beyond itself. The ego boundary, in this view, exists from birth.

With that experience of an ego boundary (or skin), the earliest ego's experience has a further quality: the object may be outside its supposed boundary, or, alternatively, inside. For instance, the feeling of hunger in the tummy locates the presence of the object inside. We might say inside the abdomen, but the baby may not be able to be so precise, merely identifying it as inside the boundary. And then, when sucking something in, the narrative of the good, satisfying object is elaborated; the bodily sensation becomes, in the narrative, the drawing of the object inside – in psychoanalytic terms, it is the unconscious phantasy, and mechanism, of introjection.

The ego possesses not only that function of locating its objects, but the active ability (in its phantasies, at least) to transport objects across this boundary, into or out of the self/ego. Such an active transport system is not just idle imagining. It is an active stimulated phantasy. The baby is stimulated into the phantasies by the sensations arising in the given bodily physiology. The baby, in actively responding, does suck in milk from a good object; it also eliminates from its anus and urethra (often simultaneously with feeding – the so-called gastro-colic reflex of the newborn). Of course, it may be said that these reflexes, suckling and gastro-colic, are automatic functions of the physical nervous system and do not require a mind for them to happen. Probably that is true: such reflexes are hard-wired into the body, just as our knee-jerk reflex is. But the question is whether there truly is an ego, or a self, in existence that can be aware of these active processes (feeding and defecating) and give them meaning. Klein would have said that such an ego does exist from birth.

The active baby

Klein emphasises that the baby is, from the start, active in creating these experiences of self and other, but it is, also, radically shaped and supported by maternal care, cradling, stroking, feeding, and so forth. The baby is an active agent in this situation, its activity being predominantly a process of introjection of such an object – a so-called "good" object, which initiates a sense of goodness of the self.

This contrasts with the view that the object is the active agent, and the ego passive. That alternative non-Kleinian view is that the baby only comes to exist experientially, as the result of the other's care. Such obscure and erudite debate is not much discussed today, because the actual baby attended to in psychoanalysis – and, indeed, in child analysis or psychotherapy – is the experience in the human much later on. Typically, therefore, the infant has a hand in constructing partly, and however primitively, his own world of experience.

* * *

Klein's view of the infant has several distinctive features:

» two basic narratives: of the "good" object and of the "bad" one;
» a symmetry in the opposite good and bad objects;
» object-relations with others from birth;
» objects may be inside or outside, and they can be transported across the boundary;
» the infant partly constructs these objects in a phantastical way.

CHAPTER FOUR

The Winnicottian babies

Jan Abram

Key concepts: Primitive emotional development; hate in the countertransference; gross impingement; patterns of relating; basic split in the personality; unintegration; compliance

---

From early on in his work Winnicott made it clear that there were two categories of babies: one who enjoys the pleasure and states of unintegration due to a good-enough holding environment, and the other baby who suffers from a grossly impinging environment in which withdrawal is the only solution for self-protection. Before examining these two different babies in more detail, let us first of all take a look at the intellectual context in which Winnicott was evolving these concepts.

Winnicott terminated analytic treatment with James Strachey in 1933, while he was qualifying as an adult psychoanalyst at the Institute of Psychoanalysis. Some time after that (around 1937), he started analysis with Joan Riviere, who was one of Klein's training analysts and a formidable thinker. He reports that as he was terminating his analysis with her (around 1942, just as the Controversial Discussions were getting under way), he found that when he spoke about classifying the environment, she was completely against any such notion. Psychoanalysis was "not concerned with the real world" (Riviere, 1927, p. 87). This refers to the area of controversy between Anna Freud and Melanie Klein and her supporters during the 1920s and 1930s and, as already stated in chapter 2, Winnicott was more in agreement with Melanie Klein on that matter than he was with Anna Freud about the practice of child analysis.

The Controversial Discussions were initiated by Marjorie Brierley, instigated by her (so-called) "Armistice Letter" to Melanie Klein in 1942 (in King & Steiner, 1991, pp. 122–123). As Melanie Klein selected her colleagues to prepare for these scientific discussions, where so much was at stake for her and the future of psychoanalysis in London, she originally named Winnicott one of her Kleinian training analysts. And, to begin with, he was loyal to her cause and attended all the meetings "conscientiously". But quite soon Klein ". . . had problems with him because he did not give her his contributions early enough for her or the group to vet them" (King & Steiner, 1991, pp. xxiii–xxxiv). So, by 1944, he was no longer considered a Kleinian (by Mrs Klein and her followers), and from his correspondence it is clear that he felt "dropped" by Klein. The Controversial Discussions were finalised between 1944–1945 and concluded with the well-known "gentlemen's agreement" between Anna Freud and Melanie Klein. In 1944, Sylvia Payne became President of the British Psychoanalytical Society, and she was involved with preparing the "gentlemen's agreement" (King & Steiner, 1991). As a result, the training was divided into the A (Melanie Klein) group and the B (Anna Freud) group. This "agreement" acknowledged the significant scientific differences between the two groups.

The aftermath of these discussions, although concluding with an "agreement", left the majority of members of the British Psychoanalytical Society, including Melanie Klein and her followers, perhaps confused, wounded, and even traumatised, mirroring the aftermath of the Second World War itself. In that precarious scientific atmosphere, Winnicott gave his paper, "Primitive Emotional Development", at a Scientific Meeting in the autumn of 1945. This paper stands as Winnicott's first seminal paper in which he sets out his particular perspective on early psychic development. It can also be read as a position statement in as much as he says he will "settle down" to clinical work in order to examine, through the practice of psychoanalysis, aspects of his theory and practice that felt true to his experience (see Part I Dialogue). The subtext of his position conveyed that he was not going to toe any party line – Freudian or Kleinian – but would rather develop his own ideas about whether they complied or not to the order of the day. This, for him, following Marjorie Brierley, was an ordinary scientific approach.

By the time he wrote this 1945 paper, Winnicott had already proposed that "there was no such thing as a baby", and I referred in chapter 2 to the years 1935–1944, which constituted Phase One of Winnicott's theoretical achievements because of two major discoveries:

1. The baby is a human being (Winnicott, 1967c, p. 574).
2. There is no such thing as a baby (Winnicott, 1952a, p. 99; see also Abram, 2008, p. 1195).

Although these discoveries were personal, my point is that they led Winnicott to create a theory of the environment–individual set-up (see chapter 6), and it is this theory (of the parent–infant relationship) that sets his work apart from the evolving Kleinian development. It also set his work apart from the Anna Freudians, who continued to see his work as essentially Kleinian. It is also true to say that there were several important Freudian analysts in New York whose work certainly focused on the early parent–infant relationship in psychic development (see Thompson, 2012).

Winnicott's use of the term "environment" refers to what I have called a "psychic" environment. The term "psychic" stresses the emotional attitude and feelings the mother has towards her baby. In that sense, the concept does not attempt to describe behaviour or the conscious and cognitive realm. Rather, it is designated to emphasise Freud's observations of primary processes and the unconscious-to-unconscious mode of relating.

Let us now examine how Winnicott came to classify the environment, because this clearly demonstrates the two kinds of babies in Winnicott's theoretical matrix. In 1952, he wrote "Psychoses and Child Care" (1952b) and illustrated the environment–individual set-up with a series of diagrams depicting two different early patterns of object relating, two Winnicottian babies: those who have been held and those who have not been held (pp. 223–224). Where the holding has been good enough, the newborn will be facilitated to develop. However, in an environment that is not good enough, the infant will withdraw. The outcome of this failure of the environment is a "basic split in the personality", which will cause a variety of psychopathologies.

The healthy pattern of relating can, for Winnicott, occur only in the context of a good-enough environment. The failure of the early environment (even though the parents may be good people) is utterly responsible for the detriment of each individual's mental health. While Winnicott did take account of the baby's "inherited tendencies" by largely accepting Freud's instinct theory prior to 1920, he simultaneously never altered his perspective about two categories of babies.

From 1945 onwards, therefore, the "self", across all of Winnicott's concepts, includes the inscription of the m/other. The psychic environment cannot be separated from the evolving self (Abram, 2007a, pp. 295–315). The parent–infant relationship constitutes the very beginnings of self-development, and, as we shall see in Part IV, the good-enough mother has to have integrated her hatred of the baby. In other words, she does not "deny" her true feelings through the defence of splitting or repression, for example, but, rather, she has to acknowledge her hating feelings. Winnicott suggested that the mother's hatred is probably sublimated through lullabies that infer aggression towards the baby, as in "Rock-a-bye Baby". In 1947 Winnicott wrote, "Hate in the Countertransference" and listed eighteen reasons why a mother hates her baby from the start – even if the baby is a boy (Winnicott, 1949). He says "even if the baby is a boy" as a rejoinder to Freud, who thought that the mother could only have love for her infant boy!

Here lies a significant difference from the theories of Melanie Klein, because for Winnicott hate is a developmental achievement rather than an innate manifestation of the death instinct. This may be put rather starkly because in our dialogues it will be seen that

Hinshelwood sees this as one of the "mythical" differences that may highlight misunderstanding about Klein's theory of the death instinct. But Winnicott stresses that to hate is a capacity that has been achieved. This achievement signifies that it has become integrated in the ego's development rather than denied.

Summary

This summary is aimed at obtaining the clearest possible account of the distinct differences between Klein and Winnicott on early development. There are a number of dimensions on which the two agree and disagree, partly or wholly. The clear common ground is that both are interested in object relations, rather than psychic energy; they focus on the earliest stages when the ego/self is in process of formation rather than the later conflictual issues (such as the Oedipus complex) that the ego must deal with. Both (with some exceptions) emphasise experience rather than objective descriptions; on the whole, though not entirely, they emphasise the temporal proximity of children's experience to the earliest stages.

Table 2 lists some of the prominent differences that need to be kept in mind throughout the rest of this book.

TABLE 2 Differences between Klein and Winnicott on early development

Dimensions	Klein	Comments	Winnicott	Comments
Experience versus observation	Baby's experience	Klein constantly focuses on the baby rather than observational conceptions	Winnicott discusses both subject and observer's point of view while formulating the infant's subjective experience	Winnicott suggests there is a rudimentary ego at the beginning as distinct from a "self" (see JA's response to RDH below). The "self" for Winnicott develops through the facilitating environment, and by around age 3 months the infant (if all goes well enough) begins to distinguish Me from Not-me

Dimensions	Klein	Comments	Winnicott	Comments
Ego boundary	Inherent boundary from birth	Bodily skin sensations may be the source of distinction of self from other	Illusion of omnipotence when the baby's needs are adapted to successfully and he feels understood. In the absence of this process, the baby has to develop a premature intellectual understanding and cannot discover externality because it is experienced as dangerous and invading	Inherent experience of being merged with the object because at the beginning there is no capacity to perceive and discern the m/other. The baby "apperceives", and due to the m/other's adaptation to needs, the baby moves gradually from apperception to perception (see "Mirror-Role of Mother and Family in Child Development", 1967b; "The Use of an Object and Relating through Identifications", 1971d).
Separation	Self	Experience of separation from other at birth	Separation of Me from Not-me comes gradually and incrementally in the context of a good-enough environment – i.e., a mother in a state of primary maternal preoccupation. By age 3 to 4 months the baby has reached "unit status".	Premature separation causes primitive agonies and unthinkable anxieties.

SUMMARY

Dimensions	Klein	Comments	Winnicott	Comments
Frustration	Result of integration, anger with the needed object	Experience of frustration is not the bad object, but neglect by the good object	Can only be experienced once the sense of self is established – i.e., "unit status"	Too much frustration can lead to a break in the "continuity of being" and premature disillusionment
Rage	Primary response to "bad" sensations,	Expression of a narrative of relationship with a "bad" object (paranoid-schizoid position)	Primitive rage in the context of a deficient environment traumatises and hampers development.	Anger is a developmental achievement once a self is established
Depth of unconscious	Deeper layers concerned with the formation of the self/ego	The ego must function before the classical psychoanalytic conflicts can be experienced and resolved	Formation of self – contingent on the illusion of omnipotence. Early is not deep.	Experience of integration and a developing sense of self due to the survival of the object (see Glossary)
External object (psychic environment)	Experienced from birth as good or bad	The nature of the external object depends on bodily sensations (i.e., the perception of inner states).	Due to the merger between Me and Not-me, to begin with the infant cannot differentiate between external and internal	The infant's state of absolute dependence on the environment and object mother is a fact
Instinct theory	Instincts are not energy concepts	Instincts result, inherently, in the experience of relations with objects (unconscious phantasy)	Freudian instinct theory is largely accepted except the notion of the death instinct	The life instinct (biological drives) is navigated and controlled by the functioning ego due to the consistent "survival of the object" which has been internalised. Thus, instincts are secondary to relationship in true self development.

Dialogue

R. D. HINSHELWOOD: Let's start this second discussion by going straight to one of the significant disagreements – the "death instinct". I agree there is a sort of squeamishness in all of us when we think of our dear little ones as seething with murder in their hearts. Hate, you have just said, is a "developmental achievement" – although not always, perhaps. Could one say that the First World War was a developmental achievement?! The many millions who died didn't gain much development from it. So, your statement may have to be qualified somewhat. I hope you might agree with that. Crudely, one can talk about the breaking-eggs-to-make-an-omelette kind of destructiveness, which has a long-term creative outcome. But not all hate is like that.

In addition, you have also conveyed that reparation coming out of guilt and concern was a point of agreement with Klein, though Winnicott didn't like to call it a depressive position. However, the implicit question is: what has set off the concern and the reparative urge? Klein had an answer to that, but I don't know how Winnicott would answer it. Klein's answer would be that the guilt comes from a kind of hate that is not worthy of being called an achievement, a hate that is simply (or mostly) destructive.

Such destructive hate is what I think we must discuss. For Winnicott, you seem to be saying, there was no destructive hate, but I can't think you would say that, and so I hope you will explain. If hate is a state to be achieved, what is the prior state from which achievement comes? Is it the primary merger, which Winnicott calls the illusion of omnipotence?

But right now, I want to explain how, it seems to me, Klein explained the move from destructive hate to the more controlled destructiveness that contributes to reparation and creativity. Frankly, I think it is wrong to rule out biological origins, but that is because, personally, I reject non-material, spiritual origins of mental events. My descriptions may not appeal to those readers who do find the greater simplicity offered by spiritual explanations preferable.

It does seem to me – with this proviso about spirituality – that our dear little offspring are biologically loaded with the capacity to scream and hate with a violence that overwhelms them completely at the outset. From the very beginning, maybe within moments of birth, a baby finds in itself the desperate means to "scream blue murder", as we call it. The early onset of this state of mind speaks to me of a biological origin. I am convinced of the innateness of that inconsolable state of mind, which also occupies the whole of the body, including its bodily states of tension, tears, and physical unapproachableness. It directly grabs the maternal aspects of all of us. Is it an achievement? Already? Or, is Winnicott's "hate" not that state of mind filled with fury and destructiveness that I describe? Most mothers would agree with me, I believe, that hate exists at moments from the beginning.

Of course, one could say it is just the work of collections of neurones that have been hard-wiring themselves into each other for nine months in utero. But I am willing to assume that other neurones, whatever they are, carry this basic circuitry into whatever functions of the brain are responsible for a "felt state of mind". I am confessing to certain assumptions from which my understanding takes off. But I would say that the vast majority of people (the majority of readers, even) would tend to make the same assumptions. The point is that it is utterly biological in origin but is simultaneously felt in some way as thoroughly experiential.

I think that there is more agreement than you allow over the movement from the primitive (biologically provoked) state of mind that is helplessly destructive to one that is guiltily reparative. How that progress goes forward may well be the dispute, instead of whether the biology of the brain is the origin.

Klein understood it in terms of a further assumption. She assumed that the early state of mind is formed on the basis of a primitive narrative of evil. Whatever the conditions giving rise to the baby's desperation, it is caused by some evil object that desires the baby to suffer that desperation.

Frustration

Now, about the developmental process for Winnicott: he would say that it is frustration of a desire, not a motivated wish by an evil object. And thus he would, indeed, see frustration as a stage beyond, on some line of development. Indeed, Klein would be willing to grant frustration a similar role and would place that experience down the line a little. Frustration, for Klein, is already quite a sophisticated experience. There is a degree of "achievement" in feeling a state of frustration. Here, we are again in danger of confusing our perspectives.

Using the term "frustration" from the perspective of the observer, we would say it is anger with someone who is recognised as the giver of some benefit (milk from the breast, say) – and without seeing the breast as pure evil. Klein would agree that this is a step on from seeing the breast as an evil object (the "bad breast", in Klein's terminology). The capacity to see the giving object as still good, still motivated to be giving, even when raging at it, is the achievement, as Klein would describe it (Klein, 1957). Winnicott's achievement is different, and we need an account of that – but I guess it is the achievement of seeing the other as separate, although, Jan, my guess needs to be examined.

A third developmental step: I have described Klein's two steps. The first is a state of mind that sees all lack of satisfaction as caused by the evil intentions of another; it is a state of mind known as the "paranoid-schizoid position". And the second step is to maintain the sense of that object as still deserving of gratitude, even though it is raged at for not providing satisfaction in the moment now. This is a developmental step and is known as the "depressive position". As Oscar Wilde (1898) wrote in his *Ballad of Reading Gaol*,

> Yet each man kills the thing he loves
> By each let this be heard,
> Some do it with a bitter look,
> Some with a flattering word,
> The coward does it with a kiss,
> The brave man with a sword

This second step is anguished and is pervaded by what is called "depressive anxiety". In effect, the anguish of attacking the one whom we still love is the origin, in Klein's frame of thinking, of guilt. It is characterised by the sense of self as evil, just as in the previous step the object was evil.

There is, however, another developmental achievement, a move on from the second step, from the rage of frustrated hating. That state of mind, the second step, is a tortured one persecuted by guilt, as it was previously in the paranoid-schizoid position persecuted by an evil object. In fact, the evil object becomes, as Freud has said, an internal persecuting object, the product of hated but loved parents. The guilt from this superego demands a punishment, an eye-for-an-eye, and so on. Now, in this further, third, step something happens to the guilt, another developmental achievement. Guilt moves from being the product of a brutal, punishing egodestructive superego to being a superego that demands that things are put right, the object repaired, atonement. This is reparation, and it has within it a potentially creative spark, instead of an essentially destructive punishment. The superego agency in any one person may occupy a position anywhere between these two poles; indeed, it may move in one direction or another at different times. The capacity for a potentially creative reparation (and away from merely punishment) is the really important achievement for Klein.

In summary, there appears to be a distinct difference between Klein's view of these earliest steps of rage as the motor of development and Winnicott's idea of hate as the end-point of some line of development. So, perhaps, I should not go further at this point, Jan, and hope that you will fill in the Winnicottian perspective on the biological origins from which the achievement of hate arises, and the steps by which it developmentally proceeds.

JAN ABRAM: Thank you, Bob, for your clarity, which is helpful because it does highlight the very different perspectives on early psychic phenomena on the part of Klein and Winnicott.

Let me first pick up on some of your points in order of appearance in your text.

1. I do not think it possible that newborn infants are, to quote you, "seething with murder in their hearts". And I do not think it is because I am squeamish about this idea!
2. The kind of hate that causes war, in my view, is hate that is split-off (in Kleinian language) and disavowed (in Freudian

language). I believe Winnicott would say that it is a result of a failing early environment – that is, an object that did not survive in the earliest stages of development.

3. Breaking eggs to make an omelette is a good metaphor for what Winnicott described as early aggression/destruction that is benign. This is a biologically driven force but not (yet) hate.

4. Winnicott was clear that the infant had to develop a capacity to feel concern, so that, in his language, the stage of concern was very akin to Klein's "depressive position". And in answer to your question, "What has set off the concern and the reparative urge?", Winnicott would answer quite simply: "the coming together of the environment mother with the object mother in the infant's mind through the experience of a facilitating object who has survived". I realise this needs unpacking, which I come to later (see Glossary). I agree it will be important to discuss destructive hate. And it is important to say from the outset that Winnicott was *not* saying that there was no destructive hate.

6. The answer to your questions – "What is the prior state from which achievement comes? Is it the primary merger, which Winnicott calls the illusion of omnipotence" – is "yes".

Let me now unpack these points.

For Winnicott the newborn is not in a position – yet – to hate, simply because he has not developed a "capacity" to hate. This is related to Winnicott's disagreement with the notion of a death instinct. The baby is born with an innate drive to live and to survive. At the very beginning, psyche and soma – Me and Not-me – are not yet differentiated. Thus, from the baby's perspective, the mother is "Me". The mother's role is to "mirror" the infant's affective states of mind and to "adapt" to the infant's needs, which includes a quality of affective reflecting as well as tending to the ordinary human biological and emotional needs such as hunger and discomfort. The mother's state of primary maternal preoccupation assists her ability to "facilitate" the infant's development in this way. Both mother and infant are actively engaged in a kind of cooperation through their mutual communication.

The reason that hate is a developmental achievement is that, in order to feel hate, there has to be a self. And for Winnicott, at the beginning there is not a self – yet. The self refers to what Winnicott described as "unit status", when the infant has reached a stage of development where it can distinguish between Me and Not-me. This would be between 3 and 4 months and is achieved only as a result of the mother's facilitating "management" of the early weeks and months. So the issue of "achievement" is based entirely on the parent–infant relationship, and without this relationship development is likely to be disconnected, leading to a pathological false self.

Hate is the other side of the coin to love. A newborn infant is not – yet – able to love. In this way, hate and love indicate, as Winnicott pointed out, an achievement of ambivalence.

The infant is a bundle of sensations, and I agree that biology must play its part, as it makes such physiological demands on the body that gradually transform into emotions. This is where the mother's role as mediator and facilitator is crucial. And this is what will be revivified in the transference of any given analysis.

And, by the way, Winnicott is not in the least bit sentimental or "squeamish" about what babies do to their mothers and how much they "wear them out". In fact, he points out in his paper on hate (1949) that there are eighteen reasons why the good-enough mother hates her baby from the start! But he is describing a hate that is the other side of love. In other words, it is integrated into the mature individual, who is able to recognise her own ambivalent feelings when the baby will not go to sleep after feeding and is able to endure (survive) the endless demands on her time, emotions, and body.

It seems to me that, for Klein (and for you, too, Bob), babies are born already feeling murderous and hateful. For Winnicott, they do not yet know what they are feeling in terms of affects because they have not yet developed a capacity to know what they feel. Rather, they are a bundle of sensations. And we know from many of our highly educated patients that there are some who have no idea what they are really feeling and need the analyst to help them articulate the painful affects they have repressed and/or split off. This, in Winnicott's theory, is always related to a deficiency in parenting that starts from the beginning and is based on a "pattern of relating".

RDH: Ok – I think we can get somewhere with this. That is to say, we can perhaps display the differences, with the reasons for each position, in such a way that readers can assess the arguments for themselves.

I think you must be right that the human infant, any infant, is born with the inbuilt biology necessary to survive. The question that has no clear answer between us, at present, is whether this is just a mechanical process – feed when the blood sugar falls – or whether there is a rudimentary experience of hunger and fear for one's survival. Psyche and soma are undifferentiated, as you say, and I agree; but the issue is which side do we, who do differentiate psyche from soma, look at it from. I think my point in the contributions hitherto is that Klein was not a biologist, and her approach was to the person's experience. And it contrasts with Freud's approach to the biology of instincts and the energy theories that have marked so many psychoanalytic theories.

I am sure we would be of one mind here. Why – you would say – why on earth did Klein then talk about instincts? Perhaps because she really did not understand what "instinct" is in biological terms. You remember I made reference, in our Part I Dialogue, to Klein's reflection, "I still cannot answer what made me feel that it was anxiety that I should touch . . .". Written in 1959, the year before she died, she still could not really sense how it was she made this choice. So I would consider that she used the term "instinct" more or less because others used it. Moreover, she needed at the outset of her career to avoid being outspoken in her views, as the psychoanalytic movement had just been dealing with the dissenting views of Alfred Adler, Carl Jung, and Otto Rank. She was at pains to avoid being labelled a dissident and had been shocked in 1926 when she was so criticised by Anna Freud for the relatively minor modifications she proposed in the theories of the Oedipus complex and the superego. Where she uses the term "instinct", I think we have to be very careful not to assume she meant it in the way Freud did.

This was my concern when I said we might find ourselves getting into a dispute over what Klein meant by the death instinct. But perhaps we do have to discuss this a bit more. For Klein, it is not a biological energy concept. It is much more like the point you were making about the biological endowment to fear of perishing. She then concentrated on how that could possibly be conceived by the infant's mind at the beginning. What she came up with, from the playing out of phantasies by children aged as young as 3 years, was that some evil presence intended them to die. The biological capacity to receive sensations from the tummy are given a "primitive" meaning, which, biologically, probably has two components: (a) "this sensation is no good to me, probably seriously bad"; and (b) "something wants these feelings in me, and wants to cause them".

It is, of course, possible that the infant does not think in terms of primitive narratives of that kind. I quite accept that Winnicott did not go along with that primitive level of thinking. He specifically, as you say, saw the baby as not having a sense of an object that can do things to the baby. The sense of an object has to be struggled for against an illusion that the baby omnipotently makes its own satisfactions. Just trying to think this through, I guess that the omnipotent baby does not enjoy the illusion that it makes its own frustrations. At the extreme, with an overload of frustration, Winnicott thought the baby loses a sense of its existence altogether – I think he says something like an interruption to the sense of continuity of his own being. But I am not sure what Winnicott would say the infant's experience of ordinary (as opposed to extreme) frustration would be.

Another alternative is that maybe the baby does not have experiences, as, for instance, many classical psychoanalysts tended to say. Babies can only be looked at from outside, with objective descriptions about the mother–baby couple, and so on. Here we come back to a point about consistency of perspective: when does the baby have subjective experiences, and from which perspective should we be describing the baby, before and after that point in development when the baby experiences?

Does Winnicott say anywhere when and how the experience of a "Me" (or a "Not-me") comes about? They have to emerge at some point in order for the paradox of Me plus not-Me objects to be experienced. So, at what point is that achieved, and how does it happen? Many analysts of the Independent group would say that it is the achievement that comes from ordinary frustration.

My main point, I think, is that, on the one hand, Klein postulated that frustration is interpreted primitively (by the baby) as a paranoid narrative threatening survival; on the other hand,

Winnicott takes the long journey around in order not to see any threat that it has to attack.

My subsidiary point is that Klein consistently saw the baby from the baby's own point of view (or she tried to – and relied on 3-year-old children), whereas Winnicott (am I right?) saw things from outside, as, for instance, a system of mother-with-baby, which we know as observers to be an illusion. Perhaps Winnicott is more realistic here, as we cannot really know the baby's point of view.

Finally, it may be helpful for the purposes of clarity if someone from a Winnicottian point of view set out what they think Klein's view of an instinct was; it is clearly different from my own understanding of Klein's view of an instinct. But we might want to be alert to how we each use the other's terminology. I guess the same may come up in Part III, when we use the term "external object". It would be a great service, perhaps, to have a list of the most misunderstood differences in the meanings of technical terms (and we have in fact made an attempt to convey some of these inter-group myths in the Appendix).

JA: I will try to address the points you're making, Bob.

First, about Klein and "instinct theory": it seems to me that Klein's work was controversial in the 1930s because she was in the process of developing her theory of object relations in which there was no place for the classical Freudian instinct theory. This was one of the main controversies between Melanie Klein and Anna Freud; Marjorie Brierley, along with Sylvia Payne and James Strachey, tried to address this and have it addressed when the extra scientific meetings were proposed that later became known as the Controversial Discussions.

I do appreciate why you are stressing the point that Klein is not a biologist. But I don't think any psychoanalyst would see that instincts, in a psychoanalytic sense, are "simply" biological. Surely what brings us all together is that we agree bodily demands cause psychic fantasies.

Perhaps we could agree with Charles Rycroft, who suggests a clear distinction between "instinct theory" and "object theory", placing both Klein and Fairbairn in the "object-theory" camp (Rycroft, 1968). As I said above, for Winnicott "biological drives" existed from the start and caused fantasies, but this entirely depended on how the infant was handled and held by the mother. Relating and the earliest relationships were crucial to the infant's development and how the infant "managed" its bodily sensations.

Perhaps Winnicott did not want to deny the value of instinct theory for the same reason Klein used the term "instinct" without really referring to an instinct (as Freudians would understand it). Neither wanted to be seen to disagree with Freud. And yet Winnicott was clear, later, that he did disagree with Freud's introduction of the "death instinct" in 1920 (Freud, 1920g). As a doctor of medicine and a paediatrician as well as a child analyst, however, he followed Klein's emphasis on how emotions and phantasies became tied in with bodily parts.

Turning to your own *Dictionary of Kleinian Thought*, you point out that Klein accepted she was seeing the clinical manifestations of a conflict between the life and death instincts in the early stages of development – and sadism, paranoia, and persecution were the manifest signs of a death instinct (Hinshelwood, 1989, p. 263). If it is not an instinct in the sense that Freudians call an instinct, then what could it be named?

There is no doubt that Winnicott disagreed with Klein about the paranoid-schizoid position. But his disagreement centred on Klein's point that it was universal. So, when you talk about an "evil presence", Winnicott's response was that Klein was developing a theory of "original sin" (see Part IV Dialogue). For Winnicott – and this makes sense to me – the paranoid-schizoid position is a good example of an early deficient holding environment. This is the baby whose object does not survive. And it is not a given that all babies will go through this particular state of mind. Therefore, the patient who is persecuted would be demonstrating that very early on in his or her psychic development the object had not survived. In other words, these extreme states of mind in which there is no ability to discern the environment as distinct from the patient's projections demonstrates internal psychic damage. This is different from the phase "illusion of omnipotence", because during that phase the infant is not capable of projecting.

When you ask about how the move from unawareness to awareness happens in Winnicott's work – from Me to Not-me – I would answer again, as above, that it was entirely to do with how the mother was able to attend to the infant's needs. She is totally responsible for the infant's development. That does not mean that the infant is passive and has no contribution to make, but it does mean that without the mother's contributions it is going to have to resort to a false self-development. The failure of the environment is absolutely at the root of all psychopathology.

As I have previously suggested, it is in his paper on the use of an object (1971d, p. 94) that Winnicott was able to identify five dynamic moments that brought about the infant's ability to move from Me to Not-me:

1. Subject *relates* to object.
2. Object is in process of being found instead of placed by the subject in the world.
3. Subject *destroys* object.
4. Object survives destruction.
5. Subject can *use* object.

There is much more to say about the above; this is a succinct fragment that I have elaborated elsewhere (Abram, 2012a).

The point about the "illusion of omnipotence" stage is that it has to be followed by a period of disillusionment in the course of development. Let me quote Winnicott, who wrote about this very point a few years before he died:

> We have to say that the baby created the breast, but could not have done so had not the mother come along with the breast just at that moment. The communication to the baby is: "Come at the world creatively; it is only what you create that has meaning for you". Next comes: "the world is in your control". From this initial experience of omnipotence the baby is able to begin to experience frustration and even to arrive one day at the other extreme from omnipotence, that is to say, having a sense of being a mere speck in a universe, in a universe that was there before the baby was conceived of and conceived by two parents who were enjoying each other. Is it not from *being God* that human beings arrive at the humility proper to human individuality? [Winnicott, 1968, p. 101]

As you will see, Winnicott stresses a sequence of development. Without "illusion", the process of disillusionment cannot occur.

So in answer to your question on the baby's "resistance" to reality – once again, I would have to answer that it will depend on the environment's facilitation so that the baby can move from illusion to disillusion, which will only, in time, strengthen the sense of self.

Finally, as will be clear from what I've said above, Winnicott was working out all the time how the infant felt in relation to the m/other, and he formulated a detailed matrix that accounted for different subjective states of mind. And although he worked with babies and children, in his late work he stated that it was analytic work with adult patients on the couch that told him far more about infantile states of mind than any "applied" work with children and/or parents and their babies.

PART **III**

THE ROLE OF THE EXTERNAL OBJECT

Chapters 5 and 6 highlight how the respective theories of Klein and Winnicott conclude with a different symbolic matrix concerning the role of the external object in the individual's development.

CHAPTER FIVE

Anxiety and phantasy

R. D. Hinshelwood

Key concepts   Constantly active unconscious phantasy; deeper layers; paranoid-schizoid anxiety; depressive anxiety

---

From early on in her work, Melanie Klein followed Karl Abraham, with an emphasis on his new class of processes in the unconscious – the primitive mechanisms of defence comprising "deeper layers" of the unconscious. She did not contrast them with the defence mechanisms of the neurotic oedipal level, as the primitive layers underlie the neurotic level.

The separate layers were not alternative to each other, and the deeper layers remained active in the unconscious. This view of the deep unconscious phantasy as constantly active was from its inception in the 1940s severely criticised. For instance, Edward Glover (one of the most vociferous of the critics of Klein from 1934 or so onwards) thought that if infantile unconscious phantasy remained active, then this ruled out the psychoanalytic theory of regression and fixation points (Glover, 1945). Though it may modify that theory, maturation involves integration of the different levels of experiencing. They converge into some sort of collaboration, the deeper layers expressed in terms of the less deep, whereas disturbed mental health suggests the coming apart of the different levels, so that the deeper layers appear without mediation through more sophisticated and reality-based transformations.

Those primitive processes involving taking-in and giving-out are responsible for the very formation of the ego and its sense of identity, as well as being the processes that deal with anxiety about identity or its annihilation and loss. The neurotic level is, however, concurrently active and takes over a dominance once the anxieties about identity and loss of self are managed in a relatively stable way. However, when conditions threaten identity, reversion to an expression of the more primitive level of anxiety and mechanisms becomes more apparent. Klein thought that as stress at a neurotic level increases past a certain level, the existence of the ego/self is threatened. Perhaps a short example is in order. Klein gave this vignette in her seminal paper on schizoid mechanisms; it is a key illustration:

> The session I have in mind started with the patient's telling me that he felt anxiety and did not know why. He then made comparisons with people more successful and fortunate than himself. These remarks also had a reference to me. Very strong feelings of frustration, envy and grievance came to the fore. When I interpreted – to give here again only the gist of my interpretations – that these feelings were directed against the analyst and that he wanted to destroy me, his mood changed abruptly. The tone of his voice became flat, he spoke in a slow, expressionless way, and he said that he felt detached from the whole situation. He added that my interpretation seemed correct, but that it did not matter. In fact, he no longer had any wishes, and nothing was worth bothering about. [Klein, 1946, p. 19]

Something literally went missing from his mind. His capacity to be aware of his feelings was lost, that function split off. Klein then interpreted this change:

> I suggested that at the moment of my interpretation the danger of destroying me had become very real to him and the immediate consequence was the fear of losing me. Instead of feeling guilt and depression, which at certain stages of his analysis followed such interpretations, he now attempted to

deal with these dangers by a particular method of splitting. [p. 19]

Klein made the point that often under stress a patient will split his object, the analyst, the one who is hated and the one who is loved; or the analyst becomes one of these – shall we say the loved one – and another, third figure becomes the hated one:

> But this was not the kind of splitting which occurred in this particular instance. The patient split off those parts of himself, i.e. of his ego which he felt to be dangerous and hostile towards the analyst. He turned his destructive impulses from his object towards his ego, with the result that parts of his ego temporarily went out of existence. In unconscious phantasy this amounted to annihilation of part of his personality. The particular mechanism of turning the destructive impulse against one part of his personality, and the ensuing dispersal of emotions, kept his anxiety in a latent state.
>
> My interpretation of these processes had the effect of again altering the patient's mood. He became emotional, said he felt like crying, was depressed, but felt more integrated; then he also expressed a feeling of hunger. [pp. 19–20]

She added that the feeling of hunger represented some element of introjection – now of a good object.

Centrally, the patient was initially occupied with rivalry, jealousy, envy, and the neurotic level of oedipal competition. But with a fulsome confrontation by the analyst, emergency protection came into operation, and the primitive mechanisms began to dismantle the ego. The splitting process exemplified this damage to the ego itself; the patient literally lost a part of himself, his capacity to have his own feelings, and for them to be significant.

However much these deeper layers of the unconscious are considered to be phantasy, such phantasies have real effects. The reality principle does not have much influence here due to introjection and projection (the transmission across the ego boundary in one direction or the other). To some extent the coherence or otherwise of the ego boundary is itself affected by what is transmitted through it. This Klein called the paranoid-schizoid position; it is characterised by the use of splitting defences to attempt to cope with the threatened loss of self and identity in the midst of conflict.

Identity

Freud's paper, "Negation" (1925h) described narcissism in the oral phase as spitting out what is bad, and taking in what is good. This, paradoxically, is narcissism expressed in terms of narratives with objects – spitting them out and taking them in. For Klein, this level of unconscious processes involving introjection (taking objects in) and projection (spitting them out) builds up slowly a sense of the ego being, or, rather, containing, mostly good things – or, if the environment is inclement, more bad things than good. If the ego starts with a profoundly felt sense of good things and bad, gradually the encounter with actual external objects will fill in more and more specific features of what is contained inside and what outside. Identity develops on this basis. Slowly, this intimate mixture of the sense of good and bad with the external objects internalised is formed and elaborated. Initially, the collection of objects inside may be very unrealistically conceived, and the reality principle works only slowly to determine the actual qualities; indeed, it is perhaps a lifelong task for all of us to gradually sort out the reality of the external objects we live with and, by introjection, that constitute us.

It is this sense of a loss of self which led to the designation of this layer as "psychotic". This process of developing a self with its specific characteristics – one's identity – can only, with some heartache, gradually include the recognition of repudiated bad parts of the self and the recognition of good parts of the other. Implicit in this view is that the origins are in the unrealistic recognitions, determined by the sense of good and bad experiences (the pleasure principle). Gradually undoing those wrong-turnings and cul-de-sacs as demanded by the reality principle, together with a slow move towards seeing oneself more realistically, is termed the depressive position.

The depressive position and the paranoid-schizoid position were posited on clinical grounds and, for Klein, are seen as an oscillating form of developmental progress (lasting, in fact, throughout life). The paranoid-schizoid position is the combination of primitive mechanisms – introjection and projection – which attempt to recreate a reality to reassure against the psychotic anxiety of a disintegration of the self and identity. The depressive position, coming along a little later, takes a harder look at the reality of the objects related to and dependent upon acknowledging good and bad.

Mixed feelings

The depressive position is a state of mind that can allow the reality of things to take precedence; the self becomes tinged with bad, and the environment with good. The meticulous spitting out and taking in has to be reined in. In addition, the infant ego performs its functions imperfectly: sometimes good objects will be spat out, and sometimes bad objects will be taken in. And this creates not just confusion but alarm.

If by mistake, or from the necessities of reality, a bad object is swallowed, the alarm is that what is good in oneself will be contaminated, spoiled, or destroyed. One's inner "good" objects are under threat (not just the self); there is alarm for the objects. It is a feature of Klein's theories that she has a place for something like altruism, not just self-satisfaction, but also a feeling for the object as another feeling person. It is a state of mind in which there is concern for the other, and a sense of responsibility for its survival. This is called a depressive anxiety – the fear for the object – and it contrasts with the paranoid-schizoid position, where a persecutory anxiety and a fear for one's own survival predominate. Of course, if a good object is allowed to slip out in some spitting frenzy, then there is also a fear that the internal goodness of self and identity is lost or compromised. Alongside the threat for the infant of taking in badness is the "mistake" of engaging goodness with retaliatory rage.

The hatred of a good object because it is good is known as envy (sometimes as Kleinian envy!), and it creates not just a storm of potential guilt but of anxiety that its satisfactions will cease. It is not a good idea for the infant to become confused in this way. However, given the need for taking in the good things, then an encounter with an external other, another mind/self who is accumulating goodness, is a threat that could unbalance the whole system. A separate other out there who is full of goodness – even one that generously offers milk, comfort, stroking, and inner satisfaction of hunger – is a provocation that is not ordinary frustration. Such a good object who is separate threatens the identity of one's self almost as if, by comparison, one's own self were bad. It brings out that aggression which we know as biting the hand that feeds you.

As the infant matures, its range of possible phantasies multiplies, and it has many alternatives to keep track of. The maturing process allows an increasing understanding of others' minds that are also managing their "spitting and swallowing", partly for the comfort of the pleasure principle and partly from the rigours of reality. The gradual admixture of pleasant and unpleasant will, in the course of maturity, growing experience, and the awareness of others, become stabilised. Reversion to the threats to identity from overwhelming destructive objects will become less frequent and less extreme. This particular kind of confusion between good and bad sets going all sorts of other confusing processes and phantasies about where good is and bad is. So complex is it that individual lines of development need to be teased out individually.

The superego

The anxiety about the fate of the object extends from those good ones felt to be inside and can then be felt about those projected outside. The experience of alarm is closely connected with a feeling of responsibility for looking after the objects and for harming them in a fit of rage. That responsibility is felt as guilt. Quite differently from Freud – who thought that the superego formed from the internalisation of a father who threatened castration for wrong-doing – Klein thought that the superego was partly triggered by the feelings for loved objects, but the guilt the superego then caused was modelled on the hate and rage that exists between the self and its threatening "bad" objects.

At the start of the depressive position, which Klein put at around 3–6 months, the superego has a lot of the blindly destructive qualities typical of the paranoid-schizoid position. However, as time goes on through the depressive position, the superego and the guilt it generates gradually ameliorate as phantasies of putting right the harm done become stronger. In normal development, therefore, there is a tendency for the superego to change slowly from a dangerous punitive internal agency modelled on "bad" objects towards a more benign, helpful object that can support acts of reparation. As this happens, guilt changes from punishment to atonement.

* * *

This chapter has tried to convey the intimate relationship with the external object and the active interchange with the environment from the beginning, subject to the abilities of the immature ego to grasp its reality. There are various features:

» defences in the deeper layers gather into two positions;
» the theoretical consequence of unconscious phantasy abolishing the theory of regression;
» the gradual mediation of the deeper layers by neurotic conflicts and defences;
» the centrality of splitting of the ego itself in the desperate efforts to survive;
» the task of a lifetime to sort out the reality of external objects from their distortion by primitive unconscious phantasies;
» the "altruistic" alarm for the fate of the object as the depressive position insists on increasing respect for reality;
» the enigma of envy, hating good because it is good;
» a completely revised view of the origins and development of the superego and guilt.

CHAPTER SIX

The environment–individual set-up

Jan Abram

KEY CONCEPTS   Primary maternal preoccupation; transitional phenomena; transitional object; facilitating environment; illusion (of omnipotence); paradox; regression; capacity to be alone

---

Paradoxically, although Winnicott's psychoanalytic concepts lay stress on the m/other's role in facilitating her infant's emotional development (i.e., the external other), the mother could never be truly external to the infant. This is why the term "inscribed" is pertinent (see chapter 2 and the Glossary). Although it is a term that is more commonly used in French psychoanalysis and not one ever used by Winnicott himself, it seems to me it best illustrates how Winnicott thought about the mother's contribution to the individual's development of a self. Let us see how Winnicott conceptualised this "inscription" on the self and how this concept relates to the transference in clinical work.

Phase Two of Winnicott's psychoanalytic evolution, from 1945 to 1959 (chapter 2), brought about perhaps one of the most innovative of psychoanalytic concepts: transitional phenomena (Winnicott, 1951). This concept, which is the major theoretical achievement during this phase (Abram, 2008, p. 1200), evolves from the notion of primary unintegration – a state of mind the newborn enjoys but only if he is in the arms of a m/other who is "ordinarily devoted" to her infant (see Part I Dialogue; see also Glossary). The good-enough mother, then, through her dedication, facilitates the infant's growth and awareness. Transitional phenomena as a concept accounts for the interpsychic–intrapsychic dynamics of the subject's journey towards the capacity to symbolize – that is, to distinguish Me from Not-me. It refers to a dimension of living that belongs neither to internal nor to external; rather, it is the place that both connects and separates inner and outer. Across his work, Winnicott uses many terms to refer to this mental dimension – the third area, the intermediate area, the potential space, a resting place, and the location of cultural experience (Abram, 2007a, pp. 337–354).

Developmentally, transitional phenomena occur from the beginning, even before birth, in relation to the mother–infant dyad. As the infant begins to separate Me from Not-me, and moves from absolute dependence to the stage of relative dependence, he makes use of the transitional object. But it must be remembered that this is on condition that he is facilitated to grow through the m/other's dedication and deep identity with his state of helplessness (see chapter 4).

A triple statement on human nature

Although Melanie Klein's work had made a significant contribution to an understanding of the infant's internal world, Winnicott's view was that her theories did not take sufficient account of the environment. The concept of transitional phenomena addresses a gap, we could say, in psychoanalytic theory and took shape in Winnicott's work in 1950. He presented his paper, "Transitional Objects and Transitional Phenomena", to a Scientific Meeting of the British Psychoanalytical Society in 1951. After acknowledging the need for a double statement about inner and outer in psychoanalysis, he writes:

My claim is that if there is a need for this double statement, there is need for a triple one; there is the third part of the life of a human being, a part that we cannot ignore, an intermediate area of *experiencing*, to which inner reality and external life both contribute. It is an area which is not challenged, because no claim is made on its behalf except that it shall exist as a resting-place for the individual engaged in the perpetual human task of keeping inner and outer reality separate yet inter-related. [Winnicott, 1951, p. 230]

Primary maternal preoccupation

Five years later, in 1956, the "ordinary devotion" of the mother was developed into the concept of "primary maternal preoccupation" (Winnicott, 1956). The two concepts of transitional phenomena and primary maternal preoccupation are related, as we shall see. The good-enough mother is able "ordinarily" to surrender to a specific state of mind, just before her baby is born, "in which to a large extent she is the baby and the baby is her" (1966, p. 6). This state of mind, termed "primary maternal preoccupation", suggested that it was equivalent to a psychiatric condition (Winnicott, 1956, p. 302). He emphasised that it usually lasts a few weeks after the birth of the child and that the mother normally forgets she had felt this, due to repressing the memory.

This state of mind in the mother contributes to many processes that her infant will gain from, especially concerning self-esteem and the capacity to develop symbolic thinking. A baby who feels his needs are met "creates the object", and this makes him feel omnipotent. Why does the baby feel omnipotent? Winnicott says the baby needed something but did not know at the beginning that he needed it. For example, the newborn who cries because he is hungry does not yet know what this hunger in his body actually means. When the breast is offered by a mother who feels completely identified with her infant's state of helplessness, and the baby feeds, he feels he has got just what he wanted. If he could speak he would say, "This is just what I wanted!" This experience gives him the illusion that he has created the world and that the world is in his control. For Winnicott, this "'illusion of omnipotence" that "creates the object" is an essential experience and is at the root of the (sense of) self. It is also at the root of a sense of trust in the environment from which the baby will get what he needs. However, this experience can only be meaningful if the baby gradually comes to realize that this "paradise" cannot continue forever. The process of disillusionment has to follow. This theory can be seen as a particular way of extending Freud's "Formulations on the Two Principles of Mental Functioning", and at the centre, Freud infers in a footnote in that paper, was the infant's dependence on the mother who facilitated the transition from the pleasure principle to the reality principle (1911b, p. 220fn.). Once these developmental tasks are achieved – that is, internalized – they then become a resource for the rest of the individual's life.

"Creating the object" and the "illusion of omnipotence" are intrinsic to the notion of the "theoretical first feed". The accumulation of infantile needs being met by a mother in a state of primary maternal preoccupation leads to what Winnicott referred to as the "theoretical first feed". The quality of needs being adapted to and met results in the beginning of symbolic thinking and imagination. For example, as stated above, when the baby is hungry, he doesn't yet know what that feeling denotes. But the mother does know, through intuition and to some extent "common sense". This makes the baby feel he is continually getting what he needs and it makes him feel he is God. But this paradise has to end, and, as the reality principle is gradually introduced, the mother helps the baby to become disillusioned. This will lead to discernment as he gradually comes to see that he is not God!

The analytic setting offers a potential space in which, through the transference, the patient regresses to stages of development that have been especially painful due to trauma. This is similar to the Freudian notion of "fixation points". I return to this notion at the end of this chapter, but before that let us examine one of Winnicott's clinical examples to see how he worked in the transference and how this example illustrates the themes related to the so-called external object.

Working with a middle-aged man who had had several therapists, Winnicott explains that despite much work having been achieved the patient complained that he had not yet reached something in the treatments, which is why he continued to search for the "something" that was missing. Winnicott writes:

> On a Friday the patient came and reported much as usual. The thing that struck me on this Friday was that the patient was talking about penis envy. I use this term advisedly, and I must invite acceptance of the fact that this term was appropriate here in view of the material, and of its presentation. Obviously this term, penis envy, is not usually applied in the description of a man.
>
> The change that belongs to this particular phase is shown in the way I handled this. On this particular occasion I said to him: "I am listening to a girl. I know perfectly well that you are a man but I am listening to a girl, and I am talking to a girl. I am telling this girl: 'You are talking about penis envy.'"
>
> ... After a pause the patient said: "If I were to tell someone about this girl I would be called mad".
>
> ... It was my next remark that surprised me, and it clinched the matter. I said: "It was not that *you* told this to anyone; it is *I* who see the girl and hear a girl talking, when actually there is a man on my couch. The mad person is *myself*." [Winnicott, 1971a, pp. 73–74]

Both Winnicott and his patient came to see that the patient had had the experience of being sane in a mad environment. The mad environment was a mother who had treated the infant as a girl when, in fact, her baby was a boy.

This is an example of how the transference relationship invokes the early psychic environment, and, if the analyst is open enough to receiving these profound communications from the patient that are mobilised by the analytic setting, then this kind of experience can be brought to consciousness.

It is also a good example to illustrate how the very distant past – a mother who was mad – will be reproduced in the present situation with the analyst in which the unconscious trauma of the past is re-lived, but this time in a setting that is designed to facilitate articulation and understanding – that is, the Freudian analysing situation. This is the stuff of analysis and should eventually, step-by-step, lead to a gradual working through.

The above clinical example resonates with what Hinshelwood has written at the beginning of chapter 3 about Melanie Klein's perspective that ". . . she would have argued that the unconscious phantasies, at whatever age, in the deepest layers, are the experiences the baby was having as a newborn". However, what Winnicott's example brings in is the (possible) reality that his patient's mother had seen her infant boy as a girl. This madness was internalised by the patient and thus remained in the deepest layers of his mind (as if it were a fact – that he was a girl) until "it" (the historic mad communication that was buried/split off/ repressed) emerged in the transference of his present analysis (the here-and-now) with Winnicott, who at that particular moment in the session felt himself to be mad (taking on the identity of the mad mother), because he was hearing his patient as if he were a girl talking about penis envy.

Unconscious phantasy, regression, and fixation points

As Hinshelwood explained in chapter 5, the notion of "unconscious phantasy" that is innate from the beginning of life was seen as controversial because it replaced (or abolished) Freud's formulations on regression and "fixation points" (King & Steiner, 1991 p. 699). The history of this controversy – between the classical Freudians and the Kleinian development – has certainly played its part in separating the schools of thought, which is why different "groups" emerged. These issues are beyond the scope of this chapter (and book) despite their relevance, and here I shall only outline Winnicott's developments on the subject of regression.

Largely based on Freudian notions of regression and strongly influenced by Klein's observations of the phantasy life of babies and children, alongside his own work with children and adults, Winnicott formulated his own theory of regression (Abram, 2007a, pp. 275–294). Essentially, he saw that the analytic treatment offered a reliable setting that would "facilitate" the patient's "regression to dependence" "as a way of re-living the not-yet-experienced trauma that had occurred at the time of an early environmental failure" (Abram, 2007a, p. 275). Applied to the clinical example above, we can see that the "environmental failure" was hypothesised as the mother's madness, understood as such through Winnicott's countertransference (that he felt mad). Thus, in the here-and-now of the transference situation, the patient could experience himself to be sane in a mad environment because it had come into consciousness in the context of the analytic relationship.

The clinical example, however, raises more questions than answers in relation to the different perspectives on unconscious phantasy and regression. The questions for all analytic clinicians who work with all categories of patients concern the issue of assessing what is coming from inside and what is coming from outside. Also, how do the two coincide and merge? And how can the analyst and patient distinguish between early environmental deficiency (failure) and deep innate unconscious phantasies? What phantasies are innate and what are created? What theories help the analyst understand these questions so that she or he can help the patient in the way Winnicott seems to have done with the above example? Some of these points are addressed in the Dialogue for this section.

Summary

TABLE 3 The role of the external object

	Klein	Winnicott
Infant's relation to the environment	Aware of the object from the start	Merged with the object from the start and unintegrated
Early distortion	Either idealised as good, or demonised as bad (paranoid-schizoid position)	Infant's illusion of omnipotence if needs adapted to by a good-enough m/other
		Unthinkable anxieties/primitive agonies if holding environment is deficient
Influence of the actual object	(a) Development of the inner world of the infant	(a) Gradual awareness of Me and Not Me (reality)
	(b) Onset of the ambivalence of the depressive position	(b) Process of reaching a sense of self (if facilitated)
		(c) Traumatised and break of continuity-of-being if environment not good enough
Effect of appropriate care by the actual object	Internalisation of a good object and an optimistic outlook	Omnipotence of illusion has to be followed by gradual disillusion (reality principle)
		Transition from merger to sense of self leading to symbolic thinking
Neglect by the actual object	A persecuting internal world dominated by a harsh superego and other objects	Unthinkable anxieties leading to psychopathological defences, depending on which age the environment is deficient (see chapter 8)

Dialogue

R. D. HINSHELWOOD: This part of the book is about another great difference of opinion – the nature of the external world – although again we may get more caught up in a difference of opinion about what Klein thought. There is a myth that Klein ignored the external object or, as Winnicott would say, the environment. But the situation is a little complex. It is true that Klein tried to see things always from the infant's point of view, and in the early days of life, the infant does not get a clear perception of the surrounding world and the others in it. In that sense, if we emphasise her own emphasis on the infant's viewpoint, then it is not always an accurate perception of the environment. At first, the infant will have a very distorted perception; not exactly solipsistic, but definitely determined by his own state of mind – and body. From the beginning, the other object is a person with intentions and experiences of its own. Those personified forms are very, very primitive, being basically the object's wish to feed the baby and to support the baby's life, or alternatively the opposite – the wish for the baby to suffer and even fragment in a terrifying annihilation.

The poles are extreme, with nothing much in between. Either the "mother", or whoever, is totally good and well intentioned towards the baby, or it is absolute evil, and wishes only harm. This engagement in the external world, or environment, is called the paranoid-schizoid position. It is, on the whole, unrealistic but is felt as a world of animate beings. Interestingly many psychoanalysts tend to believe that the baby only sees things, inanimate entities, and the sense of a living, feeling other has to be won. Indeed, this is true of many psychologists too. But Klein pictured the infant's world as an animate personalised one, and whatever the link between the body and the mind, the baby's mind relates to some supposed entity as another mind, which, of course, is not distinct from it relating bodily to another body. The capacity to treat others as things, as non-personal entities, is something that supervenes in later life.

Of course, this primitive construction of the environment does not, as mentioned in chapter 5, last very long. The reality begins to dawn on the baby, Klein would say, in the first half year of life. But it does so in a particular way, and with a crucifying experience of painful anxiety. The baby with its propensity for a double reaction – towards a life-giving other, or an evil destroyer – finds they may be one and the same person! This is a crisis, as it demands a complex set of experiences and a mediation of opposite forms of behaviour towards the environmental other. If you scream blue murder at the very person who wishes to keep you alive, what will happen? That is the crucial question long before a baby is really able to grasp the question properly or to resolve it. This kind of potential catastrophe is called the depressive position.

I have taken the opportunity to go over this sequence of events in order to clarify something about the myth of the Kleinian neglect of the actual environment. What was it that brought that myth into being, and what has made it stick against the reality of what Klein wrote and thought, and of subsequent Kleinians? It is a mystery, and maybe, Jan, you can clarify how such a misunderstanding can have such a persistent life. But first, there are two more points about this relationship with the external other, the mother, the maternal environment, or whatever we call it.

The infant's ability to cope with what I call the catastrophe of reality breaking in on the paranoid-schizoid position is so slim, and the infant so vulnerable to disaster to its life-support system, that its survival rests entirely on the ability of the environment to go on nurturing through this. In so far as the struggle to cope with the depressive-position catastrophe is a lifelong one, the individual is always dependent on his or her environment (in adulthood, it is not just the parents, of course). I know this is different from Winnicott's view of the environment as more simply protecting the infant from too much frustration. It is much more in relation perhaps, too, to Winnicott's late interest in the survival of the object, which you emphasise in your thinking – is it, Jan?

It is essential that the mother or caregiver should not be destroyed by the infant treating her/him as the evil one. Mothers are usually quite resilient, and they have a support system, if they are fortunate, with their own mother and a husband and a cohort of mothers with similar-aged children. But nevertheless, all mothers will succumb at times, and need respite, and they may at times persecute the baby in return. The mother's survival through the onset of reality (the depressive position) is crucial and is a key component of the good environment that will nourish mentally as well as psychologically. It is worth just adding here that it is the onset that is hardest, and between them, baby and carer begin to make headway in coping with the depressive anxiety. Since the catastrophe is felt to be a concrete narrative (perhaps by both) that mother will not survive, the external object – the care-giving other, reality – can also come to the rescue. If mother goes on being able to be maternal, then the reality for the baby is that mother can in fact see the baby through it. As I have said, resolving the depressive position is a lifelong task, but progress does lead to changes and the problem resolves. At first the baby expects its hatred of the evil one to be returned by the environmental other in as violent and deadly a form as the baby has hated. It is mutual persecution. The refusal of the care giver to actually engage in a return of hostilities allows a slow but steady mutation of the anxiety. At first the anxiety is a fear of annihilation, but because the infant feels it has wronged the good mother by treating it as the evil mother, there is the beginning of a feeling of injustice and guilt. We can say that, at first, the persecuting fear is a form of guilt that demands punishment – an eye-for-an-eye kind of punishment. The change that slowly takes place is an amelioration of the guilt to a less punitive form, one that demands restitution or atonement, something called "reparation".

I said I was going to discuss two more points, so now to the second. This is again complex, and it may be necessary to take up details in Part IV of the book. The scene of this narrative has been the environment with the care-giving mother or other. However, it is not only that. There is a sense in which the narrative is played out on a second stage. We have both emphasised the psyche–soma equivalence: body and mind are felt as one. Since the wellspring for these narratives are the bodily sensations – for example, hunger, being fed, being frustrated, and so on – the second stage is the sense of these narratives being played out between self and objects actually inside the body. The sensations from the tummy are felt as a narrative of a good mother or a bad mother inside causing these sensations. There is a constant interchange between the two arenas, internal and external, and in Klein's view this builds up the sense of identity – the sense of having substance and life and, indeed, relationships inside. They may be very remotely unconscious, but not entirely. Most of us do quite consciously talk in our minds to important others. Of course, that is usually at a rational or at least sophisticated level, but for Klein it was a distant echo of much more primitive narratives played out at deep layers of the unconscious mind.

Well that's enough, I think, for the moment. Please give us a Winnicottian take on this development process I have tried to convey, and where it may need more elaboration.

JAN ABRAM: Winnicott did not disagree with Klein about the depressive position, and, as I wrote in chapter 2, he states that Klein's depressive position was equivalent to Freud's Oedipus complex in terms of advancing psychoanalysis. But he did not agree with the name and so renamed it the stage of concern, and his re-vision of Klein's work outlines parallel features to the ones you've identified above (Winnicott, 1963).

So there are many similarities, but also specific differences. One of the main similarities is that Winnicott identifies that for the infant there are two mothers at the very beginning – the environment mother and the object mother. The environment mother is taken for granted; she is the mother of the quiet times. The object mother is the mother of the excited times. At a certain time, the baby has to bring these two mothers together, and he starts to see that the mother of the excited times is the same mother of the quiet times.

Now the difference is that, for Winnicott, as long as the baby has been held and has experienced the illusion of omnipotence, there is no evil mother – because Winnicott did not agree with the innate hateful and persecuting object. However, an evil persecutor may well exist for the infant who had not been held. But this would be entirely the responsibility of the environment if the baby were to feel this. Moreover, there are truly pathologically cruel mothers who do feel and act sadistically towards their infants. This fact complicates internal processes. But I think there are profound differences.

The object mother in Winnicott's theory is different from the quiet mother and makes the infant feel excited and agitated, which probably relates to the mother's varying states of mind. The subjective coming together of the two mothers – environment and object – was the major task for the infant as he was reaching the stage of concern. Subsequently, the baby starts to feel a sense of responsibility towards the mother he appreciates as well as the mother he may blame or reject or feel excited or agitated by. Winnicott was trying to add nuance to the infant's experience because he felt it was not a simple matter of good or bad. In fact, the Kleinian terminology was what he was rejecting when he came up with the term "good-enough" mother. His focus, different from Klein, was that there was a real mother who was either good enough (not perfect) or not good enough. The "enough" stressed that all women are human beings and fail but that there is a difference between a failure with a small "f" and a Failure with a capital "F".

In response to your point about the "myth" that Klein ignored the environment – I am unsure from your description of how the infant moved from the paranoid-schizoid position to the depressive position. How does Klein theorise this development? You have said above that it depends on the environment, but where in Klein's work does she write about that? I have the impression that it wasn't until Bion that Kleinian theory started to acknowledge the role of the environment for the infant's development with his introduction of the container-contained in "A Theory of Thinking" (Bion, 1962b).

So I'm not at all sure it is a myth that Klein ignored the environment. If there is no theory that depicts the environment, then it would follow that she would be perceived to be ignoring its role.

RDH: I think we may have covered some of this in the previous discussion. But you touch on two main areas of interest. About the great myth: I am interested in how tenacious it is. As you know, Klein wrote on weaning (in 1936), for instance, and I rather think she became disheartened by the lack of interest that others were displaying in her view on the reality principle and made little effort to counteract the gathering myth that Bowlby (1940) and Winnicott (1945a) and others seemed to create. In any case, after her paper on the depressive position published in 1935, the British Psychoanalytical Society was much more interested in trying to sort out Klein's concept of the "internal object". It puzzled them a great deal, and, for ten years, more British papers were published in the *International Journal of Psychoanalysis* on the internal object than on any other topic (Hinshelwood, 1994). Nevertheless, it is fundamental for Klein that at around 4 to 5 months of age, there is an increased accuracy of perception (perhaps it is a biological development of the senses), and reality becomes increasingly present. That is the depressive position – as you say there is a realisation in both Winnicott's and Klein's babies of the reality of the object (mother or other), and partial perceptions have to be put together: Klein's "good" and "bad" mothers, Winnicott's "environment" and "object" mothers. Really, Klein's conception of this work of the depressive position is her version of the reality principle. And the focus on the internal world that was provoked by her 1935 paper on the depressive position was really about the ways in which the internal world of objects and relations matched, or did not match, the external world of objects and relations.

It is the distorting effect of the internal world which is the focus of primary importance – that is, it is just as much a study of the distortions of the external world as an observer might see (and the subject might come to see as time goes on). As you know, Ernest Jones concluded his Exchange Lecture in Vienna in 1935 in a slightly chiding vein:

> I think the Viennese would reproach us with estimating the early phantasy life too highly at the expense of external reality. And we should answer that there is no danger of any analyst neglecting external reality, whereas it is always possible for them to underestimate Freud's doctrine of the importance of psychical reality. [Jones, 1935, p. 273]

It was a comment that could also be directed at the reproach Winnicott and his followers make of Klein. The issue we are debating, I think, is the interaction of the internal world, coming from the inherent "factory settings" of the newborn infant, as it has to reset itself slowly to the true realities. Maybe this is a mythical construction, as all our debates about these early experiences have some element of myth about them, don't they? But, it may also be mythical that the infant actually can realistically tell if mother's "neglect" is accidental (she just hasn't got the bottle warmed up enough yet), or if it is neglect with a capital N because she's just bloody-mindedly making him wait for bit. I'm quite sure the baby will sense something different in the two cases, but what sort of differences does the baby have available to think with at the earliest stages?

The second area I want to ask about, the really interesting thing, which I hope you'll explain more, is the differentiation between an "environment mother" and an "object mother". On their own, they don't give the nuancing of the baby's experiencing, as you suggest they do – can you elaborate what Winnicott sees the baby experiencing in each case?

JA: I'd like to respond to your two main points, Bob. You reference Klein's 1936 paper "Weaning", and it was a pleasure to return to this paper while preparing my response for this section. The paper is a clear example of how Klein does indeed bring the environment into play, and I can see what you mean about her wish to address the way in which the infant moves from the pleasure principle to the reality principle. I wonder if you realised, when you cited the paper, that in fact it is in that paper that Klein footnotes her gratitude to Winnicott "for many illuminating details on this subject". It comes after a significant paragraph she writes on the importance of the mother's care when introducing the nipple to the infant at the earliest moments of life. She says that the "good contact between mother and child may be jeopardized at the first or at the first few feeds" if this situation is not handled with sensitivity (Klein, 1936, p. 297). And Winnicott writes about these early moments also in several places throughout his writings.

My sense is that the myths remain "tenacious", as you say, due to the way in which theories have become polarised. In addition, although it is true that Klein acknowledges the nature of the object in assisting the weaning process, there are also many references to the baby's internal phantasies from birth, and perhaps this emphasis in her work rather detracts from her comments on the role of the real external object. The Kleinian development after she died does lay such a powerful stress on the internal world, which must be another factor contributing to this "tenacious myth".

Following on from that point, it seems that Klein and Winnicott (as well as you and I) do come together again on seeing that (to quote you above) "the depressive position was really about the ways in which the internal world of objects and relations matched, or did not match, the external world of objects and relations." And your Ernest Jones' quote is helpful too, because it highlights the difficulties between the Viennese (classical Freudians) and the British analysts many of whom were following Klein's innovations on object relations. So it is interesting to see how we may just be agreeing on the points you have made above, as you have answered my previous question about where Klein writes about the environment. However, let us now examine how this theory is translated into technique.

Although we can now agree that Melanie Klein did take account of the external object/environment in relation to the infant's development, in many of her writings, I think it important to see how this was applied to the clinical situation. For example, let us compare Klein's clinical example with Winnicott's as cited in our respective chapters in this section. In Klein's example, she highlights the importance of interpreting the patient's anxiety as a manifestation (due to his associations) of his envy and grievance towards his analyst in the transference. The patient's response was to agree that she might be right but that "nothing was worth bothering about". Klein's next interpretation showed the patient that he was afraid of losing his analyst because of his destructivity. Then Klein asserts that her "interpretation of these processes had the effect of again altering the patient's mood. He became emotional, said he felt like crying, was depressed, but felt more integrated . . .". The "processes" she was analysing, I assume, are those related to the paranoid-schizoid position. This seems to me to be a classic example of Kleinian technique, and I can see how it may be helpful for some patients depending on how the analytic work has evolved. But if this technique is applied too soon in an analysis, particularly with narcissistic/borderline patients, it may either make them compliant (as we might say this patient did after the initial interpretation), or it may wound them to such an extent they would leave the analysis possibly traumatised and confused. I wonder if this may be what Bowlby and Winnicott were referring to when they criticized Klein – they were actually criticizing her technique, which did rather focus, at least in this example, on the internal world only. What do you think, Bob?

Now, if we compare Winnicott's clinical example, we see how his interpretations implicated the environment/analyst for the madness the patient was feeling in the session when Winnicott interpreted that he heard a girl talking about penis envy (despite the fact that there was a middle-aged male patient on his couch). We also see clearly how Winnicott was finely attuned to his countertransference in making this interpretation, whereas Klein was more focused on the patient's internal anxieties related to his envy and grievance.

The notion of regression can be mentioned here because Winnicott's example also illustrates how his patient had regressed to an early stage of infancy and how his analyst (Winnicott) seemed to have felt this in the countertransference. Klein (who rejected the notion of the countertransference), on the other hand, was attending to early psychic processes which could be seen to bypass the object's responsibility for the patient's anxiety at the beginning of the session. Thus, Klein's clinical example illuminates her focus on the patient's internal world.

I will now say a bit more about the difference between the "environment mother" and the "object mother" in Winnicott's formulations concerning the stage of concern. Winnicott was trying to get away from the polarisation of good and bad. As I wrote above, the environment mother is related to the whole atmosphere of the family (parents, siblings) that the infant is born into. The mother's capacity to be in a state of primary maternal preoccupation aids her psychic attunement to the baby's emotional states. The object mother comes into focus during the excited times – which may not necessarily be bad or persecuting. The bringing together of these two aspects of mother are the result of maturational processes being facilitated by the mother who endures (survives) the infant's instinctual impulses – that is, the phase pre-ruth when the infant is "ruthless" (Abram, 2007a, p. 104).

RDH: Just quickly about the interpretation by Klein being purely "internal": it may be we see internal and external in different ways. It seems to me that the interpretation was exactly about the patient's relationship with a rich and creative external object. He relates to that object. Now, that is his reaction to her – it is internal in that sense, but that ignores the fact that he is relating to a real external object. There is the other side of the relating which is important: it is an external object with its own rich internal world.

In fact, to borrow a phrase from Winnicott, Klein's interpretation described an internal–external "set-up". But then, it may be we speak different ideas with the same words.

PART **IV**

THE PSYCHOANALYTIC CONCEPT OF PSYCHIC PAIN

Chapters 7 and 8 examine the different developments on the notion of psychic pain as a concept. There is an examination of how the theories impact on psychoanalytic technique.

CHAPTER SEVEN

Melanie Klein and internal anxiety

R. D. Hinshelwood

Key concepts   Concern; persecutory anxiety; splitting; destructiveness; mental breakdown

---

I think it is true for both Winnicott and Klein that they approached their work and the anxiety their patients were suffering, or the point of urgency as Strachey (1934) called it, by confronting it with reality . For Winnicott, it seems it was more to do with capturing and stabilising an existential sense of "self".

Observing children's anxieties

At the beginning of her work, when she merely made observations of her own and other children, Klein was interested in the pain of learning. For instance:

> For Fritz, when he was *writing*, the lines meant roads and the letters ride on motor-bicycles – on the pen – upon them. For instance, "I" and "e" ride together on a motor-bicycle that

is usually driven by the "I" and they love one another with a tenderness quite unknown in the real world. Because they always ride with one another they became so alike that there is hardly any difference between them, for the beginning and the end . . . of "I" and "e" are the same, only in the middle the "I" has a little stroke and the "e" has a little hole. [Klein, 1923, p. 64]

As she commented, "They [the letters] represent the penis, and their path coitus" p. 64). These unconscious connections to serious matters of relationships and development create a very inhibiting impact on curiosity and learning. At that time, she was using the psychoanalytic theory of the Oedipus complex to show how it had to be managed as best the little child could, in the learning situation.

However, as her work became more systematically psychoanalytic in the 1920s when she tackled the treatment of disturbed children, she was impressed with their aggression and with a fear of doing harm to the loved parents because of hatred when seeing them together. Klein described at that time a particular figure that she thought the children tried to indicate to her, and which she named the "combined parent figure". It was a term to represent the child's tortured experience of seeing, or imagining, the parents in oral or genital intercourse together. The parents' intercourse was seen as occurring with a cruelty, the degree of which corresponded to the rage the child felt about the excluding intercourse. In turn, the child's pain was commensurate with its fear (guilt) that it had caused such aggression to, and between, the parents.

Klein, watching children play out their crises of anxiety (and the inhibitions that followed), thought she was shown how anxious they became in specific relational situations. In particular, they were frightened that the crises could spiral dangerously towards being out of control. She therefore thought that it was the children who emphasised destructiveness as the source of anxiety. It was an anxiety because it was their loved ones they had to protect from their own destructiveness.

Anxieties in the depressive and paranoid-schizoid positions

However, in the course of her later work and thinking, her conception of psychic pain moved to a different register, and I think this coincided with Winnicott's closer association with her in the 1930s and 1940s. We have seen that she began to consider deeper levels than these oedipal neurotic ones. From at least 1934 onwards she started to consider that these were deeper levels and involved specific mechanisms of defence; at first she called them "early repression mechanisms" (Hinshelwood, 2006). But by 1946 this had evolved into an understanding of the specific "schizoid processes" – that is, the splitting up of the ego or self, as opposed to repression. Splitting works as a defence by "annihilating", as Klein said, the ego-function that produces the intolerable experience, and it is different, therefore, from relegating the experience itself to the unconscious.

At this time too, she had understood that the core of psychic pain had become the degree of disintegration of the ego. However painful the oedipal conflicts, the fragmentation and loss of the sense of self overshadowed the Oedipus complex. You cannot even have an Oedipus complex until you have an ego that is functioning well enough (and is integrated enough) to recognise the conflict.

A loss of self is an existential terror, for which I believe Winnicott used the term "the loss of the sense of the continuity of being" – a very apt phrase. However, how they each came to think this existential disaster came about was quite different. Here I restrict myself to Klein, and point back to the brief example in chapter 5. In the vignette, the troubled man was confronted with the hate and envy he felt towards his analyst. He could only cope, even temporarily, by completely divesting himself of the capacity to feel anything of importance at all. His mind went blank, and he felt nothing mattered. He had, in a real sense, lost vital aspects of his self, or ego.

For Klein, psychic pain is phantasy, inside the self, in so-called internal reality. It has two forms. First, the pain of anguish about the state of the loved parents – or, we might say, the capacity for concern, which I think Winnicott strongly agreed with. Second, the fear for one's self, one's own identity. Winnicott too followed Klein here, but he radically disagreed with the processes and mechanisms, which established, and sustained, the sense of self (as discussed in Part III). These painful anxieties exist in the infant's mind in terms of the narratives that he composes, and tells himself, unconsciously.

These concerns, in the depressive position, take the form of the phantasy that love may not be strong enough to protect the loved ones. This amounts to the infant's anxious phantasy that his destructiveness prevails and overwhelms the loved ones (the good objects). The end result is the redoubled effort to protect and, in fact, restore them (she called this reparation). Frequently, this psychic pain of the depressive position is evaded by a particular category of defences called the manic defences. These defences work by distorting the object-relations so that those important ones that the child fears to lose are dealt with by denigration – that is to say, the child gets into a state of mind where he denies their importance and says to himself, "They are no loss to me, I don't need them!" This entails an illusion of great omnipotence.

The other painful anxiety, which she called persecutory anxiety, is when the self feels in danger of some threat. The fear is for the self, that the subject will not survive. In terms of the unconscious phantasies, the self feels a lack of capacity to live adequately, to pursue a life, because it seems to have more bad objects inside than can be coped with by the good ones. The sense of self is deeply formed from the sense of this balance – or imbalance – within. The pallor and weakness of life is indeed felt like that, as an inner lack of living substance and energy, and an impoverished inner world. That danger and impoverishment may, even in adults, be felt as physical symptoms of pain or disease in body or limbs. The unconscious experience then connects the threat to specific diseases inside; notoriously, cancer is consciously made to represent the internal threat.

One of these mechanisms, projective identification, is indeed, very important in impairing or destroying the sense of self. The phantasy Klein articulated entailed the evacuation of parts of the self. This added to Abraham's (1924) previous discoveries about introjection and projection, which he described as omnipotent phantasies by which the ego moves its good and bad objects in and out. Klein's addition was that the ego could move parts of itself in and out in the same way. Identity is then formed or distorted by this process. Parts of the self are seen as someone else. When two people bump their cars, it is always the other driver who must feel the guilt. This is a simple example of how, even in ordinary life, projective identification can be used in a situation of fear and stress. This configuration represents the paranoid-schizoid position and exemplifies how, throughout life, the ego may slip between one or other of the two positions.

Projective identification typically shows how these early mechanisms against the persecutory anxiety of the paranoid-schizoid position must rely on splitting of the ego. In the example of the two car drivers, the function of the ego to feel guilty is lost and aroused in the other – or that is the attempt. The term "projective identification", however, has been taken by many analysts of various other schools of thought (though not Winnicott) and imported into quite different conceptual contexts.

When processes that are intended to protect against the fear of annihilation depend on splitting, the initial anxiety about fragmentation may then be enhanced. This can become a cyclical process, which in later life forms the essence of a freewheeling impetus towards a mental breakdown. In this condition, the disintegration is increasingly seen as threats from outside (due to projection) when in fact much of the problem is the self-destructive, ego-splitting aspects of the mechanisms employed by the ego. Of course, this is strongly determined by an environment that does supply unfriendly and persecuting or abusing carers. The Kleinian position would be that onslaughts on the integrity of the ego by carers may have various effects. That is to say, we must grasp why some people are especially vulnerable to an inclement environment, while others are much more robustly resilient. Those more prone to schizoid mechanisms will be the ones less resilient to environmental neglect.

The ailments of the ego manifest as the anxiety of one or other position. Phantasy problems with body and mind are not difficult to develop, given the vivid imaginations of human beings. And people can spend a good deal of time and energy – and money – on remedies to bodily ailments that are based sometimes on quite obviously phantastical conceptions of our bodily functions. These forms of conception of the ways our bodies work, together with the more scientifically realistic theories of orthodox medicine, can be imbued and saturated with the significances and meanings that percolate from the unconscious and its roots in inner reality.

Primary destructiveness?

Klein's concern, ever since her earliest work in developing a play technique with children, was the intense anxiety and stress that human beings have over the balance between love and hate. And it is when a settled balance is disturbed that forms the primary source of psychic pain, according to Klein. Often this is taken as a commitment to a primary "instinct" of aggression. There is no doubt that aggression is readily felt in relation to frustration. A baby screams, we say, "blue murder" when hungry. But this is intuitively not remarkable. In fact, it is intuitively understandable that a baby should be full of bliss and love when it is satisfactorily fed. There is no reason why we should object to either of these reactions – the love emanating after satiation, and the hate from frustration. Both are innate and bodily in origin – and present in the newborn from the beginning. The fact that certain objects or certain occurrences bring out a blistering hatred is no more remarkable than the fact that some objects and some occurrences bring out the most passionate and tender love. It is not really possible to object, in my view, to Klein's understanding of the death instinct – but . . . instinct is not necessarily the full energetic concept of instincts, which Freud had proposed.

* * *

As I described in chapter 1, Klein focused on the psychic pain of children, rather than on instinctual drives and energy. This has led to an ever-increasing attempt to refine the detailed understanding of anxiety and its various forms of expression:

- » The pain of the Oedipus complex pervades all aspects of life, including thought and learning.
- » This view of the oedipal couple could, Klein thought, take many forms, including a terrifying, monstrous sort of hybrid "combined parent figure".
- » Klein then saw that psychic pain was more than an oedipal conflict but was fundamentally the conflict between love and hate.
- » It emerged, too, that it was not just the pain of the contents of mind, but a terror that the structure of the mind itself was in jeopardy and could undergo serious impoverishment and disintegration.
- » Moving to the pain of the depressive position, there is a powerful avoidance by denial of the importance of the important objects – a defensive strategy known as the manic defences.
- » Another extremely common method of evasion is to attribute all mental (as well as physical) pain to bodily causes.
- » In all forms, Klein traced psychic pain to the balance of love against hate, and the difficulty of establishing a stable equilibrium.

CHAPTER EIGHT

Donald Winnicott's concept of aggression

Jan Abram

KEY CONCEPTS   Use of an object; survival of the object; stage of concern; fear of breakdown; communication; dependence; mirror-role of mother; creativity; playing; unthinkable anxieties; primitive agony; antisocial tendency

---

The notion of psychic pain in Winnicott's work is related to the timing of the environmental failures at each stage of development. In 1962 Winnicott set out six stages of dependency to illustrate the effect of environmental failure at specific developmental phases to show what kind of mental health problem would be caused by failure:

(a) *Extreme dependence.* Here conditions must be good enough, otherwise the infant cannot start the development that is born with him.
Environmental failure: Mental defect non-organic; childhood schizophrenia; liability to mental-hospital disorder at a later date.
(b) *Dependence.* Here conditions that fail do in fact traumatize, but there is already a person there to be traumatized.

Environmental failure: Liability to affective disorders; antisocial tendency.
(c) *Dependence–independence mixtures.* Here the child is making experiments in independence, but needs to be able to re-experience dependence.
Environmental failure: Pathological dependence.
(d) *Independence–dependence.* This is the same, but with the accent on independence.
Environmental failure: Defiance; outbreaks of violence.
(e) *Independence.* Implying an internalized environment: an ability on the part of the child to look after himself or herself.
Environmental failure: Not necessarily harmful.
(f) *Social sense.* Here it is implied that the individual can identify with adults and with a social group, or with society, without too great a loss of personal impulse and originality, and without too much loss of the destructive and aggressive impulses that have, presumably, found satisfactory expression in displaced forms.
Environmental failure: Partly the responsibility of the individual, himself or herself a parent, or a parent-figure in society.

[Winnicott, 1962c, pp. 66–67]

This list illustrates, once more, the extent to which Winnicott saw how responsible the environment was for certain forms of mental illness. The "failure" would mean that the infant has been psychically traumatised. The earlier the failure, the more catastrophic for the mental health of the baby. Therefore, "psychic trauma", which constitutes psychic pain, relates more to parental failure (as we saw in the two different early patterns of relating discussed in chapter 4).

In his last decade, Winnicott's final major theoretical achievement, I have suggested (see chapter 2), was his concept of the use of an object (1969a). Elsewhere I have proposed that this is his final theory of aggression (Abram, 2012a). As has been made clear, Winnicott, like many Freudians, did not agree with Freud's theory of the death instinct. Melanie Klein's development of the death instinct concludes with a different concept from that of Freud's, which can be confusing for the student of psychoanalysis (see Glossary). Winnicott, in my view, offers a very different rendering of how the individual deals with his or her innate aggression. To begin with, as already stated, Winnicott considered that it was the life instinct that was driven by a benign aggression – that is, a life force or energy, we could say.

So, for Winnicott, the way in which the infant experiences his forceful movements towards the object (the foetus's involuntary kicks in the womb, for example) will have an effect on the foetus's subjective states of its body-self contingent on how mother responds to the kicks. Did she respond as if the foetus was intentionally setting out to hurt her? Or did she respond by understanding that the developing foetus/infant was unable – yet – to know what he was doing when kicking?

This area of Winnicott's work – how the infant's innate aggressive impulses developed in the growing personality – was resolved, he said, when he wrote "The Use of an Object" (see Abram, 2012a p. 308). He theorized a sequence of object relating for the newborn infant in order to illustrate what role the environment had to play so that the baby could be facilitated to move from object relating to the use of an object, which was the "momentous developmental step" equivalent to resolving the Oedipus complex (Freud) and reaching the depressive position (Klein). The main point in his paper is the issue of "destruction" and "survival". He writes:

> After subject relates to object comes subject destroys object (as it becomes external); and then may come "object survives destruction by the subject" . . . A new feature thus arrives in the theory of object relating. The subject says to the object: "I destroyed you", and the object is there to receive the communication. From now on the subject says; "Hullo object!" "I destroyed you". "I love you". "You have value for me because of your survival of my destruction of you". "While I am loving you I am all the time destroying you in (unconscious) *fantasy*. Here fantasy begins for the individual. The subject can now *use* the object that has survived. [Winnicott, 1969a, p. 713]

As we have seen since chapter 2, it is the quality of the psychic environment that is essential for the baby to develop. This does not mean that the baby has nothing to bring to the table (so to speak). Inherited tendencies and biological drives – that is, innate self-preservative instincts (as first suggested by Freud) – activate the baby and have a huge impact on the m/other, who will respond to her infant's raw emotions in an infinite variety of ways. So, for Winnicott, the infant's psychic pain is caused by a failing environment that will be internalized by the infant, as opposed to psychic pain being caused by anxieties that are the result of the innate death instinct (or destructive drive) in the Kleinian infant.

This makes the concept the "use of an object", I have argued, a theory of aggression, and Winnicott emphasises and demonstrates that it is object relating that structures the core of self rather than the Freudian instincts.

In his very late work, Winnicott tries to show that while he acknowledges the importance of libidinal and aggressive drives in psychoanalytic theory, what he wants to illuminate is that from his extensive clinical experience and "careful research" he has evidence to show that "there is phase prior to that which makes sense of the concept of fusion" (1969b/2013, p. 293). The first drive is (potentially) "destructive", he says, in that it can be equated to fire. Through "survival of the object", the infant is able to move from object relating to object use. "Survival" essentially means that the object does not retaliate (Winnicott, 1969a, p. 714) (see Glossary).

Summary

TABLE 4 **Psychic pain**

	Klein	*Winnicott*
Oedipus complex obstructs development	In her earliest work	In line with the Freudian Oedipus complex – that it occurs later – but extended because it is a stage of development and therefore not a given
Psychic pain arises from love being threatened by hate of the loved object	The depressive position	The stage of concern achieved when environment mother and object mother are seen as one and the same person
The structure of the mind itself is in jeopardy	Pain is from the loss of mind	Psychic pain is rooted in deficiencies of the early psychic environment – premature loss of the other that cannot be processed
Avoidance of depressive anxiety through omnipotent denial of the importance of the important objects (manic defence)	Omnipotence is secondary	Illusion of omnipotence is not a given and will only occur through mother's devoted attention. Lack of early devotion could lead to a defensive omnipotence
Relation to the body	Experienced as a narrative of internal objects	Integrated psyche-in-dwelling-in-the-soma comes about from holding, handling, and object presenting by a good-enough real mother. Deficiency of good-enough beginnings leads to body–mind dissociation

Dialogue

R. D. HINSHELWOOD: Well, starting off again with what comes immediately to mind as I read your chapter, there are two main things. The first I want to deal with is the sense of responsibility as it is played out between infant and environment; the second is the question of what is innate. But it occurs to me that both are caught up in an issue, which is not always clarified, about whose point of view are we looking from, and whether we are being consistent about it.

Well, there is in Winnicott, it seems, a strong claim, all through the six points of dependence–independence you quote, that the environment is what counts. It is true that there is a real and near total dependence of a baby on the caring other. And mothers feel that – with some ambivalence. It burdens mothers as well as giving a sense of immense purpose to life. I hesitate to define a mother's experience and should say that this is my understanding (based on being the father of four children). The point that occurs to me is that responsibility may not be so simply assigned. There is a responsibility of the environment, when the baby is born, but as I understand it Winnicott, unlike Klein, claims that the baby's experience at first is that of omnipotently achieving everything, and thus the responsibility is totally his when the breast comes: the baby feels it has created it. This is a matter of "points of view". The question of who feels responsible will be answered differently by different players.

More than this, from an objective point of view, the baby is in fact partly responsible for this creation of its feed at the breast. Usually the baby cries to establish that it needs a feed. Then mother's responsibility comes in, and she takes responsibility to feed the baby (or fail, if she is an irresponsible mother). From the mother's point of view, there is a negotiated sequence of steps in an actual sharing of the responsibility. Then, from the point of view of Winnicott's objectivity, the neutral position of the observer, the mother is responsible for responding or not responding, and the baby's responsibility in telling mother when to feed appears to be discounted. I'm not sure if it matters so much if there are wide differences in the separate points of view, but it probably does matter that descriptions should all be from one point of view, and should not move around without it being stated why the point of view needs to change.

Of course, a Winnicottian arguing for the total dependence of stage one might claim that the baby is not really responsible for crying in order to stimulate mother's awareness and her prolactin. It is just an automatic reflex when he is hungry. Here is the problem of innateness. It may be that the baby feels responsible for crying, and indeed that is what Winnicott described – the baby feels omnipotently powerful, causing everything. It seems intuitively likely that, despite so much of the baby's behaviour and actions being reflex, the baby still has an experience of doing it for himself. This capacity to feel a sense of agency so early may not be a valid theory, but since our two protagonists we are comparing would both agree on the baby's sense of responsibility, this is not a point for dispute between them. It does, however, leave Winnicott with the need to sharpen up the account of the perspectives he is using: when he refers to the baby's perspective (omnipotent and responsible for everything), or when to the objective observer (total dependence, with mother responsible).

I don't know if this clarifies the unclarity. In a nutshell, the question is that Winnicott is claiming that the first phase is (a) total dependence and (b) the baby's perception of omnipotence. There needs to be some order about when we use (a) and when we use (b). To be explicit, the first phase of dependence–independence is seen as total dependence by the observer, but when we move to the second phase, it seems the point of view changes; now it is the baby's point of view that is important – the struggle to accept a degree of dependence, as the baby would see it. Have I got this wrong?

Moving now to Klein, for whom, like Winnicott, the baby is responsible because from the baby's point of view he feels he is. For Klein, however, the responsibility a baby feels is of a different kind from the omnipotent one. The baby feels he has an agency that is directed to preserve its own life, and this is manifest in hunger, feeding, and all the usual things he gets from his "good" mother. Moreover, he feels responsible for dealing with the intruding hatred from bad objects that causes his discomforts, and he must challenge and disarm those bad objects as best he can. So, the baby, for Klein is the agent responsible, and frankly there seems a consistency in sticking to a specific point of view.

I suppose my concern here is not just in the difference in the concepts each party uses, but in the way the concepts are actually used. Am I possibly off track? I'm sure you will put me back on track again.

Now, since we are talking here about perspective in relation to psychic pain, I want to make a point through asking, whose pain? For Klein, patients – and especially the difficult patients – create a situation in which both parties suffer. In the 1940s and 1950s, the time when Winnicott was defining his views in relation to Klein's, she was concerned about the countertransference as felt by the psychoanalyst with patients with schizophrenic conditions. She said in an intervention at an IPA Conference:

> To turn now to the schizophrenic patients, the fear of his hostility in some cases where he is actually dangerous is no doubt an influence on the counter-transference of the analyst, even where precautions are taken. With schizophrenic patients who are not dangerous, but who direct their silent, non-co-operative and deeply hostile attitude towards the analyst, his counter-transference is inclined to be a negative one. [in Hinshelwood, 2008, p. 111]

She continued with an important point about these patients who take desperate measures, including projective identification, to use the analyst's personality itself in order to cope with their suffering:

> [They] stir in the analyst very strong counter-transference feelings of a negative kind. He may get tired, he may wish to go to sleep, he feels assailed by the patient intruding into him and may fight against this intrusion. In my view, this fact, more than any other, is the reason why, in such situations, analysts have always been inclined to alter the situation by reassuring the patient, by trying to bring about a positive transference, by not touching on the deepest anxieties of the patient, etc. [in Hinshelwood, 2008, p. 111]

But also, I'm sure you are aware of the paper, in 1956, by Roger Money-Kyrle, about a case – not psychotic at all – where a man who suffered with a harsh superego left the analyst feeling useless and criticised at the end of the session:

> A neurotic patient, in whom paranoid and schizoid mechanisms were prominent, arrived for a session in considerable anxiety because he had not been able to work in his office. . . . [He] soon began to reject them all [my interpretations] with a mounting degree of anger; and, at the same time, abused me for not helping. By the end of the session he was no longer depersonalized, but very angry and contemptuous instead. It was I who felt useless and bemused. [Money-Kyrle, 1956, pp. 362–363]

Klein had developed an awareness of how the suffering of the patient is something both have to handle – preferably together, though it is tempting for both to leave it to the other.

Klein's approach technically to the suffering of psychic pain presented this important argument that the analyst is in emotional contact deeply with his patient. This view undermines the classical view of the analyst, who unperturbed maintains a neutral stance like Freud's surgeon, "who puts aside all his feelings, even his human sympathy, and concentrates his mental forces on the single aim of performing the operation as skilfully as possible" (Freud, 1912e, p, 115). Much better known in this respect is Klein's one-time follower, Paula Heimann, who in 1950 argued convincingly for the countertransference as an important means for understanding the transference. Klein was not too happy about Heimann's ideas, as she thought, "that such extension [of the use of countertransference] would open the door to claims by analysts that their own deficiencies were caused by their patients" (Spillius, 1992, p. 61). She said this in a recorded interview with a number of students in 1958, where she also ironically commented, "I have never found that countertransference has helped me to understand my patient better. If I may put it like this, I have found that it helped me to understand myself better" (quoted in Spillius, 2007, p. 78). In fairness, Heimann did concur with that concern about the misuse of countertransference in a subsequent paper, in 1960.

This debate about how psychic pain is shared out between the two participants is important and has been the focus of significant technical developments in the clinical practice of psychoanalysis right up to the present. These developments subsequent to Klein (after her death in 1960) are not the direct interest of this book, but it is worth noting that such developments start with Klein. She was clearly reticent about publishing her views very widely, or outside her own group, and perhaps that was to do with a growing divergence of opinion with Heimann. These developments in understanding the interpersonal vicissitudes of psychic pain she left to others, from Money-Kyrle's 1956 paper onwards.

JAN ABRAM: The first thing that strikes me when I read your response to my chapter 8 is that I feel I have not made my points clearly enough. So I re-read my chapter and then thought to myself that I did make my points as clear as I possibly could! This led me to think that what I perceive to be your misunderstanding of what I wrote (which I will come to soon) may relate to something that many critics of Klein, including Winnicott, have said about her work on the infant: that too much development is imbued in the newborn infant. I think this is where we may be having difficulty in understanding each other, because it seems to me that in following Klein's theories you also imbue the infant with more sophistication than Winnicott sees. This relates to your first two points about the relationship between "responsibility" and "innateness". The other point you make is about the theories that relate to the distinction between subject and observer. I will try to say more about these three points in response to your comments.

You rightly say that "the environment is what counts" in Winnicott's theory. That is precisely what I have been trying to convey since chapter 2 and I believe is precisely what Winnicott was theorizing up until his very last piece of work. You follow this by saying that you understand that the environment (mother/parents) takes appropriate responsibility for the infant because of the baby's intense dependency (as I cite Winnicott in chapter 8). By the way, I don't think that this is necessarily a "burden" to the mother. Rather, I think this term would refer to a mother who is not psychically ready for the birth of her infant. Of course, there would be days and periods of time, depending on the infant and the vagaries of living, when the new mother may feel burdened because the responsibility is so intense to begin with, but as long as she has good support it may be that the feeling of "burden" is not experienced. In other words, I don't think it "normal" that the mother would feel burdened or indeed that she is, de facto, "ambivalent".

You then say that you understand Winnicott to say that "the baby's experience at first is that of omnipotently achieving everything, and thus the responsibility is totally his". I think this is a misunderstanding of what (I am trying to convey) Winnicott says. There is a difference between feeling that you "get what you need when you need it" and feeling responsible. The feeling of being God is an illusion (of omnipotence), remember. And this is distinct from "delusion". I think what Winnicott is getting at is that the mother's ability to "adapt to the infant's needs" facilitates the infant feeling that he is God, and it is precisely that feeling, Winnicott says, that is at the root of imagination, the ability to play, and also the sense of trust that the infant can make a contribution on an interpersonal level.

Let me say something about the meaning of certain terms in the context of the language of psychoanalysis. Winnicott uses the term "omnipotent" to denote a feeling of power in the infant – not for power's sake: there is no awareness at this stage of even remotely wishing to be powerful. Perhaps a better term or a term that may qualify the meaning would be "agency": that the baby has a sense of his own agency when he gets what he needs. This feeling will initiate and lead on to a sense of trust that he is able to get what he needs from the outside world (environment).

The confusion perhaps comes about because in Kleinian terminology the term "omnipotence" is, as I understand it, always related to psychopathology and usually refers to a defensive position in which the patient becomes "omnipotent" as a defence against feeling small and dependent (see Glossary).

In Winnicott's matrix, the reason the baby cannot "feel responsible" is because he has not yet developed a capacity for concern – and once again I want to emphasise, "yet". Therefore, "feeling responsible" comes later in development for the Winnicottian infant. The stage of concern occurs during the stage of relative dependency (from 4 to 6 months, which correlates with Klein's depressive position) when the baby is developing a capacity to control urges as he really does start to develop a sense of guilt (Abram, 2007a, pp. 101–113).

When you move to Klein and confirm that she believes that the infant "feels responsible" for "the intruding hatred from bad objects", I have the impression, from your previous chapters and my reading of Klein, that good and bad objects are innate – not biologically, as you have emphasised, but psychically. And Winnicott would argue that "good" and "bad" are just not yet integrated into the newborn infant's emotional vocabulary.

Turning to the issue of what is innate and what is not innate, Winnicott does refer to "inherited tendencies" in each infant, and he endorses the notion of the life instinct as a "drive". Later, he refers to "primary creativity", which I have interpreted as his way of elaborating on Freud's life instinct. It adds the psychic dimension, and in that sense all psychopathology, for Winnicott, is to be seen as a result of a failing environment – as we can see in the list of the six stages of dependency at the start of chapter 8.

When Winnicott refers to the facilitating environment, he means that the innate, creative drive has to be facilitated to grow. He even offers the analogy of a bulb that requires certain conditions to develop, grow, and flower. It's a simple metaphor, but it demonstrates that without the right conditions (primary maternal preoccupation, for example), the potential in the bulb (newborn) cannot grow and/or will be distorted (psychopathology). I have the impression that in Klein's theory this does not have the same emphasis as in Winnicott's theory.

Let me now address the issue of perspective. You emphasise that Klein is always seeing things from the infant's perspective and you argue for consistency in this regard. I have found this helpful because I wonder whether this is why Klein's work may seem confusing at times because of her use of language and particular focus. For example, the use of the term "evil" suggests that she believes in "evil". But perhaps your point is that she is saying it is the baby who believes in the "evil object" – rather than the "evil object" actually existing. Have I got that right? The issue of the existence of innate "evil" is very suggestive of the death instinct, which is always associated with negative emotions in Kleinian and post-Kleinian theory, is it not? I should add here that I do appreciate now that, for Klein, the "death instinct" was not actually a drive in the sense of Freud's economic theory, and this is something I feel I have learnt through the course of our work on this book. However, as I said above, it does seem that Klein seems to be saying that the baby is born with the good and bad objects already in place – that is, innate.

I would like to say one more word about perspective. I find it helpful when Winnicott alternates from the observer's perspective to the infant's or patient's, because it aids understanding from both perspectives, which seems of paramount importance when working in the analysing situation. For example, when Winnicott says that the antisocial tendency is a sign of hope, he shows how this tendency irritates and makes the environment want to punish the individual who commits the antisocial act. But then, when he illustrates how it is motivated by inner deprivation and that the patient's acting out has an unconscious message – that is, that the analyst should recognise the patient's inner turmoil related to the past failure of the environment – the analyst is hopefully more able to reflect and think in the face of the antisocial act. An example in everyday analytic treatment is when the patient keeps forgetting to pay the fee! So it seems important to me that, as analysts, we are able to move from the observer's perspective – that the patient is behaving badly and provokes negative feelings in us – to appreciating the patient's inner drive to repeat a past trauma by forcing the environment to react. I think this relates to my final points related to your citations of both Melanie Klein and Roger Money-Kyrle. Again I found these citations clarify our different positions – you coming from the Klein frame of reference, and me from the Winnicott frame of reference.

The first two quotations of Melanie Klein, who writes about the analyst's negative countertransference feelings when working with schizophrenic patients, resonate deeply with my own clinical practice over the past thirty years. However, I would not say that I have experienced these feelings towards patients who were diagnosed as "schizophrenic". It is a term that needs some explicating, I think. Is Klein referring to patients where paranoid and schizoid mechanisms dominate – as Money-Kyrle described? Or were the patients she described psychiatrically diagnosed as schizophrenic?

My experience of these kinds of negative emotions have related to certain patients whom I would describe as "borderline". What I mean by that term is that in the analytic setting they show signs of functioning at quite a literal level and have not reached a capacity for concern and so struggle with discerning between Me and Not-me – despite having some ego functioning. These patients struggle with making use of the transference as an "illusion" and tend towards a "delusional transference". But I would agree with Melanie Klein that it is crucial not to try to "reassure" the patient, and in my clinical practice I have always attempted to get to the deepest anxieties the patient seems to be communicating often through their enactments and actualisations. In one particular case I have written about, I almost terminated the treatment because of the patient's violent acting out. In that paper, I try to show that when I was able to interpret the patient's deepest anxieties, after a period of not having survived his attacks, he was able to emerge out of a delusional transference and subsequently ordinary analytic work followed (Abram, 2007b).

Let me comment on the short quotation from Money-Kyrle. When I read this, I have to be honest and say that my heart sank. There is a sense that the analyst blames the patient. Moreover, there is also a sense that the analyst is blaming the patient for not accepting (or understanding) the analyst's interpretations. And here we are in the area of a long-held critique of Kleinian technique and approach to patients.

I think it is a common experience for analysts to feel that their patients are not accepting the good nurturing interpretations they offer because *de facto* the analyst is good. But, from my point of view, not just following Winnicott's approach but following on from my trainings in both psychoanalytic psychotherapy and psychoanalysis (and I believe similarly to many analysts from all schools), I take the view that if the patient leaves me feeling useless then he has succeeded in getting across how he or she (the patient) feels in the transference. Doesn't it say more about Money-Kyrle's countertransference to the patient's transference? And wouldn't this be a good example of *Nachträglichkeit* (or "deferred action", as Strachey translated the word)? For example, if Money-Kyrle were to follow up on this example by saying how he went on to make use of his countertransference to address the deep anxieties the patient must have been feeling to react so defensively, then he would be following what Klein advocates in the first two citations you selected. I happen to strongly believe that if a patient is angry with me and leaves me in that way, then I have not managed as their analyst to "analyse" what needs analysing. This is what I have named as a revivification of the non-surviving object, and all analyses have to go through something of this because it is naturally part and parcel of the transference (Abram, 2005).

One final point in reference to your last quotation from Klein. I think that all contemporary analysts, from all schools of thought, are trained to be in "deep emotional" contact with their patients. You state that the Freudian perspective implies that aiming to take a neutral position is equal to being "unperturbed". I understand that this is a quotation from Freud himself, but there is too much in the Freudian literature to disqualify your interpretation and I'm sure many classical and contemporary Freudians would be up in arms! The analyst's aim is to stay neutral (retaining an observing area of the mind) in the face of feeling (on occasions) intensely perturbed. That is the essential quality to develop as an analyst, and I think that infant observation, as a prelude to clinical work in British psychoanalytic trainings, is a crucial component in analytic training to develop our capacity to "observe" when feeling in turmoil. I imagine you agree with this.

It seems very important to cite what Klein says about not finding that the countertransference helps her to understand the patient better but, rather, helps her to understand herself better. At first glance this seems to contradict the first two quotations in which she refers to the negative countertransference instigated by schizophrenic patients. Could you clarify this? I had the impression that Money-Kyrle aimed to highlight the patient's problem for not accepting his good interpretations rather than seeing that the patient's reactions had something to do with Money-Kyrle's approach that made it impossible for him, Money-Kyrle, to attune himself to the patient's deepest anxieties and thereby make a comment that made the patient feel understood. Although I know that that is easier said than done, nevertheless the analyst has to keep trying to show the patient that she or he, the analyst, is attempting to understand the deepest layers, and I think this is the approach Winnicott not only advocated but also advanced.

RDH: I think a lot gets clarified by what you write, Jan, as well as the clarifying questions you open up. One of the difficulties in our dialoguing, fruitful though I believe it to be, is that it is so difficult to remove from one's mind that one of our protagonists is "right" and the other "wrong". So there may be a sort of reactiveness to each other's attempts to get things clear. I think we really have been trying to engage with each other's positions, rather than merely state a point of view which does not engage the other – a much easier project. So, having said that, I should like to go through just a few points where I have a sense that we may still have got each other's positions a bit wrong – not many, perhaps.

First, there is an issue about how sophisticated a baby is in its perceptions and actions. It is, of course, not possible to know the infant with sufficient certainty to decide this question, but I think we both have the view that babies probably do experience from birth; Winnicott would say a baby experiences an "illusion of omnipotence", and Klein that a baby experiences good and bad sensations to which it gives a meaning (in object-relations terms). These primary experiences are different conceptions in the adult minds of psychoanalysts. I am not sure if it is really possible to judge who is the most sophisticated. If a baby is "programmed", as it were, by its biology to feel satisfactions and dissatisfactions, this is not really sophisticated. What is, however, added in the Kleinian perspective is the capacity of the baby to "interpret" these sensations as coming from somewhere – somewhere other than itself. This is more sophisticated. But is it more sophisticated than attributing the power of self-satisfaction via the illusion of omnipotence?

I have been very influenced by experiences I have had over the last fifteen or so years, which clarify what I am trying to think out – can an innate biology be sophisticated? My wife began to keep horses, and we had a number of foals – six in fact. I stretched back in my memory to many years before, when learning obstetrics at medical school. What struck me was how the newborn foal was, from the beginning, starting a search. And within about forty to forty-five minutes it was sucking at the mare's nipples. This is not so easy for a foal, because in order to reach the nipple it has to be standing under the mother and using its four legs. Nor does the foal have the benefit of a dextrous mother who can manipulate the nipple and mouth to come together. The foal does it largely on its own – a process of finding the use of its legs, and straightening them to stand on, finding out how to balance on them, and then searching with its lips and nose for the right place to find the nipple (presumably with feel and smell, maybe sight), and then sucking. The foal even has some innate knowledge that the nipple will be in the angle under one of mother's legs, because sometimes it roots around under the wrong legs – at the front of the mare rather than the back. All this seemed to me quite a sophisticated accomplishment, invariably, as I say, in less than an hour after birth.

The point I want to make is that there must be an awful lot of biology in that primary accomplishment. For the human infant, there is a similar, though simpler, accomplishment, but there is still a biology that directs the suckling reflex to the nipple. My involvement with the birth of foals taught me that there is a lot of sophistication in the given biology – even in a species of mammal we might judge as a lot less sophisticated than humans. So, it is difficult to see how an argument on the basis of "too sophisticated" can work. The more telling argument would be to challenge whether the baby (foal) has an experience of doing these things in the moment that these biological reflexes are happening – but then I think we stand together in defending the view that the infant does experience from the beginning.

I think you may be right that the question of responsibility might better be put in terms of agency. The infant's ability to experience itself as chasing away a bad sensation (such as hunger, cold, etc.), and sucking-in (milk) as a good experience, would be seen as the experience of agency – and though I put it in terms of the phantasies the Kleinian sees, the sense of agency is not so different from the illusion of omnipotence that Winnicott sees.

Now, you make a distinction between biological innateness and psychic innateness. If I have it right, this is interesting. I had not thought of such a distinction. It is so foundational in Kleinian thinking that what is innate (say, instinctual) is also mentally represented – as unconscious phantasy. As you know, this is Susan Isaacs's (1948) central contribution. The biology and the mental representations are indivisible, at least at the beginning. And I am not sure how one might divide them. From a materialist perspective, which I think both Klein and Winnicott took, it would seem that psychic experiences are totally founded on some material, physiological processes – not that we have much idea about that foundational material–mental relationship. But then, of course, during development mental experiencing does seem to gain some sort of autonomy; there is some degree (though not complete) of emergence of mental activity from the strictures of physiological reflexes. These are deep questions and go beyond where I am able to follow; perhaps they do not matter too much for the practice of psychoanalysis.

Now, both frameworks accept that some moral quality enters into the psychological experiencing at some point – and at roughly the same point, from age 4 months or so on. Perhaps it does not need repeating that from a Kleinian point of view this occurs when perception has become accurate enough to realise that nothing is all good (Winnicott's iconic designation, "good enough"), and then there is a crisis over hating objects that are only partly bad, but also carry a lot of the good. And Klein thought that, in a complicated way, self-condemnation for this is represented internally as the relations with a bad object (a harsh superego) that seeks to hurt and harm. As you may know, in his 1942 book the embryologist C. H. Waddington was interested in how Klein's psychoanalysis (and Freud's) can allow the understanding of a "natural ethics" – that is, that ethics comes ultimately from nature, from biology, and not from religion. Waddington set some theologians and philosophers to argue with this. I don't think Winnicott could have followed Klein here, as he did not accept that the baby feeling pain could hate it – that is, hate the "it" that was the cause.

About perspective: I'm afraid I am not sure if I do yet understand how to manage an observational perspective of total dependence (your first of the six phases) and the infant's perspective of the experience of causing all things. Those two perspectives, the infant's and the observing psychoanalyst's, seem more or less irreconcilable. You question whether the term "omnipotence" implies pathology. Perhaps it does at stages when the reality principle is up and running, because then omnipotence is a chosen illusion. But, as you say, one can take two attitudes to such an illusion anachronistically occurring later in development: either we can call it diagnostically pathology or, alternatively, we can seek to understand what sort of struggle with the intolerable creates the need to sink into an illusionary state. I have a sense that Winnicott might not agree and would want to add a third alternative. It is true that we do all use illusions, all the time, and they are not pathological, nor are they absolutely realistic. When in 1929 René Magritte, the surrealist artist, painted a picture he called "The Treachery of Images", it was the image of a tobacco pipe under which he wrote *Ceci n'est pas une pipe* [this is not a pipe]. Indeed, it was not a pipe, but paint and canvas. This ambiguity in representations is, in fact, the basis of all culture and civilisation, which I believe Winnicott recognised in his paper "The Location of Cultural Experience" (1967a). And did he follow Segal's (1957) understanding of symbols?

Given the emphasis on the external world, perhaps it is more natural to speak of normality. After all, from a more internal perspective, "normal" means nothing, since to an infant who does not yet "know" the external world, "normal" is just everything that "is" (from the infant's point of view). Of course, this not to say that Kleinians do not have a sense of "normal", just that it may be less readily applied.

Your example of your reaction to the Money-Kyrle example may be a case in point. My reading of the words, which made your heart sink, was different from yours, Jan. I did not think that Money-Kyrle was actually claiming his interpretations were "good"; he only spoke in an ironic sense. I read his words as saying he was mistaken and that the patient needed to use the analyst's mistakes to communicate a sense of uselessness. The analyst failed, in his own terms, by not understanding the patient's need to communicate until after the session was over. It was, in the psychoanalytic jargon, an "unconscious-to-unconscious communication", and Money-Kyrle, as I read it, was rueful about his own failing. I am sorry I was not clear here. As you said, it would be important what Money-Kyrle communicated in the next session in his interpretation. In fact, he interpreted that the patient was reversing the situation he'd experienced with his lawyer father, and he had the analyst "on the mat". And, as Money-Kyrle stated, the patient's "response was striking":

For the first time in two days, he became quiet and thoughtful. He then said this explained why he had been so angry with me yesterday: he had felt that all my interpretations referred to my illness and not to his. [Money-Kyrle, 1956, p. 363]

Money-Kyrle concurred with the patient's assessment of the analyst's "illness". I hope this clarifies a little how the Kleinian analyst makes efforts to experience the roles assigned, by the patient – in this case, the analyst is ill with uselessness, and it is not entirely a false observation by the patient. Would I be mistaken if I thought that, for Winnicott, it is the analyst who assigns the roles, by "being" the mother who allows the illusion of omnipotence?

I strongly agree with you that we do have to be so very careful with our language, as both sets of analysts have evolved their words and terms, and without much thought of how to translate them to each other. Hence our efforts here. I suspect we are not doing this perfectly, but hopefully it is a start.

JA: I agree it's helpful to be challenged on elaborating concepts so that one can work further on clarifications. I acknowledge how easy it is to feel that one is being perfectly clear and that it's the other person's problem if they don't get it!

You have brought up several points, and I will respond to those that I feel require a further word from me.

Yes – it is a danger to slip into arguing for what is right and what is wrong in the developments of both Winnicott and Klein. This is one of the major pitfalls that we're trying to avoid. However, we ought to feel free to be honest when we do actually think one or the other is wrong. I think it's striking, for example, that Winnicott found Klein's way of describing pathological states of mind – that is, the paranoid-schizoid position – helpful when working with a patient where these processes dominate. And I must say I find that too in my clinical work where one can witness such clear examples of Klein's vivid descriptions of these processes. Nevertheless, Winnicott considered it absolutely wrong to apply these processes to the newborn infant. By the way, I think he must have been influenced by Edward Glover who, among other criticisms of Klein, said exactly that (Glover, 1945).

Winnicott could not agree that Klein's paranoid-schizoid position is a universal phenomenon felt and experienced by the newborn and that the "screaming blue murder", as you put it, demonstrates massive anxiety and helplessness. In addition, I cannot accept the infant's demonstration of those kinds of raw feelings as a clear sign that the baby thinks the "evil object" is about to kill him. I would say, rather, that it is a clear sign that the infant is upset because of the sensory experiences he is having and that he is not yet equipped to deal with them. This is where the infant is absolutely dependent on mother to mediate, as it were, by translating what it is he needs at that moment. Edward Glover, and Elizabeth Zetzel a little later, both referred to Klein's theory of "evil" as equivalent to the religious belief in "original sin" (Glover, 1945; Zetzel, 1956). Winnicott and many others followed this view.

A different perspective tends to indicate that one side considers the other wrong, and clearly Klein did not agree with several points that Winnicott made, and he did not agree with her on some specific points either. I don't really have a problem with you agreeing or disagreeing with my perspective. What would be unacceptable is if either of us were to dismiss each other simply on those grounds. And unfortunately that is what occurred during the Controversial Discussions and beyond. For example, although I find the Glover and Zetzel papers helpful in their critiques of Klein's theories, I had a visceral reaction to the angry tone in both papers.

How sophisticated is the human infant?

Yes – I think we can agree that, for both Klein and Winnicott, the baby is active from the beginning. And I also think Winnicott would agree that the baby starts to "interpret" how he is being held and fed and changed and so on. In fact, I think that the "illusion of omnipotence" constitutes the infant's "interpretations" of mother's ordinary devotion. But, an important difference in Winnicott's theory from Klein's is that the infant is not straight away able to differentiate between what is happening in his body (say hunger) and what happens externally (mother offering the breast). Winnicott said that instincts "can be as much external as can a clap of thunder or a hit" (Winnicott, 1960, p. 141). This means that at the beginning the newborn is not equipped to differentiate between a pain inside the stomach or an external noise. It is only through the mother's psychic and bodily care that gradually the baby is able to distinguish between inside and outside.

I'd like to add a word also about the "illusion of omnipotence", because it is not a given in Winnicott's theory. It will only occur if the mother is good enough. The "failure" of the environment at the beginning means that the infant will not have experienced illusion, which will consequently impair his ability for authentic interpersonal relationships for the rest of his life. This is where psychoanalysis as a treatment comes in, because it offers an opportunity for the patient to address these psychic deficiencies.

Let me also add a word about the use of illusion and delusion. Illusion is not psychotic, whereas delusion is. The analyst depends on illusion to work in the transference, whereas a delusional transference is very difficult and even dangerous because the patient really is feeling that the analyst is the object he or she may be projecting. This is why assessment for a psychoanalytic treatment is so crucial. So, illusion in Winnicott's language refers to the third area of the mind that we all depend on to "live creatively" (Winnicott, 1970).

I think this is another important difference between Klein and Winnicott in terms of creativity. For Winnicott, creativity was not only about reparation, as it seems to be in Kleinian theory. This is what I have understood from the work of Segal, who stresses that the roots of the creative drive are reparative (Segal, 1957). In his late work, Winnicott referred to "primary creativity", which I have proposed relates to a "primary psychic creativity" and an elaboration of the Freudian life instinct. This is also different from the Freudian view of sublimation, which stresses repression. For Winnicott, this drive is psychically innate and, in that sense, relates to the way in which the baby "interprets" the world from the beginning (Abram, 2007a, p. 114). It is important, though, to see that Winnicott does make a distinction between "creative living" and the "creative act". A successful artist therefore may not be "living creatively".

Biology and mammals

I suppose your example about the foal's innate biological, instinctual knowledge highlights something about "equine nature" that might be transposed to human nature. Winnicott was rather dismissive of Bowlby's work on attachment theory because of his reference to mammals to illustrate human nature. While I agree that the infant must be "hard wired", as you term it, it seems to me that psychoanalysis is more interested in the psychic function – the "imaginative elaboration" of bodily functions, as Winnicott (1988) termed it. However, I think this is different from saying that the baby can differentiate between inside and outside at the beginning. It might be so, but from clinical experience of working with psychotic patients (as Winnicott wrote about), who regress to infantile states of mind in which their environment was indeed deficient, the analyst is able to assess that it is most unlikely that the newborn infant is already equipped to differentiate, despite the fact that he must be experiencing on a sensory level.

The sense of agency, we seem to agree, is something that the infant feels quite early on. But I would have to add that this would be contingent on the good-enough environment, otherwise the infant will be impaired from having a sense of agency. If I think of some analysands in analysis who go through phases of paranoia, I would say they have no sense of agency, which I think may be one of the reasons they feel so acutely paranoid. So again, this references how Winnicott delineates between a healthy beginning and a beginning that is simply not good enough and leads to psychopathology.

Biological and psychic innateness

Winnicott referred to the "psyche-indwelling-in-the-soma" and "psychosomatic collusion", which describes the integration of mind and body through a process of what he termed "personalisation" that occurs as a result of the mother's "handling" of her infant during the holding phase (Abram, 2007a, p. 263). It seems to me that this rather infers that Winnicott went along with the Kleinian perspective of unconscious phantasy from the start of life. Again though, as I have just stated, it would depend on the mother as to whether the infant's psyche became integrated with the soma or not. A deficiency of good-enough "holding and handling" at the beginning would lead to a mind–body split and a state of depersonalisation, Winnicott proposed.

Yes, Winnicott does acknowledge and appreciated Klein's theory of the depressive position, as I have stated above, but in his late work he revised the elements and stressed the "development of the capacity for concern" that emphasised the infant's development. In terms of morality, Winnicott did write a paper on this topic, "Morals and Education" (1963c), and argued that it was pointless teaching a child morality unless the child had already reached a "capacity" for a sense of morality emanating from the success of the early parent–infant relationship. The thesis in that 1963 paper may well link with Waddington's argument related to "natural ethics".

Illusion and imagination

When you mention that illusions are not pathological and then give an example of Magritte's *"Ceci n'est pas une pipe"*, it is precisely what I think Winnicott is getting at. I referred in chapter 6 to the "theoretical first feed" that relates to the early initiation of the infant's development of imagination. Without illusion there would be no art, no theatre, no creativity, no literature, and, moreover, there would be no psychoanalysis. We depend on our patient's capacity to play in the illusion of the transference during everyday psychoanalytic sessions, even if this capacity is tenuous for many borderline and psychotic patients.

I am glad you elaborated on Money-Kyrle's paper, but perhaps it goes to show how careful we all have to be when explaining a particular way of working. There would be more to gain from discussing this example, but perhaps it's beyond the scope of this Dialogue.

RDH: It is hard not to have the last word – and perhaps I am not trying hard enough! But I'll say one short thing. In relation to your last point, it is interesting that you say it took a while to realise that the reference to "evil" is baby talk. And that you read it as Klein herself attributing evil to the baby/patient. It does convey that there is a really witch-like view of an improbably persecuting Klein. It's very strange how she (or any analyst) can be constructed as such a mythical bad object – it almost makes one believe in the paranoid-schizoid position! Let's get down to writing our Appendix on our mythologies about each other.

JA: Let me clarify further, Bob, because I did not mean that I thought Klein herself was an evil witch! But – and I don't think I'm alone in this view – her writings, along with those of many Kleinians, do convey a belief that the baby is born with innate evil due to the "innate death instinct". It comes across as rather literal. For example, as I mentioned above, the papers by Edward Glover and Elizabeth Zetzel do rather portray Klein's developments in this vein. But, as I said, their tone is angry, and I can see how Melanie Klein the woman must have felt hurt as well as misunderstood. I think it very likely that Winnicott, in his early days as a newly qualified analyst, would have heard these arguments and later I'm sure he would have read the papers.

From what you have said, I think I have now learnt that this "innate evil" is an aspect of the innate unconscious phantasy that includes the two unconscious narratives of good and bad – that is, the dynamics that go to make up the paranoid-schizoid position. And that this is a universal phenomenon with each and every baby. The depressive position, subsequently, represents a hard-won battle to perceive that there is no such thing as evil (or absolute good or bad, presumably), but, rather, a human being who struggles with internal good and bad objects in order to discern the other person – the external object – as a human being who can never be totally good or bad. Am I beginning to get this right now?

RDH: Ok, let me just add one more thing (or two)! I think the point about judging who is evil and who is good is the polarisation of primitive paranoid-schizoid functioning. We all do it, of course, all through life – when we read tabloid newspaper headlines we are invited to involve ourselves in an outrage over something. When our nation goes to war, or we "hate" extremism, we are so invited, and frequently accept the invitation, to think in good–bad polarities. So I think there is openness on your part to see that Kleinians view us as born into this "primitive" functioning, and we have the lifelong job of growing out of it. So, if a Winnicottian wants to see Klein as an old hag, assaulting innocent young children with interpretations of their destructive badness, it is tempting to do so; and if Kleinians want to see Winnicott as slapping Klein callously in the face when she was down, it can be tempting.

Having said this, there is a point about perspective. The Kleinian view attempts (not always successfully) to stand alongside the patient's perspective, which includes his or her experience of evil. However, none of us is averse to lapsing into such a good–bad perspective, just as patients may be as good as us in rising above that level when necessary. It is just that in a clinical session, a patient has a license to relinquish the effort, whereas the analyst does not have such a license (what we do with each other is another matter!).

And to round off another point, about illusion and delusion. Yes, I agree with your distinction, but then I think you conclude that Kleinians regard symbolism as driven by reparation, and you make reference to Segal. The exact train of thought is not clear. But what you attribute to Klein is not exactly what she thought. As always, Winnicottians need to be careful what they attribute to Klein. You are not wholly accurate when you say, "For Winnicott, creativity was not only about reparation, as it seems to be in Kleinian theory". Nor was it for Klein only about reparation. And until Segal came along with a more sophisticated view, Klein thought that symbolisation was a simple matter of displacement.

I do understand your comment, as I remember discussing this with Hanna Segal, when she picked me up for saying what you did. The ability to use toys for expression has a lot more to it than reparation. Though the creation of literature or a work of art may be reparation, and may be a narrative about reparation, the use of symbols is a creative form of expression in its own right. And various Kleinians have searched in Keats and Coleridge and others for an understanding of the creative process.

I would have thought that this mixture must apply to Winnicott as well. It must be not only his ideas on symbols as illusions, but also his idea of the stage of concern that must have creative, or at least caring, elements as well. Your attribution to Klein is a little too restrictive. There is a certain irony that people congratulate Winnicott for his stress on "playing", while hardly noticing that it was Klein who developed the "play technique", recognising the creative expressiveness of play comparable to an adult's use of speech. Would such Winnicottians claim that using words "was only about reparation" do you think?

JA: As I wrote in chapter 2, Winnicott was impressed and clearly influenced by Klein's technique with children concerning the small toys. But his theory of playing evolved in his late work – the third phase I referred to in chapter 2 – and emphasises the "process" of communicating and the "search for a sense of self" which Winnicott says can only occur in relation to the other. You seem to be saying that Klein's theory of creativity (followed by Hannah Segal) is also not only about "reparation", and it would be helpful to understand more about that dimension in Kleinian theory.

When Winnicott referred to "primary creativity" and "formlessness," during the third phase of his work, alongside his thought on the concept of playing, I think he was developing some conceptual ideas that related to the patient's need to contact states of "being" within the analytic relationship in which primary creativity could potentially have a chance to breathe and grow – probably for the first time in the patient's life. I think this is different from the concept of reparation in Kleinian theory, which emanates from a sense of guilt. Primary creativity and the capacity to play emanate from the capacity "to be", which is a space in which there is no sense of guilt. It may well be associated with Freud's "oceanic feeling" (1930a, p. 64), which is probably at the root of Winnicott's concepts of illusion related to the early merger of mother and infant.

RDH: You seem to be asking for clarification on a "non-reparative form" of creativity. I don't think Klein (or Segal) were so interested in the kind of model building that Winnicott was doing here. So I can't be definitive. But thinking about it now, it does seem that representing the inner world in verbal, visual, or other forms is a capacity enjoyed by human beings from an early age; perhaps it is primary. But unconscious phantasy in represented form – whether children's play, a novel, an academic treatise like ours, an innings at cricket, or whatever – seems a natural activity in human beings. I suppose it is about illusion: the meeting of a representation with the thing represented has inspired linguistics since de Saussure (1916) wrote on the signifier and signified and invented the discipline of semiotics.

The relevant point is that the act of playing, from childhood onwards, is creative because it results in representations with which to connect with others.

Actually, semiotics has had little influence in psychoanalysis, and what influence it has was sequestered into the Lacanian version of psychoanalysis. Instead, in a Kleinian development, the interest has been in the intercourse of the parental couple and its product – on the one hand, hatred and envy, and on the other, new children. Whatever is creative in the ordinary sense depends on the unconscious phantasy of intercourse between the internal parents. It is a product of objects relating (internal and/or external objects), as one might expect from an object-relations theory. Creativity is then so often the acting out of this unconscious phantasy, but at the same time the content of the acting is the same unconscious phantasy. But this gets us into serious complexity. So I'll stop there.

PART V

PRACTICE AND THEORY

In the final part of this book, we concentrate in chapters 9 and 10 on the issues around working in the clinical session, as we sum up some of the important questions we have attempted to address throughout. Both Klein and Winnicott were dedicated practitioners of psychoanalysis and gained their ideas directly from thinking about the material they were confronted with in the clinical encounter.

CHAPTER NINE

Whose reality? Whose experience?

R. D. Hinshelwood

KEY CONCEPTS   Transference; reality principle; point of maximum anxiety; response to interpretation; priority of patient's experiences

---

Klein's technical approach came from the early days of psychoanalysis, and not so long after Freud's attempt to formalise his method in his Papers on Technique, around 1913–1914. She accepted the need for a setting that maximised free expression, with interpretation of what is expressed but not consciously known. In addition, she accepted that the person of the analyst is a player in the clinical process. Winnicott's own development was mostly twenty to thirty years later, when he was deeply immersed in the much more nuanced debates about the transference and, eventually, countertransference. His analyst, James Strachey, published his own landmark paper on the mutative interpretation in 1934, the year that Winnicott qualified as a psychoanalyst.

Certain theoretical assumptions followed on from the concept of the unconscious: these were transference, the inherent benefit of insight, and the dynamic anxiety-defence structure of the unconscious. As Robert Wallerstein (1988), when president of the IPA, argued, clinical theory is where we agree – it is metapsychology that divides us as psychoanalysts. But there may be significant differences in clinical practice between Klein and Winnicott, even if their theories are not too distant.

Klein, who had trained first and foremost as a clinical observer before being therapeutically engaged, emphasised certain things. First, she was interested in what seemed troubling to the people (actually children) she saw.

And then, when she conducted therapeutic analyses, she became interested in what actual impact interpretations had. It was very important to her that an interpretation felt right *to the patient*, rather than merely feeling right to the analyst. She was not the only analyst to be interested in the clinical process of immediate change and benefit. However, she was particularly interested in it, perhaps because her work was so dismissed by certain colleagues from the mid-1920s onwards. Consequently, her case reporting does demonstrate a considerable "evidence base" for her approach. The tradition of looking carefully at the small details (the microprocess) of the clinical material has remained a prominent dimension of Kleinian writing to the present day.

I shall say a little about each of two aspects of working with clinical material: the point of maximum anxiety, and clinical validation.

Anxiety

As indicated in Part I, Klein chose to explore the anxiety of her earliest patients, and, indeed, from her earliest observation work. She found that her child patients were open about their distress, and they could, using their set of toys, tell narrative stories about it. In chapter 1, we saw that this was an alternative approach to studying the probable course of energy flow through the psychic apparatus. However, it also set the approach as one focused on the experiences of the patient, rather than on the theories of the analyst. These narratives, played out with toys, demonstrated to others in the child's world the phantasies that emerged as immediately preoccupying in the moment. Though the child was not explicitly making communications to the therapist, it was as if play were a messaging system. The child seemed to be making manifest in the external world something vital of his or her inner thinking. Where we perhaps take it for granted that words used in adult psychoanalysis are communications between two people, the play of children expresses something more about the communicative processes between an inner world of "phantasy" and the outer world of symbols and reality.

Displacement from inside to outside in the immediate analytic session has, clearly, survived as the principles of "unconscious phantasy" and "here-and-now" interpretation, which have been so emphasised by Kleinians for many decades. That process of displacement into the external world, with the serious possibility of distorting it and misrepresenting it to oneself, is central to the Kleinian (and, indeed, Freudian) theory of transference; however, it may seriously clash with Winnicott, who, it seemed, started with the external world, the environment.

Where they come close, I guess, is in the issues that both consider are the important ones in practice. For Klein with her emphasis on the deeper layers, these displacements, in and out, comprise the basic processes for building and shaping the identity of the self, or ego. Winnicott too, but in a different way, places the emphasis on the development of a sense of self.

The big difference, however, which has pervaded all through this book, is a quite different focus. For Klein, the focus is on the point of maximum anxiety. Direct interpretation of the anxiety modifies it (Isaacs, 1939). Klein was less interested in the defences against the anxiety and more in the content of the anxiety which could be displayed as narratives in the play or, in adults, as phantasies in dreams and enactments. This approach was directly in line with Freud's view of insight, a view he derived from the earliest work with Breuer when Anna O's symptoms diminished or disappeared once her abreactions under hypnosis made it consciously clear what anxiety was behind the symptom (Freud, 1895d).

So, Klein's interest from the beginning was on the subject's (child's or adult's) experience. That experience was shaped always by her observations of children's play as narratives, and especially as narratives of their unconscious phantasies. It is her claim that she *discovered* that children were anxious about their aggression, the harm they could do to important figures, and the fear of aggression and harm to themselves from evil others. The insistence in the mythology of many non-Kleinians that Klein got her emphasis on aggression from Freud's theory of the death instinct is simply not true. She was not that much of a theoretician nor that much of a conformist. In fact, Klein did not employ the concept of the death instinct in her writing until her book in 1932, whereas she reported the disturbing phantasies of aggression in children in her first papers in 1919 (before Freud postulated the death instinct in 1920).

It was her discovery, not her allegiance to Freud, that put aggression centre stage in her views on human experience. She did not at first think that this in any way disputed Freud's oedipal theories, since murder is central; it is murder consequent on sexual rivalry and jealousy. Only later, especially with the influence of Abraham, did aggression became extremely important for understanding how the structure and constituents of the ego formed. Incidentally, Abraham, from whom Klein derived these later theories, never indicated any interest in, nor allegiance to, the death instinct.

It is a long path from her early observations of the point of maximum anxiety to the understanding of the paranoid-schizoid fear of being annihilated by some evil other, or by one's own self-destructiveness. But consistently, the uniting thread is the fear of aggression getting out of hand.

The question of validity

Klein felt so strongly criticised by Anna Freud's 1926 book that the *International Journal of Psychoanalysis* published a Symposium on Child Analysis in 1927, formed of contributions from six British psychoanalysts who largely agreed with Klein and attempted to rebut Anna Freud. So when Klein came to write her book (*The Psychoanalysis of Children*) in 1932, there are many exemplary vignettes showing her claim that significant changes occur after an interpretation and thus serve to confirm the correctness of the interpretation. I give one very striking example:

> ... Ruth, aged four and a quarter, ... was one of those children whose ambivalence shows itself in an over-strong fixation upon the mother and certain other women on the one hand, and a violent dislike of another set of women, usually strangers, on the other. Already at a very early age, for instance, she had not been able to get used to a new nursemaid; nor could she make friends at all easily with other children. She not only suffered from a great deal of undisguised anxiety which often led to anxiety-attacks and from various other neurotic symptoms, but was of a very timid disposition in general. In her first analytic session she absolutely refused to be left alone with me. I therefore decided to get her elder sister to sit in the room with her. [Klein, 1932, p. 26]

The sister (actually her stepsister) was some twenty years older than Ruth, and the idea was that the sister would enable Ruth to feel secure and enable a positive transference with the analyst, with the hope that she would then feel able to talk and play with the toys. Eventually the analyst could then continue on her own with Ruth.

> [B]ut all my attempts, such as simply playing with her, encouraging her to talk, etc., were in vain. . . . The sister herself told me that my efforts were hopeless. [p. 26]

Klein is describing here how the attempts at reassurance are not enough, and she was keen to show that interpretation achieves more:

> I therefore found myself forced to take other measures – measures which once more gave striking proof of the efficacy of interpretation in reducing the patient's anxiety and negative transference. One day while Ruth was once again devoting her attention exclusively to her sister, she drew a picture of a glass tumbler with some small round balls inside and a kind of lid on top. I asked her what the lid was for, but she would not answer me. On her sister repeating the question, she said it was "to prevent the balls from rolling out". Before this she had gone through her sister's bag and then shut it tightly "so that nothing should fall out of it". She had done the same with

the purse inside the bag so as to keep the coins safely shut up. Furthermore, the material she was now bringing me had been quite clear even in her previous hours. I now made a venture. I told Ruth that the balls in the tumbler, the bits of money in the purse and the contents of the bag all meant children in her Mummy's inside, and that she wanted to keep them safely shut up so as not to have any more brothers and sisters. The effect of my interpretation was astonishing. For the first time Ruth turned her attention to me and began to play in a different, less constrained, way. [pp. 26–27]

Klein emphasised in a footnote to this vignette that "[I]nterpretation has the effect of changing the character of the child's play and enabling the representation of its material to become clearer" (Klein, 1932, p. 54n). Two changes, taken together, indicate a correct interpretation. Klein was not scientifically trained, but she found a logical method for demonstrating the use of empirical data. As I imply, these were unusual circumstances – the direct challenge to her method and her set of findings. At the time, it was usual for psychoanalysts to be quite circumspect in debating each other's findings.

Even today, this method of supporting one's claims, by showing that an interpretation effects relevant change, is less used than might be expected (see Hinshelwood, 2013). Instead, correctness of an interpretation is claimed by making an appeal to what makes sense according to a theory that a psychoanalyst holds. And this, of course, convinces only those who happen to hold to the same theory as the analyst making the claim.

* * *

In this chapter, I have discussed two principles of Melanie Klein's approach to clinical practice. One is that her theories could be said to come from her patients and, in particular, that her emphasis on aggression is directed there by the patients' emphasis; the second is that there needs to be a method that can convince someone that a theory is correct, even though the person may not hold to that theory.

CHAPTER TEN

Holding and the mutative interpretation

Jan Abram

KEY CONCEPTS   Holding; interpretation; human nature; environment–individual set-up; transitional phenomena; the use of an object; survival of the object; primary creativity

---

As we have seen, Winnicott was fourteen years younger than Klein and started his work in psychoanalysis at a point when she was already in a senior position in the British Psychoanalytical Society. It is striking that Winnicott qualified as a psychoanalyst in the same year that his analyst, James Strachey, published his paper on the therapeutic action of psychoanalysis – 1934. This classic paper (referred to in Part I) on technique could be said to exemplify the way in which the majority of British-trained psychoanalysts work today regardless of what theoretical orientation they adhere to. Wallerstein's point, as cited by Hinshelwood in chapter 9, that analysts differ more on their metapsychology than in their practice resonates for me as a British analyst because I find that, in discussing clinical work with my colleagues from all schools of thought, we are often in agreement about our formulations concerning the patient's psychopathology. And analysts from the same school of thought, on occasions, disagree with each other about technique. While this is inevitably true, there are, nevertheless, significant differences in approach that emanate from each analyst's basic assumptions related to the paradigm from which he or she works. This means that most scientific papers can be identified as aligning to one of the three schools of thought, and how the analyst speaks to the patient – in tone and language – is often an indication of the analyst's theoretical orientation.

As we have seen from previous chapters, Melanie Klein found that interpretation of the patient's unconscious content made a huge impact on the patient's sense of relief from anxiety. It is generally true to say, following this clinical finding, that the majority of Kleinians privilege "interpretation" as a sine qua non for each analytic session. Analysts from the Contemporary Freudian and Independent school tend rather to focus on listening and assessing at which level the patient is communicating from. This should not be construed as meaning that interpretation is not important for non-Kleinians but, rather, that interventions must be paced and timed so that the patient will be able to make use of it. Thus, a tendency of approach can be identified in most presented clinical material. To interpret in the transference, however, is the common ground that all British-trained analysts share as that which distinguishes any given psychoanalytic treatment from psychotherapy.

My aim, in this final chapter, with its focus on analytic practice, is to highlight some of Winnicott's clinical innovations (Abram, 2012b). I have already commented on how Winnicott's work evolved in the rich and controversial discussions that were current during the 1930s onwards. And although he was quite clear that he was going to "settle down to clinical work" after 1945 (which implies that he did not want to get too involved with the political and scientific conflicts), he could not help but be engaged in reflecting and responding to the Kleinian development. He was passionate about psychoanalysis and very committed to the scientific life of the Society of which he was president on two occasions (see Chronology).

It is a mistake to think that Winnicott's work focuses on the environment. His primary focus, and indeed his most significant clinical innovation, is on the environment–individual set-up. As I try to make clear throughout this book, it was this concept that made the Freudian concept of primary narcissism a clinical concept. This is Winnicott's original clinical innovation (see chapter 2) – the inscription of the parent–infant relationship – and it advances the concept of the subject in psychoanalysis.

Like Freud, Winnicott was very influenced by Darwin and therefore understood psychoanalysis as a science – a human science. In 1945 he emphasised, by citing Darwin, that "living things could be studied scientifically, with the corollary that gaps in knowledge and understanding need not scare . . ." (Winnicott, 1945b, p. 7). And he maintained this position, as shown in his response to Ella Sharpe who described the psychoanalytic method as an art, when he wrote in a letter to her in 1946:

> I am not certain that I agree with you about psychoanalysis as an art . . . from my point of view I enjoy true psychoanalytic work more than other kinds, and the reason . . . is bound up with the fact that in psychoanalysis the art is less and the technique based on scientific considerations more. [in Rodman, 1987, p. 10]

Throughout Winnicott's writings, he stays loyal to the Freudian principles of psychoanalysis while at the same time amplifying and extending theory in relation to his clinical findings. This is the true definition of any scientist's work. Pearl King (1972) said of Winnicott that he was "firmly rooted in the spirit of the psychoanalytic tradition, rather than the letter of it . . ." (p. 28), and this meant he was at the cutting-edge of psychoanalytic discoveries. There is absolutely no doubt, as can be seen in this book, that he was deeply influenced by Klein's clinical work and her theories. I have previously stated how I think that his discourse with Klein sharpened his thinking and led to the clear divergences we witness in his final theoretical matrix.

The aims of psychoanalytic treatment

In his paper "The Aims of Psycho-Analytical Treatment (1962a), Winnicott outlines his approach to "standard analysis" and suggests that there are three phases. This is in line with classical

Freudian analysis. In the first phase of analysis, the analyst's "ego-support" helps to develop the patient's ego-strength. Then, adding to classical theory, Winnicott parallels this process with another one derived from his recognition about the earliest parent–infant relationship. This was based on his clinical findings and results in relating and relationship taking precedence over instinct theory in his formulations. He writes that the analyst has to be prepared to be the mother of the earliest phases of life as well as the mother and father of the later stages of development (in Abram, 2012b, p. 1464). This emphasis crucially includes the importance of the "holding" environment, and an interpretation will not be effective without analytic holding (I will come back to this point, and it is also be referred to in the subsequent Dialogue). In the second phase of treatment, the longest phase, he writes, "the patient's confidence in the analytic process brings about all kinds of experimenting . . . in terms of ego independence". And in the third and final phase the patient is able to "gather all things into the area of personal omnipotence, even including the genuine traumata" (Winnicott, 1962a, p. 168).

There are two points that I wish to examine concerning Winnicott's notion of "standard analysis". The first is that, for Winnicott, there is always an infant in the patient on the couch. This is why the analyst has to be prepared to be the mother of the earliest phases of life. Green referred to this phenomenon as the "clinical infant", as I discussed in the Part I Dialogue. Therefore, the analytic interpretation has to be offered when the patient is able to listen. This is explicated later through a clinical example.

Winnicott's increasing clarity about his theory of emotional development meant that he felt it was absolutely crucial that the analyst should not "interpret" before the patient was ready to hear the interpretation. Emerging out of his work with evacuees during the Second World War, he developed the notion of "holding". This is a term that signifies both the physical and psychic holding the infant needs. The analytic setting constitutes something akin to the early holding environment and replicates the mother's capacity to "hold the situation". The verbatim sessions in Winnicott's book *Holding and Interpretation* (1986) offer an insight into his clinical technique, which involves a sensitivity to the patient's need to be "held in time" as a preparation period before hearing the interpretation. An interpretation that came too soon and aiming to reach too deep could potentially preempt the patient's process and could be traumatic. In "The Use of an Object" from his late work, he writes:

> The analyst feels like interpreting, but this can spoil the process, and for the patient can seem like a kind of self-defence . . . [Winnicott, 1971d, p. 92]

Winnicott advocated that the analyst "wait" to see how the patient was responding to being in the analytic situation. This was founded on his conviction that it was the patient, and only the patient, who had the answers.

Perhaps it can be discerned that the subtext of his writings on technique alluded to his experience that analysts were tending to interpret too much and too soon as if it were the analyst who knew the patient's answers. At best this could lead to the patient's compliance, at worst to indoctrination. Winnicott's thoughts on psychoanalytic technique aimed, through free-floating attention, to facilitate the patient's process. Thus, the patient, "in the ripeness of time" starts to reach his or her own answers and in his or her own way. This is an area of difference in technique, because often Klein's writings indicate that the analyst knows more than the patient knows. But it is one of the major pitfalls in psychoanalytic practice for all psychoanalysts, because the patient often longs for the analyst to "know". Three years before he died, Winnicott wrote that he derived more pleasure in seeing patients find their own answers than he ever did by giving "clever interpretations" in his early practice.

Dependency and regression

Winnicott maintained that ". . . the dependent or deeply regressed patient can teach the analyst more about early infancy than can be learnt from direct observation of infants, and more than can be learned from contact with mothers who are involved with infants" (1960, p. 141). This endorses Freud's original argument that innovations in psychoanalysis can only evolve in the context of Freudian clinical methodology – that is, the analysand on the couch in high-frequency analysis. André Green argued that Winnicott's thought emerged from a close examination of his countertransference in the analytic situation rather than from his paediatric work (Green, 1975). And, following Freud and Green, I have argued that a clinical innovation can only have value as an authentic psychoanalytic advance if it emerges out of the transference–countertransference matrix of the analytic situation. This is probably a point that is also an aspect of the common ground between Klein and Winnicott – despite some of their different conclusions.

Ordinary formal regression inevitably occurs during the course of analysis and is a way of "re-living the not-yet-experienced trauma that happened at the time of an early environmental failure" (Abram, 2007a, p. 275). Thus the analytic setting provides the potential for the patient to experience a holding environment for the first time. In that sense, analytic treatment constitutes a method that offers the patient a place in which to grow emotionally in a way he or she was not facilitated to do in his or her early psychic life.

> The regressed patient is near to a reliving of dream and memory situations; an acting out of a dream may be the way the patient discovers what is urgent, and talking about what was acted out follows the action but cannot precede it. [Winnicott, 1955, p. 288]

Talking about what was acted out cannot precede it because the patient is not functioning at a symbolic level. Thus the analytic work may have to enlist "modifications" in analytic technique. This seems very parallel to the situation Melanie Klein was in with her small patient, Ruth (see chapter 9). She acknowledged that the little girl needed, at least temporarily, her elder sister to accompany her in the early sessions of the treatment. Thus Melanie Klein's adaptation to the child's need gradually paid off. This seems to me to correlate with Winnicott (1955) pointing out that a certain amount of "acting out" might be necessary to begin with and therefore has to be tolerated, as long as it is followed by "a putting into words of the new bit of understanding" in the post–acting-out period.

The belief in applying "modifications" to ordinary psychoanalytic technique led Winnicott to work quite differently with a small proportion of patients. For example, he held a patient's head when he believed she was going through the physical memory of being born (Winnicott, 1949). He also gave a patient an extended session (up to three hours) because he saw that she had never had the experience of "formlessness" in her early months of life, and the ordinary session time could not offer sufficient time for her to reach a state of mind like "formlessness" (Winnicott, 1971b). And for Winnicott, this three-hour session did indeed facilitate the patient, who seemed able to reach something in herself that felt truly authentic. These ways of working have been admired by some analysts but have been seen by others in a critical light. While Winnicott was clear that the "modifications" should only take place for a brief phase of the work, it seems to me that this way of working has to be based on a deep conviction in the analyst that this is what the patient needs.

There is no question that some of Winnicott's clinical examples are controversial. But it must be true to say that it is highly unlikely that there is an analyst who has not "modified" classical technique for some patients at certain times during the course of the treatment.

From all accounts it seems that Winnicott may have become too invested in feeling able to help some of his patients. Despite this, I have the strong impression from many people who knew him that his attempts were honest and were based on his deep belief in psychoanalysis as a treatment model due to the power of the transference.

Summary

TABLE 5 **Summary of key issues in psychoanalytic practice**

	Klein	Winnicott
Focus of fundamental problem	Anxiety	Parent–infant relationship
Disturbance/psychopathology	Balance of love over hate	Failure of early holding
Expression in analysis	Pre-symbolic narrative (toys and enactments)	Acting out/actualisations in the transference
Validation of method	Interpretation reduces resistance/inhibition	Holding and interpretation to facilitate patient's awareness
Mutative factor	Insight through interpretation	Experience of self-development through analyst's psychic survival
Timing	As patient's unconscious presents	Patient's ability to listen and receive through the mutative process

Dialogue

R. D. HINSHELWOOD: Yes, Jan, I do think you have the advantage of me here, as we have established that we will measure our two protagonists against each other in terms of their core principles. But they evolved those principles at different times: Klein between about 1924 to 1946, and Winnicott between 1945 and the late 1960s. These are different periods in the history of psychoanalysis, and many different preoccupations were struggled with in the 1950s and later that had not loomed into view in Klein's heyday. One of the issues (but only one) was the development of clinical technique, and particularly in relation to the immediate relationship of transference and countertransference in the session. After the difficulties that Jung and Ferenczi got into with their patients in the very early days, the problems of emotional intimacy in the psychoanalytic encounter were pushed away to a distance, at least in mainstream psychoanalysis. But during the 1940s, culminating in 1950, the issue of the analyst's personal intimacy, and what to do with it, began to come to the fore. Perhaps the paper by Alice and Michael Balint in 1939 was a pre-echo of this recognition of the real emotional being of the analyst as present – as other – in the session. And, of course, Winnicott's 1949 "Hate in the Countertransference" was a powerful part of that swing towards a revision of technique (Hinshelwood, 2016).

This revision did not affect Klein, and the paradigm shift in the view of countertransference which we associate with Winnicott and Paula Heimann left Klein behind. The Kleinian developments in technique were very much without Klein herself, even before she died in 1960. This hampers a comparison between Winnicott's clinical practice and a Kleinian one we would recognise today. Therefore, I have to step out of the role of spokesman just for Klein and indicate at least how she cast her light before her into the future others made.

It is clear that her clinical descriptions in 1946 of the schizoid mechanisms were foundational for others. That paper allowed attention to fall even more strongly on the relationship in the session, just as Balint, Winnicott, and Bowlby were emphasising the importance of the relationship with the "other". But Klein did not go with them. It was Rosenfeld, in 1947, who explored Klein's ideas in terms of the interaction of his psychotic patient Mildred with the analyst's own identity and self; and Segal, in 1950, who explored how Edward (her psychotic patient) collapsed his symbol-formation function through destroying the relation with the external world.

These manifestations of the disrupted reality principle of patients in psychotic states were a quite different avenue of approach to understanding the relationship with the external world. It must, I think, have prompted Winnicott to capture his own, and rather different, alternative understanding of the psychotic's existential anxiety, or loss of the continuity of being as Winnicott tended to put it; this is a very nice and evocative expression of the core anxiety in psychosis. As the idea of containing emerged out of the work the Kleinians did on psychosis, Winnicott developed another alternative conception, that of holding. Maybe it is for another occasion to consider the exact relation between Winnicott's notion (from the mid-1950s) which keeps the idea of the continuity of being in place, and Bion's notion (from the mid- to late 1950s) of containing.

Bion's development in understanding how mother (the environment) together with her infant do a similar job with the primitive psychotic anxiety pointed to a very different view of the psychoanalytic process and relationship (Bion, 1959). This striking step forward has put to use the subjective experience the analyst has of the immediate relationship. When in your quote from Winnicott about the timing of interpretation he says an analyst "feels like interpreting, but this can spoil the process" (1971d, p. 92), the Kleinian of today would entirely agree about that possible spoiling. And the provenance of that concern about the process is indeed Winnicott. Perhaps he did not have the opportunity to follow that up, because today this feeling of the analyst would not be dismissed. Instead, it would be regarded as a part of the process, if only the analyst could grasp it as such. Today we would all accept that the subjective feeling of the analyst says something about the context he or she is in, and that context is the analyst's relationship with his or her patient. What we do about it might be different – to recognise it either as telling us something about the patient (Kleinian), or as an indicator that the analyst must hold back and wait (Winnicott). That is, if I have got it right . . .

Winnicott did not live to see that development (made by Joseph 1975, 1989, and by many others), just as Klein did not live to see the full blooming of her descriptions of the schizoid mechanisms. We cannot know what Winnicott would have made of the developments in the forty-five or so years since he died; nor what Klein would have made of those developments in the fifty-five-odd years since she died. At this point, we are writing the history of the present.

JAN ABRAM: It's interesting and important to note the point you make, Bob, about Klein and Winnicott developing their theories and techniques at different moments in the evolution of psychoanalysis. And although we have spent some time, inevitably, discussing technique and clinical work in previous chapters, so far we had not taken this fact into account. However, does this fact really "hamper" the comparative work we are attempting? Do you think that Klein would have changed her mind about the use of the analyst's countertransference had she lived longer? Indeed, would she have changed her mind about her position in general? As I pointed out in Part IV, your clinical example of Klein discussing the extreme negative countertransference in work with psychotics does rather contradict her statement that countertransference told her more about herself than the patient. Perhaps it does illuminate that she was already beginning to make use of the concept? She was certainly aware of how the patient's projective identifications penetrated the analyst – which is another way of discussing the countertransference.

Despite this contradiction, I personally think that Melanie Klein had a good point in being cautious about the concept. It is easy for all of us to mistake our own emotional responses as "countertransference" when it may very well be more to do with our particular "transference" to the patient. One could say that it is one of the major pitfalls of the concept, and I have recently argued this point in a Contemporary Conversation in the *International Journal of Psychoanalysis* (Abram, 2016b). So I think this is one example that demonstrates Klein's position as helpful for all analytic clinicians today, and in that respect I'm not sure she was "left behind" by the developments, as you indicate, coming from Heimann and Winnicott in the late 1940s. Because the awareness that analysts were responding on deep emotional levels to their patients occurred during Klein's heyday, it seems to me. It was Marjorie Brierley's paper, "Affects in Theory and Practice", in 1937 that could be seen to have initiated the concept of the analyst's use of the countertransference, even though Brierley did not use that term in her paper (see Abram, 2015a; Green 1977). Brierley emphasises that the analyst must find her way into the patient's unconscious ". . . by following the Ariadne thread of transference affect . . ." (Brierley, 1937, p. 257). My impression is that Melanie Klein must have been observing many of these developments. Winnicott was writing about holding and interpretation from the mid-1950s when she was still alive, and his work on regression, as you know, was very much disapproved of by Klein, Segal, and Joseph. I have a sense that Klein would never have gone along with many of the developments after she died because the evidence suggests that it is unlikely she would have changed her mind about her formulations. Therefore, while recognising the difference in age between Klein and Winnicott, I consider it important and valuable to compare their perspectives despite the age and epoch discrepancy.

Following on from that, as I indicated above, in my recent work I have tried to demonstrate how I consider that Winnicott's difference of opinion with some of Klein's concepts instigated some of his most significant advances because he was always in some sort of dialogue with the Kleinian development, in theory and technique, up until his death. And it was that scientific dialogue, in the context of his psychoanalytic and paediatric experience, that, I have suggested, "sharpened" his original contributions about the parent–infant relationship and its application to the analytic setting (Abram, 2013).

This takes me to comment on your points concerning present-day Kleinian technique following Winnicott's cautionary advice about the timing of interpretation, and your recognition that its provenance belongs to Winnicott. This is an important point because I think the Kleinian school in general have rarely acknowledged that Winnicott's contributions to psychoanalytic theory and technique have made any significant contribution to the Kleinian development of technique. This brings us to the work of Bion and his development of the concept of "container-contained" and your response related to psychosis.

The disrupted reality principle

Let me first of all refer back to my chapter 4 concerning Winnicott's two babies and remind the reader that one baby is enjoying and profiting from the continuity of being. This is the baby who has received a "good-enough holding" from the environment from the very start and during the most formative stages of emotional development. Of course, it's important to say here that this does not mean that the growing infant does not have "issues" and "problems". It only means that the infant is more equipped, as it were, to sustain a general level of health. The other (unfortunate) baby, however, suffers from a break in the "continuity of being" caused by the deficient environment. The break (in the continuity of being) is equivalent to what Winnicott terms "unthinkable anxieties" and "primitive agonies". For Winnicott, therefore, psychosis is an environmental-deficiency disease. He adds to this by stating that psychotic processes are a defence against those unthinkable anxieties. This is why, in his view, the paranoid-schizoid position is a description that depicts the psychic result of a failing environment rather than it depicting a universal phase of development for all babies.

As I have tried to show in chapter 1, from 1945 onwards Winnicott developed a theory of the parent–infant relationship – "there's no such thing as a baby" – and "holding" as a concept grew out of his ongoing work on formulating the essentials of "emotional development". This work was at least a decade old before Bion conceptualised his "theory of thinking" and developed his particular concept of the environment – that is, container-contained. Bion did not acknowledge how much Winnicott's work on the environment–individual set-up influenced his own developments, which is something you have pointed out. However, we both agree that Bion's theory of the environment in his conceptualising of the container-contained is different from Winnicott's concept of holding, although there are many overlaps. These scientific matters unfortunately became "political" issues and still reverberate in psychoanalysis today.

The separate evolution of the different schools of thought in the British Psychoanalytical Society – Kleinian, Contemporary Freudian, and Independent – gradually evolved after 1945, and more often than not each author referenced his or her own school. As you pointed out, Winnicott cited Bion only twice and Bion never cited Winnicott's work. These facts have their history, and, while many "myths" may have emerged out of them, I think some issues still hold true.

For example, you have just accepted that Kleinian theory and technique today has been influenced by Winnicott's "The Use of an Object" (1969a), which stressed the sensitivity in timing the interpretation. But at the same time, you write (mistakenly, I think), that Winnicott was developing the concept of holding as an "alternative" to Bion's concept of containing. I hope my above observations illustrate that the evolution of a theory of the environment and the crucial impact it has on emotional development is primarily Winnicott's provenance. As you pointed out in Part IV, Melanie Klein agreed with Winnicott on this point and acknowledged it in her 1936 paper.

In preparing this book, I understood that we both felt it was important to acknowledge how Klein and Winnicott and their followers influenced each other – where their theories converge and where they diverge. The "politics" and acrimonious history are issues we both wanted to avoid in discussing the theories, because we were attempting to find a more neutral way of exchanging views on different theories. Perhaps we sensed that this project was fraught with dangers of repeating the difficulties related to the unconscious group dynamics, as you have pointed out. But, at present, there is a real and lively interest in this kind of discourse – on an international level, too – which is not only stimulating but also essential for the continued evolution of psychoanalysis.

As can be seen in chapter 8, Winnicott very much believed, from his experience as an analyst, that the deficient environment caused psychopathology. But in his technique he was keen to advocate that the analyst's task was to decipher the patient's meaning through the transference matrix. So, although you are correct in saying that we don't know what Winnicott or what Klein would have made of developments in psychoanalysis after their deaths, I do think we can make an informed guess on the basis of where they got to with their respective theories.

RDH: I think Klein was in a difficult position during the 1940s, and Winnicott's presentation of his notion of the transitional object in 1951 went completely against Klein's view of the relations in early infancy. This blow to Klein coincided with Heimann's original conception of countertransference, which also went against Klein's allegiance to the classical approach to clinical work.

Independence from Klein

It had been an unfortunate moment for them to display such differences. The Controversial Discussions (1943–1944) had devastated Klein. She had lost her position as the major original thinker in British psychoanalysis (endorsed by Ernest Jones) to become a relatively minor fragment of the British Psychoanalytical Society, with a mere handful of supporters and students. And the development of something called the Independent group at this time (the late 1940s) created a visible organisational distance from all those supporters she had relied on before the arrival of the Viennese in 1938. Within ten years she had lost almost everything – at least in her view. She refused both Heimann's paper on countertransference and Winnicott's on transitional objects for her 70th-birthday festschrift (published in 1953 in the *International Journal of Psychoanalysis*). Was that just childish spite? I think that would be a bit uncharitable, though there were many who perhaps saw it that way, including Heimann and Winnicott, who took that moment for independent thinking (Winnicott a lot more successfully than Heimann).

You may be right, Jan, that Winnicott did contribute to the development of Kleinian (as opposed to Klein's) thinking. But it was probably only in the sense that Kleinians wanted to show that they also had explanations that were both possible and plausible. That may not be a particularly good motive, but challenges are the seeds of originality.

I was surprised by your example of Winnicott giving the evidence for an interpretation on the basis merely of one feeling he had in his countertransference – that he felt insane to see his middle-aged male patient as a young girl (chapter 6). It seems exactly the kind of over-confident use of the countertransference without any check that Heimann in 1960 warned against. It is certainly a countertransference feeling, and one not to be dismissed. But it is a rather immediate and incautious interpretation, isn't it? The patient agreed consciously, but we know that conscious agreement is exactly what we must not be led by. In addition, it goes against Winnicott's principle that an over-soon interpretation spoils things, which you quote in chapter 10.

The micro-process

It may be useful to take that up now, as it contrasts so directly with a contemporary Kleinian view of working with the countertransference. I want to clarify what I said early in this Dialogue about Winnicott's experience that he might "spoil" things if he made an interpretation. The view of many Kleinians right now is that an experience like Winnicott's (that he might "spoil" things if he made an interpretation) could be taken as a really important indicator of something in the patient's experience at the moment. What does it mean that an analyst advises himself not to make an interpretation (the one leverage allowed him in his work)? It could be an indication that the connection with the patient is very fragile – which it might be. Or it could be a communication that the patient himself feels threatened by the analyst's effectiveness; or it could come from the analyst's sense of his own destructive aggressiveness in relation to the negative transference. Furthermore, it might appear that the analyst's superego is brought into play at this point, for some reason making him aim for perfection. Winnicott, without seeming to give himself the time to consider all the possibilities, assumed that the patient needed to feel a control, needed to be given the experience of the unspoiled illusion of omnipotence. Maybe Winnicott was correct, but how could we know that, given the alternative possibilities that could have been interpreted (and no doubt more of them that have escaped me)?

The meticulous descriptions of this kind of detailed interaction is sometimes called the "micro-process", in connection with the developments in clinical practice recommended by Betty Joseph (1989) and which have come from her more cautious attempt to consider the possibilities of the countertransference communicative system.

The corrective emotional experience

At this point, I might introduce another hesitant concern about Winnicott's practice. This might count as a part of the Kleinian mythology about Winnicott, and maybe you can illuminate this, Jan. When Winnicott confided that he felt he could spoil some delicate situation, he seemed to be proceeding in a technical way with some explicit notion in his mind as to how he "should" be proceeding – as a mother indulging the baby in a feeling of omnipotence. A contemporary Kleinian might instead take an alternative stance; he or she would attempt a full examination of what that notion in one's own mind signifies. Given that one is working in a specific context, and the context is the mind of another person, it seems likely (though, of course, not completely certain) that the notion arising in the analyst's mind is something or other to do with the context. Even though no doubt it is to do with the analyst's mind as well.

If it is true that the analyst reacts to his context, then he will react in his own way. In the case at issue, he reacts with something like a superego injunction not to spoil. It is that conjoined coupling which has to be carefully considered, as Money-Kyrle had to in the example referred to a number of times. A particularly significant operating principle that I find myself referring to a lot is: "If there is a mouth that seeks a breast as an inborn potential, there is, I believe, a psychological equivalent, i.e. a state of mind which seeks another state of mind" (Brenman-Pick, 1985, p. 157). It cannot be difficult to flatter the analyst into the comforting view that he is doing better than the original mother – which, of course, a psychoanalyst cannot actually be in many respects. To "be" an illusion is a radical approach and entails collusion, which a Kleinian would say is better examined than enacted, if or when possible.

What does this mutuality between patient and analyst mean if a superego figure makes its spectral appearance for the analyst? That, it seems to me, is a question that needs to be pondered rather than reacted to. Here I would agree that psychoanalysts do get caught up in debates with each other in which the group ideal of one group establishes a confrontation with that of another, though spoken through the mouths of the individual persons in each group. We are reactive people like anyone else. And I do believe that Klein also was not above this kind of accusational, and self-accusational, thinking.

This vulnerability to a professional superego leads to attempts on all sides to comply with a correctness, derived from the governing power of the analyst's superego, adopted from our own personal analysts, supervisors, and the group we eventually join. When Winnicott, nearly fifty years ago, cautioned against spoiling a psychoanalytic treatment with a too-soon interpretation, he seems to be requiring that we observe an ideal method – one aimed at creating a specific experience in the patient, the persistence of an illusion of omnipotence. And it may be that those historical expectations of professionals trapped Winnicott in his own times, as they did Klein, perhaps.

The contrast between a corrective experience of being mothered as new-born, and the search for new knowledge, could perhaps only have been clear a generation or two after both Winnicott and Klein. As I have indicated, the approach that follows a superego instruction, as Winnicott seemed to (and Klein in her approach to countertransference seemed to), needs to be contrasted with the alternative – that the superego imperative is itself to be considered. Where does it come from, and why? Winnicott's dedication to a corrective emotional experience is not at the same level of thought as the analyst's attempt to understand why he is prompted by his professional superego, at that moment.

Here I have, for the sake of clarity, to turn briefly to Bion. It may be true that engaging in a project with the patient to develop new knowledge is itself a new and corrective experience. However, Bion (1962a) thought he could make a distinction between, on the one hand, knowing, with its corollary being known, and, on the other, loving and hating. These are different categories of relating (he preferred to call them links).

Then subsequently he had to distinguish between two categories of "knowing": one a "knowing about", which comes from sensuous perception, as a doctor knows when a patient has an appendicitis; and one that he called intuiting, which has more the character of empathy. Exemplifying, he contrasted a patient with a broken leg, which the doctor (or others) can see is broken, and a broken heart, which one knows from the inside, as it were. The crux is, do we know about our patients from our theories, or do we know about them from an intuited understanding of "their" theories (even if those theories are their unconscious phantasies). I believe this distinction was not adequately available to either Winnicott or Klein during their lifetimes.

About provenance

I do understand you want to set the record straight, and maybe that should indeed be done, but I do think it interrupts our efforts at conceptual comparisons. Well, I have pursued this far enough. It has been extraordinarily productive to engage in this teasing out of our differences like this. It has been food for thought for us, I think, whatever it provides for the reader.

JA: These dialogues are certainly proving to be illuminating! It had never occurred to me that Melanie Klein could have been upset by Winnicott's paper on transitional objects. I don't think I really understand why. Did she feel it compromised her innovations on internal objects? I did know that she had not wished Paula Heimann to present her paper on countertransference because of her views on that concept, as we discussed above. Paula Heimann's paper in 1950 is often seen as the pivotal paper that launched the concept, but of course it was in 1949 that Winnicott published

"Hate in the Countertransference" in which he discloses a dream through which he is able to understand the mind–body split of his patient. But again I want to cite Marjorie Brierley's paper of 1937, "Affects in Theory and Practice", because it seems to me that this paper, as I already stated, really initiates the way in which analysts start to reflect on their emotional responses towards their patients before the concept was termed "countertransference".

I have always appreciated that Melanie Klein must have felt devastated in the wake of the Controversial Discussions, but I had assumed it would have been because her daughter Melitta Schmideberg had rallied against her so passionately during the Discussions alongside her (Schmideberg's) analyst Edward Glover. But by 1945 it was Edward Glover who resigned, and Melitta Schmideberg left for New York with her husband. Even Marjorie Brierley, who had been instrumental in setting up the Discussions, retired and moved to the Lake District. The British Psychoanalytical Society must have been quite traumatised, and I've always thought that, post-Discussions, the atmosphere must have been tense and difficult. What is clearer to me now, from what you are pointing out, is that Melanie Klein's continued developments from 1945 onwards were possibly emanating from a wounded position. The Kleinian development became quite militant on a political level in the Society, and gradually, there is no doubt, the Kleinian group took its ascendancy, not just in the Society but also on a global level.

I can only imagine that Klein did not wish the contributions from both Winnicott and Heimann for her festschrift because she did not agree with the concepts, rather than it being "childish spite", as you ask, or because she felt so narcissistically wounded by their new developments. Was this really the start of the "Independent" group? Not officially, I think, though it must have sown the seeds. But it was Edward Glover who coined the term "Middle Group" in reference to the majority of indigenous analysts who did not wish to align with either Freud or Klein when the "gentlemen's agreement" was instated after the Controversial Discussions. It was not until 1968 that William Gillespie led the way for a more official "Independent Group", which Winnicott refused to join because he felt that the setting-up of groups was divisive.

My point about Winnicott's analytic contributions to Kleinian development was aimed at highlighting the issue of provenance. It seems to me incumbent on all analytic authors to take account of contemporary developments, and this is something that has been a long-standing issue for both Freudians and Independents about many Kleinian and post-Kleinian formulations. This complaint may also come from a wounded position, because there is no doubt that, when colleagues ignore valid contributions or speak badly about fellow analysts, people will inevitably feel hurt as well as angry.

In the British Psychoanalytical Society it has been noticeable that, in the past decade or so, the referencing of other schools of thought different from the author's has gradually started to occur. But there continues to be quite a political divide between the different schools that reflects the scientific differences as well as indicating unresolved historical events.

Hopefully this book will have a constructive effect that will lead towards more dialogues occurring between different theoretical positions that will be discussed not from a wounded position but in the spirit of genuinely wishing to dialogue with different perspectives. This is how we both set out, I feel. We have already seen that, since our first workshop on Klein and Winnicott at the University of Essex in 2013, there is present interest in comparing Bion and Winnicott – especially on the concepts of holding and containing. And at the end of 2017 we conducted a workshop on Bion and Winnicott in Warsaw.

Winnicott's clinical vignette

I was struck and surprised by your reaction to Winnicott's clinical example because I consider it to be one of the most moving and convincing clinical examples in the psychoanalytic literature. Moreover, I think, as it stands, it exemplifies the Strachey technique and the meaning of the mutative interpretation. Let me take the opportunity to outline what I mean, by citing the sequence as Winnicott describes.

The first interpretation Winnicott makes is already unusual:

> "I am listening to a girl. I know perfectly well that you are a man but I am listening to a girl, and I am talking to a girl. I am telling this girl: "You are talking about penis envy." [1971a, p. 73]

This interpretation does not come out of the blue. The analysis, we learn, has been in process for some years and the patient is experienced at "being" a patient, with substantial experience of the analytic method. Something in the way of psychic change, however, has not yet occurred for the patient, and Winnicott tells us that good work had been consistently destroyed. This suggested that, for the patient and analyst, there was still something to discover in the depths of the patient's unconscious.

Following Winnicott's interpretation, there is a pause, illustrating that the patient is processing Winnicott's interpretation. Then the patient responds:

> "If I were to tell someone about this girl I would be called mad."

Winnicott says that things could have been left there but he found himself going further when he (Winnicott) said something that surprised him (Winnicott):

> "It was not that you told this to anyone; it is *I* who see the girl and hear a girl talking, when actually there is a man on my couch. The mad person is *myself*."

This interpretation "went home", Winnicott says. The patient felt it to be true and said:

> "I myself could never say (knowing myself to be a man) "I am a girl". I am not mad that way. But you said it, and you have spoken to both parts of me."

Winnicott goes on to say that his feeling mad enabled the patient to "see himself as a girl *from my* [Winnicott's] *position*".

Here, then, we see an incremental lead-up – as Strachey describes – towards the mutative interpretation when Winnicott says that it is he who is mad. At that moment, he is talking from the position of the patient's archaic object of the m/other who looked at her infant boy and saw a girl. Moreover, Winnicott is also doing precisely what Strachey (1934, p. 149) advocates because he is responding to the moment of urgency in the session (which was also following the technique Melanie Klein was advocating at the time).

This is why, for me, the exchange between patient and analyst in this example illustrates a convincing description of the *après coup* (*Nachträglichkeit*) that has been totally facilitated by the analysing situation.

Let me briefly compare this with Money-Kyrle's clinical vignette that you quote in chapter 8. For me, the two examples illustrate how both analysts were working from their deeply felt emotional responses (countertransference) and in so doing they were allowing themselves to (analytically) become the archaic object. Money-Kyrle realises that his affective response to his patient illustrated how he was feeling like the patient at the end of the session, which seemed to be as a result of falling into the (countertransference) trap of behaving like the patient's father. I think the comparison of both clinical examples tends to demonstrate how, when analysis is working well and the analyst is open to being placed in the position of the archaic object, there is little distinction – apart from theoretically – between a Klein or Winnicott way of working. So that although at first my heart sank (as I put it) when I read your Money-Kyrle clinical example in chapter 5, once you had added the next part of the material, and I had subsequently studied the paper, I realised that he was working in a similar way to Winnicott in the example I referred to. A more detailed compare-and-contrast of these specific clinical examples could be fruitful.

The micro-process you cite of Betty Joseph's seems to me to be very similar to Strachey's description of the analytic process in his seminal paper. At the same time, I take your point that if the analyst has an urge to "do something" for the patient, it is important to understand that urge and to work out how it relates to the patient's internal world. The patient will inevitably draw the analyst into something that has to be reflected on rather than acted out. The "proof of the pudding", I think we agree, is the patient's response to the interpretation and subsequent use of the analytic setting.

Illumination on Winnicott's technique as "corrective emotional experience"

I am also struck by the way in which you seem to be interpreting Winnicott's aims for psychoanalysis when you refer to the "corrective emotional experience". You seem to be implying that Winnicott tried to "compensate" the patient for a failure of early maternal caring by offering the patient something he had never had before. This, though, is not what he meant, because across the whole of his work he did not lose sight of the transference and the importance of interpretation and technique. Let me quote Winnicott from a 1963 paper (so only eight years before he died), in which he writes:

> . . . no analyst *sets out to provide* a corrective experience in the transference, because this is a contradiction in terms; the transference in all its details comes through the patient's unconscious psycho-analytic process, and depends for its development on the interpreting that is always relative to material presented to the analyst. [Winnicott, 1963a, p. 258]

He follows this statement by saying that "the practicing of good psycho-analytic technique *may* in itself be a corrective experience . . .". I think he means here that one of the good side effects of analytic treatment may be "corrective", but that it would never be enough because the early failures have to be brought right into the transference. He concludes:

> So in the end we succeed by failing – failing the patient's way. This is a long distance from the simple theory of cure by corrective experience. In this way, regression can be in the service of the ego if it is met by the analyst, and turned into a new dependence in which the patient brings the bad external factor into the area of his or her omnipotent control, and the area managed by projection and introjection mechanisms. [p. 258]

When Winnicott writes that the analyst has to be "prepared to be the mother of the earliest phases of life as well as the mother and father of the later stages of development" I think he is specifically referring to the analyst's ability to receive the patient's communications during any given analysis. In other words, the analyst has to be able to work in the context of the maternal and paternal transferences that are intrinsically part of the analytic process. So I believe he was referring to the psychoanalytic meaning of being mother and father rather than behaving as if he were the mother or father. This is just as we see in the Money-Kyrle example you cite when he recognised he was becoming the patient's father, in the context of the transference, and was left in the same state of mind that the patient's father had made the patient feel in the past. Winnicott's way of working in a "standard analysis" is demonstrated in several clinical vignettes as well as the verbatim sessions of an analysis in his book *Holding and Interpretation* (1986).

My reference in chapter 10 to the papers in which he wrote about "modifications" to technique have always made me feel uncomfortable. I would not wish to avail myself to working in this way. But, as I wrote, I believe that Winnicott sincerely believed that it was this way of working that the patient needed at that particular moment in the treatment, and he may have been right about that.

Winnicott's clarity about his ideas on regression tended to give him the reputation of wishing to make his patients regress and advocating a literal holding as the solution. It seems to be a frequent misunderstanding that Winnicott thought all patients had to regress. He disputed this strongly and simply argued that patients do regress during the course of treatment, and therefore the analyst should be ready to meet the regression to dependence in the context of the analytic setting (Winnicott, 1955). We address some of these themes in relation to misunderstandings and misperceptions in the Appendix.

RDH: One last comment on the issue of regression as corrective. It is not altogether clear how this is not a corrective emotional experience. You seem to be saying that because the patient needs (or wants?) to regress in order to bring the external object "into the area of his or her omnipotent control" (Winnicott, 1962a, p. 258), as you quote, therefore it is not a case of the analyst providing an experience. It seems to me if the analyst does allow this kind of regression, then he is offering an opportunity for a correction to the "incorrect" traumatising of the original mother. You make this comparable to Money-Kyrle's "mistakes", when patient and analyst unconsciously enacted a scene of someone being "on the mat", as Money-Kyrle put it. In fact, there is, I think, a real difference, since Money-Kyrle was offering an opportunity for the patient to recognise the painful truth that he was confusing the object in the session with the paternal object in his mind. That is, I agree, in line with Strachey and a potential reality-test for the patient's use of phantasy to define what he expects from the other. In Winnicott's case, he is allowing the phantasy expectations to be curative per se.

Allowing illusion (or phantasy) to be the truth of the moment, is different from recognising the need to confront the internal objects and phantasy as distinct from the external object. Paradoxically, one could almost say that, in the Kleinian framework, there is more respect for the importance of the external object than in Winnicott's paradigm!

JA: I have that *déjà vu* feeling that once more I have not made myself clear enough, Bob! Let me try again, as it seems so crucial to try to clarify the similarities and differences to complete this final dialogue of the book.

First, let me reiterate my view of Winnicott's meaning on regression. Following Freud, Winnicott saw that the nature of the analytic setting mobilised regression for all patients. This is different from a conscious intention on the analyst's part to instigate regression, which Winnicott advocates against, as I showed from the quotations above when he says "no analyst *sets out to provide* a corrective experience in the transference, because this is a contradiction in terms". He goes on to outline that the transference evolves "and depends for its development on the interpreting that is always relative to the material presented to the analyst" (Winnicott, 1963a, p. 258).

There are differences in technique, you're right, in the clinical examples. Money-Kyrle's "interpretation" at the beginning of the subsequent session was stated from the analyst's position, who was able to comment that the patient was feeling anxious that he had made his analyst feel as the patient had felt with his father. This "interpretation" helped the patient feel more thoughtful and thus relieved. And I agree with you that, in this way, Money-Kyrle was bringing to consciousness for the patient the painful truth that, in the previous sessions, the patient had "confused" his analyst with the paternal object. But, Money-Kyrle also makes clear that before he could say this to the patient, he as the analyst had to work on why he was feeling useless and bemused and, moreover, why he had not been able to reach his patient through interpretation. When he, Money-Kyrle, recognises that his state of mind after the session was similar to his patient's feelings with his father, he writes that he felt a "relief of a re-projection" (1956, p. 363). This in turn helped him find, we could say, the "corrective" interpretation in the subsequent session. In other words, the interpretation helped both analyst and patient see what had been played out in the transference in the previous session. I see this as the ordinary, everyday working through in the transference of all analyses that are in process.

As I said above, I consider that there are some significant similarities with each approach while at the same time differences in technique. The common ground in approach is that both Money-Kyrle and Winnicott are receptive to their patients' unconscious communications. Moreover, they both avail themselves to "becoming" the archaic object – maternal or paternal – knowing that this is intrinsic to the transference situation. Both are acutely aware of their "countertransference" reactions. In his conclusions to that same paper, Money-Kyrle admits that what he names the "disturbance" in the countertransference "probably takes up more time than we readily remember or admit" (p. 365).

You say that Winnicott allows "illusion (or phantasy) to be the truth of the moment". I think that is a good way of describing what Winnicott is able to interpret to his patient from the position of the archaic object when he says, "The mad person is myself". But here is the real paradox, it seems to me: by stating that he the analyst is mad, Winnicott locates the patient's dissociation (of feeling like a girl) intersubjectively (Goldman, 2012, quoted in Abram, 2013, p. 353). This is a good example of how Winnicott sees psychoanalytic practice as "playing" in the transference, which he identifies as illusory. But it is crucial to recognise that this way of "playing" in the analytic session is in the service of self-development. Through the incremental experience of this kind of playing in the transference, an increasing deepening of insight occurs (cf. Zilkha, 2013). This, in turn, will lead to the liberating capacity to discern and distinguish between the intrapsychic, interpsychic, and interpersonal in the analytic dyad.

While neither Winnicott nor Money-Kyrle was aiming at the corrective experience, perhaps there would be agreement among many analysts that the outcome of a good analysis could be seen as "corrective", despite it being a long way from what Alexander (1946, p. 66) had designated the "corrective emotional experience". I think that's what Winnicott meant.

RDH: Oh, I'm sorry if you feel I'm not getting it – even at this late stage of our dialogue. And I hope we are not just playing with words. It is interesting that we have homed in on a point that started in our first dialogue (Part I) where you corrected my attribution to Winnicott's theory of a phase of primary omnipotence (it is an illusion of omnipotence). You talked there about mother's "capacity to tune in to the baby's needs that made the baby feel he was God". It is what the baby "needs", and you repeatedly conveyed that for those people traumatised, and with an ensuing identity problem (false self), it is necessary for them to find an analyst with the capacity to make them feel like God.

When Money-Kyrle (1956, pp. 363–363) found that he had been playing the part of a humiliated junior to a patient who became a critical legal figure, it may be that the patient did feel like God. But it was hardly the analyst's intention in the way that it might be a mother's intention to "worship" her little baby. What Money-Kyrle and the patient were acting out unconsciously was some contest about who was ill – and the patient won the contest. And, next day, Money-Kyrle could lay out the drama to the patient, as a means that the patient had developed for managing his own kinds of experience – legally criticising or else feeling humiliated.

It really seems to me that Winnicott's interpretation (1971a, pp. 73–74) was similarly presenting back to the patient the mad idea that the patient could think himself both a girl and a middle-aged man. It is a sort of double vision, which the patient could see as mad. But it is still not clear where the omnipotence comes in, in that sense of Winnicott as meeting the need of the baby.

For Money-Kyrle, it is clear, there is a replay of a repeated unconscious drama with the legally critical father. One party is humiliated and the other is God-like in his criticism. In the analytic setting, the analyst and patient unconsciously agree to play the roles according to the patient's convenience.

The therapeutic strategy is, like Strachey (1934), to expose the drama for comparison with the reality.

The therapeutic strategy for Winnicott may be different. But first there is a question. What exactly is the god-like figure in the drama that Money-Kyrle's patient brought? It could be the lawyer father whose power the patient can exert when he criticises the analyst. But this is not quite right, because one cannot generalise, as Winnicott wants to, about the need of patients *in general*. So it would seem that what is more likely from Winnicott's point of view is not the actual role of God in the unconscious drama, but the fact of getting the drama unconsciously replayed by the analyst.

I would agree there is something very powerful about getting the analyst to respond in a role the patient assigns from his unconscious, whether that is the humiliated person in the case of Money-Kyrle's patient, or the fumbling inability to confuse a girl with a middle-aged man in the case of Winnicott's patient.

The difference comes then in how the analyst should handle it. Well, first of all he has to spot it. But assuming the analyst does, in either case he has a choice of how to proceed based on his view of infant development.

For the Money-Kyrle analyst, there is a task to be achieved in pointing out to the patient the misperception (enjoying an illusion), and to do so with a tact and pace that can allow the patient to apprehend what has happened unconsciously.

For a Winnicott analyst, there would seem to be a sense that he has already accomplished something for the patient, by meeting the need of the patient to misperceive, or to hold to, an illusion.

So this brings us to an important point of difference: how to see and handle the situation. On the one hand, as Kleinians would perceive Winnicottians, you allow the patient to indulge in an "untruth", the illusion, as a sort of recompense and to continue for as long as the patient needs – and perhaps this is not a kindly view of a Winnicottian analysis. Or, do you berate the patient with negatively toned interpretations for getting the reality wrong, as Winnicottians believe Kleinians do?

There is a difference between the two camps, and each camp can justly criticise the other.

Maybe we have to leave it at that difference – or, possibly we could write another book of dialogues on what to do when you find yourself going along with the transference illusion!

JA: Yes, Bob – we have agreed that we may need to leave this Dialogue at that difference. However, let's clarify what we really disagree on before we decide to call it a day, because having re-read your last comment above to my further comments, and having let it percolate somewhat, I think I can see where we might be talking at cross-purposes. It seems to me that some misunderstandings may be arising due to Winnicott's use of words, especially "illusion" and "omnipotence". So let me try once more to clarify some of the points I was trying to make before your very last comment above. I shall address four main points you make:

1. Omnipotence: normal and/or pathological.
2. What is reality in the transference?
3. Illusion and delusion – truth and untruth.
4. "Going along with the transference illusion."

Omnipotence: normal and/or pathological

Winnicott's use of the term "omnipotence" has led to serious confusion in the psychoanalytic literature and in our Dialogues. Before he evolved his theory of illusion in the late 1960s, the term "omnipotence" almost always referred to a defence that was pathological, especially in the Kleinian literature, and this is still the case today. Thus there are two kinds of omnipotence: Winnicott's refers to a normal stage of development at the start of life, whereas pathological "omnipotence" refers to the patient's defence against feeling small, humiliated, and ashamed.

You pointed out that, throughout this book, I have emphasised the notion of the illusion of omnipotence, and you also say that I have "repeatedly conveyed that for those people traumatised, and with an ensuing identity problem (false self), it is necessary for them to find an analyst with the capacity to make them feel like God". I don't recognise this as a point I have tried to make, because it indicates "intention" in a rather psychological and behavioural way, which was certainly not intended. Because, while I have stressed what Winnicott means by "illusion of omnipotence", I had not intended to convey that this is what the patient needs to feel throughout the course of analysis. I don't think any analysis could make the patient feel like God. However, through the normal course of analysis – holding and interpretation – the patient can start to feel in contact with a core self if he or she is able to "work through" the early psychic deficiencies. A good-enough holding – that is, the analytic setting – can really offer this opportunity to a patient.

Now, if we look at Winnicott's work, especially in *Playing and Reality*, he did see that modifications in analytic technique with a certain category of patient could offer a sense of formlessness, related to the early psychic stages, which they may never have had the opportunity to experience before. So perhaps you are right that he was offering a new therapeutic experience related to illusion. But it is important to emphasise that he did not set out to make the patient feel like God in a pathological way but, rather, in a way that meant he or she felt understood and seen.

When you refer to Money-Kyrle's patient feeling like God, I felt you meant the pathological kind of omnipotence that is a defence, and you suggest analyst and patient "were acting out unconsciously" a contest about who was ill. As you point out, the patient won. But, and I wonder if you agree with this, it was a "playing out in the transference" that is inevitable in any given analysis. Money-Kyrle, in this early paper on countertransference, designates what happened to him as a "disturbance" in the countertransference, but he concludes that paper by implying, I think, that such "disturbances" occur quite frequently. I don't know what you think about this, but it seems to me that this kind of example is what I would call an "ordinary" countertransference experience that leads to insight on the part of both analyst and patient.

Then you say that Winnicott's interpretation "was similarly presenting back to the patient the mad idea that the patient could think himself both a girl and a middle-aged man . . .", implying that he was working in a similar vein to Money-Kyrle. But, as I tried to show above, it was quite different, because when Winnicott "presents back" to his patient, he takes on the patient's projections of the early mother or, in Strachey's terms, the archaic object, and speaks from that position: "The mad person is *myself*". But wasn't

Money-Kyrle also experiencing himself as the archaic object at the end of that first reported session?

You then ask where the omnipotence comes in with Winnicott's example. I would say that what I think Winnicott illustrates is how he is working at a deep psychic level that we could name the "unconscious illusion" of that session. Thus he felt he was embodying the early mother, without trying to, through being psychically available, like Money-Kyrle. It seems to me that both patients had been helped, in slightly different ways, through the analysts' receptivity to their transferences of a traumatic past-object–relation dynamic. That, in and of itself, was therapeutic. It might not have made them feel they were God, but could we perhaps agree that they both felt seen and understood in a way that made them feel more in contact with their core selves? The patient's "need" is to have the experience of "creating the object". This is what most patients are able to feel when the analyst is able to identify the central unconscious hidden trauma within the context of the transference–countertransference matrix, as Strachey suggests. Thus the "therapeutic action" of analysis constitutes a mutative process.

What is reality in the transference?

When you say that the therapeutic strategy is to "expose the drama for comparison with reality", I think it raises the question of how we define "reality" in any given analytic treatment. It seems to me that both patients felt that their analysts helped them to see a psychic reality that could then be distinguished with the reality of the present day. Winnicott's patient knew he was not a girl but felt Winnicott had spoken to two parts of himself: the one who felt he was being seen as a girl (the mad mother in the past), and the one who knew he was a man (his analyst in the present-day situation). Money-Kyrle's patient became confused about who was ill, his analyst or himself, which played out his experience with his legal father's (pathological) omnipotence. It seems to me that through exposing the psychic reality of the past, as it is re-played in the *après coup* of the transference, the reality of the present starts to emerge. The patient is then able to place the past in the past and hopefully move on and be in the present.

Illusion and delusion – truth and untruth

In the last part of your comment you suggest that misperception is "enjoying an illusion". I don't really understand this, Bob. For me, "illusion" is related to psychic reality and therefore contains a layer of truth. Winnicott's patient felt "as if" he was a girl because his mother looked at him "as if" he were a girl, when actually he was a boy. He had to grow up with this experience of being seen (and treated) as a girl. This had a psychic reality and truth to it (even though it was mad), as Winnicott discovered in the transference. But it is crucial to note that the patient could hold both "realities" and "truths" – that is, that he was a man who felt like a girl (because of his mother's "delusion"). Therefore, different from what you seem to suggest (that misperception is an illusion), illusion of the transference brings psychic reality (what happened in the past) to consciousness. I don't mean to "play with words" here but, rather, highlight different meanings of the same words.

"Going along with the transference illusion"

I was struck by your last comment about "going along with the transference illusion". For me, as I hope I have illustrated above, the transference is inextricably linked with the stuff of "illusion" associated with Winnicott's late concepts on "creating the object", "creative living", and "primary psychic creativity". Thus, to "go along with the transference illusion", for me, equates with any given psychoanalytic treatment. Money-Kyrle, it seems to me, had no choice but to go along with the transference illusion – but it wasn't a misperception. On the contrary, what his patient experienced with his analyst repeated what had happened earlier with his father – or, rather, what he had made of what had happened with his father. The paternal transference was repeated in the transference–countertransference dynamic of the analysis, which in turn was processed by his analyst and re-played back to him through interpretation.

Both patients, it seems to me, were working quite well in the ordinary transference. If there had been a delusionary transference, neither would have been able to grasp the analyst's interpretations.

Technically, then, each analyst would be confronted with a much more complex problem, as is often the case with psychotic and borderline patients.

I do hope Bob, that this time I have managed to clarify some of your important questions.

RDH: There is a real risk of going on too long with this discussion, which is already long. And yet, at the end of this Dialogue, it is as if we are just getting near to the heart of the matter. So, I should like to risk extending this further.

I think it is a very complex situation and revolves around the meaning of the term "illusion". I was meaning that it is seeing something as if it is something else, like an optical illusion. And that "as-if" capacity is the basis of all symbolism, and so on, a thoroughly creative capacity of the mind, as we discussed in relation to Magritte's painting, "The Treachery of Images". However, you're saying something a bit different; that there is some truth in an illusion. It is the truth of inner reality and therefore has a genuine place in the external world in terms of the transference in an analytic treatment.

That inner reality is what Kleinians would call unconscious phantasy, something that gives the emotional meaning (all meaning) to the external world. From a Kleinian point of view, the external world is just something perceived; it has no meaning except in terms of the internal world – what is seen externally is "in the eye of the beholder", as folk psychology would say. In this sense, any meaning is illusory, obviously, because the world is made to stand in for currently sensed aspects of the internal world. However, that use of "illusion" is not a strong use, as it just means everything meaningful.

The arrival outside the womb demands a representation of what the world is. If, in the inner world, there is hunger, it is conceived in terms of the interpretation of sensations from the abdomen. And the external world is a presence that exists in those terms, and must have the properties of being satisfying, frustrating, needy, dependent, appreciative, and so forth. That is the reality that is most meaningful to the Kleinian baby.

Freud thought that there is some sense in which the meanings given to real external things and events can come to be approximated, to a greater or lesser extent, with how they actually are as real external objects. This is so often imagined as the task of objective observation and, ultimately, of the empirical sciences. But there is something different when the external object is not physical, but is the mind of an "other". Another person's mind is not a consistent object like a lump of physical matter – shall we say a lump of coal. Nor are the minds of several others necessarily similar, in the way lumps of coal are roughly similar in their properties. The external world – made of other minds – is not just a set of meaningless things, as the material world is.

This leads to the one important point (to my mind) that the US relational psychoanalysts stress: a patient relates to a unique psychoanalyst. For instance, Money-Kyrle's patient related to an analyst who had a susceptibility to being confused cognitively. That patient had become adept unconsciously at engaging with that precise part of the analyst, his confused states. And the patient could use that aspect of his analyst to display the transference–countertransference drama, which he could not fully convey in words. Winnicott's patient was adept unconsciously at engaging with a part of Winnicott concerned with gender identity, it seems.

But then Kleinians get scolded for expressing how (and why) the patient is needing to use the analyst, and Winnicottians get praised for how they allow themselves to be "played" with in this way for the sake of the patient "creating his object", as you say. There is here a considerable difference in the end between describing an internal reality dramatised in the transference, and a playing-out of a past experience, as an after-shock as it might be called. I would agree that the latter, the Winnicottian model, is in fact closer to Freud's view of the transference.

Extending from this, it is as if the inner world for Winnicott is then the product of past trauma getting in the way of a meaningful external world, which would be perceived unproblematically – except for the problems of trauma. However, for Kleinians, the perception of those senses that deal with the outer world (such as vision) are initially formed on the basis of the internal receptors – for hunger, say. Nevertheless, it has to be said, the experience of the external world for what it is seems to be present, to some extent from the outset, given the example of the new-born foal. But even the foal is in some way integrating its search of the external world with an awareness of an internal world (being hungry) that exists before trauma. This question of reality is perhaps, as you say, the crux of the matter – for Klein reality has to be won, for Winnicott it appears to be waiting to be perceived.

Finally, your four points of disagreement: I agree in principle with this summary. However, I would like to avoid the term "pathological" and would want to stick closely to the analytic frame of anxiety and defence. Otherwise I think the points are right, and I may (or may not) have expanded clarifyingly here.

Although, as I say, I have risked this further comment, we may just be rehearsing a disagreement about what we disagree about! But it might just be helpful for us – and for our readers.

JA: Thank you, Bob, for this, which I find helpful because, although we could easily continue, I feel that what you have said concludes our book, as we are indeed getting to what you say is the "heart of the matter": the very subtle and abstract distinctions between Klein and Winnicott on the concept at the heart of psychoanalysis – the transference. It's good to leave this final Dialogue open to further questions and to feel hungry for a further investigation on this very topic.

APPENDIX

The mythologies and misperceptions

One of the really interesting outcomes of our work together has been the realisation that many of the differences that appear to separate the followers of both Winnicott and Klein is that there are misperceptions about each other's concepts. Such misconceptions have often seemed hard to dispel, and they persist in a tenacious way, transforming into what could be called "factions" – that is, fictions based on historical events that have been misconstrued and become mythologies. While it must be acknowledged that the Kleinian development since 1945 has grown exponentially, it is also true that there has been a systematic dismissal of Winnicott's contribution by many analytic thinkers of the British Psychoanalytical Society, not only Kleinians, but also Freudians. In a general way, this applies also to the work of analysts who are identified with the Independent tradition of the Society.

Recently this has been changing, and several authors whose theoretical allegiances may be Kleinian or Freudian are beginning to reference Winnicott's work. And so we thought that it was worth devoting this Appendix to outlining what we see as the key myths as they have emerged throughout the preparation of this book.

1. Freudian instinct theory

Klein, as emphasised in this book, never makes reference to psychic energy, nor to the economic model. She uses the term "instinct" almost certainly because it proclaims an allegiance to Freud and his libido theory at a time when she was becoming a psychoanalyst and there was considerable concern about dissenters.

Abraham described the early mechanisms as both an instinctual impulse, like oral introjection, as well as a phantasy of incorporation; however, despite her devotion to Abraham, Klein only takes up the phantasy side of these mechanisms and emphasises the phantasy as one of relating to objects.

Although it appears that Winnicott adhered to Freud's instinct theory, as Abram points out in Part 1, his contribution emphasises the psychic environment and relationship as primary and instincts as secondary in the evolution of the self (see Part 1 Dialogue).

2. No external object

There is a tenacious assumption that Klein did not give importance to the environment, as Winnicott called it. In fact, Klein's earliest work with children showed them occupied with objects in their minds, and these objects were modelled to a greater or lesser extent on those in their world around. The mental internal objects were never exact replicas of the external objects, and they were always coloured by the preoccupations of anxiety the child was managing at the moment. In fact, Klein's model of infancy could perhaps emphasise the external even more than Winnicott's model, since Klein believed that there was an ego boundary between self and other from birth.

There is, however, an important factor here. Winnicott distinguished the "environment mother" from the "object mother". The environment mother is the one the observer sees, who functions to provide the mothering in an objective sense. The environment mother is taken for granted by the infant if she is "good enough". The object mother, however, is the mother eventually experienced by the infant, from around age 4 months, with all the potential distortions that might be expected for an infant mastering its capacities for perception, and interfered with by the pressures of needs arising from the life instinct.

Both Winnicott and Klein therefore thought the infant was, from around 4 months, deeply involved in grasping and coming slowly to terms with the reality of the world around. What is different is that before age 4 months, Klein understood the baby to be struggling with an external world and its objects largely constructed on the basis of meanings given by the internal perceptions of the state of its body. Winnicott, on the other hand, saw the baby in these earliest months as part of a multi-object system comprised of two (baby with mother), while the baby apperceived the system as only one object. This is the merger. It is important to recognise Winnicott's binocular vision: his view of the mother and baby, and the baby's view (see Point 4; see also chapter 6).

3. Persecuting interpretations

There is a persisting mythology about Klein's theories of aggression leading to premature and persecuting interpretations that deal only with the rather reprehensible levels of aggression in the patient, giving rise to the constant arousal of guilt throughout an analysis. In fact, Klein did not focus on aggression and destruction without a balanced focus on love and creativity. Her emphasis on the worrying threat that destructiveness posed to life and love came, she argued, from the patient's guilty anxiety about his or her aggression, and what it might do, and how to put it right with their capacity for loving.

Klein did lay a stress on destructiveness, and its place as negative transference, because she was persistently critical of other schools of analysis that shied away from acknowledging that the analyst could be seen as "bad" (Klein's mythology of other analysts, perhaps!). Moreover she saw these preoccupations with aggression as presented first by what she saw her small patients doing and demonstrating.

In defence of her interpretations causing guilt and anxiety, she constantly gave examples of how her interpretations that her patients worried about their aggression actually reduced anxiety.

The interpretation led to a stronger sense of the positive transference and opened up new areas of material.

4. The model of infancy is real

Klein created a model of infant development which, she claimed, derived from the phantasies of patients, both adults and children, as expressed in their clinical psychoanalysis. There is a tendency for her to think that her model is not just explanatory, but suggests the real experience of the infant. The misconception here is rather subtle.

Whether Klein's model is really how actual infants do feel and conceive, or not, is of less importance. In practice, Klein and her followers understand these infantile experiences as coming from the deeper layers of the unconscious, now. They are not exact repetitions from the past. In fact, the idea of continuously active unconscious phantasy got the Klein group into a lot of trouble in the Controversial Discussions in the 1940s, as it seemed to rule out fixation points, regression, and therefore key ingredients of Freud's model.

The misconception, then, is that these deeper layers of unconscious phantasies equate with actual infancy. However, for practical purposes in a psychoanalytic treatment, the important issue is: what phantasies in the unconscious are active today – and right now, here, in the moment of meeting? Because these phantasies often approximate to those of the primitive mechanisms, this layer of the mind might be regarded as the infant in the adult (or in the child), without necessarily being an accurate repetition of the past.

5. Winnicott encouraged his patients to regress

Winnicott followed Freud's theory of regression and considered that regression – simply returning to a former state of mind that belonged to an earlier stage of development – was part and parcel of the transference in analysis. Like Ferenczi before him, he experimented with a certain category of patient. For example, if he felt that the patient was not able to work in the symbolic area of illusion – which constitutes the transference – then it was necessary to "modify" technique. In other words, he saw it as a necessary adaptation to the patient's needs, otherwise the treatment would be ineffective because the patient had not developed a capacity to make use of interpretations. The concept of regression between Klein and the non-Kleinians continues to be a controversial issue (see Part V).

6. *Winnicott believed in the "corrective emotional experience" in his technique.*

This is an issue that arose in Part V, and in the Dialogue Abram attempts to illustrate how this is wrong. Through citing Winnicott's rejoinder to some of the criticisms of his day, she demonstrates the difference between working in the transference and the more behavioural approach known as the "corrective emotional experience".

7. *Winnicott's theory focuses on the external object*

Winnicott's major disagreement with Klein focused on the issue of the role played by the early environment in emotional development. His stress was on his realization that "there's no such thing as a baby" and that the individual's development is intrinsically and inseparably associated with the psychic environment. This took the focus of his theories to the primacy of the parent–infant relationship rather than a focus on the environment.

GLOSSARY

This Glossary aims to define some of the specific terms that are used throughout this book by both R. D. Hinshelwood and Jan Abram. For more in-depth definitions of Kleinian and Winnicottian terms, the reader is advised to turn to the two main textbooks by the present authors – Hinshelwood's *A Dictionary of Kleinian Thought* (1991) and the second edition of Abram's *The Language of Winnicott* (2007a).

Aggression

The concept of aggression is one of the main points of divergence between Klein and Winnicott associated with the DEATH INSTINCT.

RDH: Klein saw aggression as the origin, from the beginning, of disturbance. Both love and hate were provoked, as Freud described, from bodily sources such as the erogenous zones. In an initially rather simplistic way, Klein identified aggression as resulting from frustration, but later she identified ENVY from more psychological sources. Anxiety and psychic pain was reinterpreted by Klein as the fear that anger would overwhelm loving feelings, and defences were aimed at an equilibrium state of balance between loving and hating feelings.

JA: Winnicott conceptualises aggression at the start of life as synonymous with activity and motility. He refers to "primary aggression" and states that instinctual aggressiveness is originally part of appetite. So this is a concept of benign aggression, which is the engine of the life instinct. Aggression changes in quality as the infant develops, and the change will absolutely depend on the kind of environment in which the infant finds itself. With good-enough mothering, aggression becomes integrated into the personality and sense of self. But if the environment fails, aggression will manifest itself in a destructive and/or antisocial way. Winnicott's concept of aggression evolved, and in his late work it is pivotal in all of the most celebrated of his concepts – the antisocial tendency, creativity, the good-enough mother, transitional phenomena, true and false self, and, finally, the use of an object (Abram 2007a, pp. 15–40; 2012a).

Anxiety (psychic pain)

RDH: Klein came to see that the most important anxiety was the fundamental issue about the survival of self and of others (though this became embedded in the neurotic level of oedipal anxieties as described by Freud) [see DEPRESSIVE POSITION, PARANOID-SCHIZOID POSITION].

JA: For Winnicott, there were two fundamental qualities to the subjective experience of anxiety, and both were caused by the psychic (environment). If the (psychic) environment was deficient at the earliest stages of life, then primitive and unthinkable anxieties occurred. The deficient early environment therefore led to psychotic defences (see chapter 6). Due to a good-enough environment, the second quality of anxiety was oedipal – that is, castration anxiety.

Child analysis

See PLAY TECHNIQUE/CHILD ANALYSIS

Clinical paradigm

The term "paradigm" follows the ground-breaking work of Thomas Kuhn, who published *The Structure of Scientific Revolutions* in 1962. Kuhn's theory of scientific revolutions has been applied by Zjelko Loparic, a Brazilian philosopher, to understand the "paradigm change" from Freud to Winnicott (Loparic, 2010).

We have added the term "clinical" to the title of this book to emphasise the crucial nature of clinical practice that, for both Klein and Winnicott, was the sine qua non of the formulation of psychoanalytic theories and technique. Thus a "clinical paradigm" refers to a set of "guiding principles" that are founded on clinical practice.

Concern

RDH: The feeling of concern is a significant affective state of mind for both Klein and Winnicott. Klein regarded concern as central to the depressive position, and it was the expression of love in a form that recognised some damage had been done to the loved one. It is closely connected to GUILT.

JA: Winnicott largely agreed with Melanie Klein's conceptualisation of the depressive position and refers to this term in many of his writings up to 1960. However, in his late work, after 1960, he revised Klein's theory by focusing on how the infant comes to acquire a "capacity" for concern. Winnicott's emphasis on the development of the capacity for "concern" relates to the coming together of the environment and object mother (see Part III Dialogue). This description differs from Klein's stress on the "good" and the "bad" division in the mind in the PARANOID-SCHIZOID POSITION.

Containing

RDH: Strictly speaking "containing" (or container-contained) is not one of Klein's concepts. It was developed by Wilfred Bion from about 1959, and the term was taken from Jung. However, the concept is so closely connected to Klein's major discovery of projective identification that containing cannot be separated today from Kleinian psychoanalysis.

The idea is that psychological development proceeds from the very earliest days through a process by which the mother/carer will internalise the baby's mental states – when the baby cries, for instance, and mother becomes alarmed – and proceeds to give those a meaning. She then conveys the meaning to the baby through appropriate action – for example, feeding if the baby is crying with hunger. The baby learns by this process what meaning its sensations have.

There are many similarities between Bion's concept of container-contained and Winnicott's concept of HOLDING, but essential differences that should be carefully acknowledged.

Countertransference

RDH: Initially (always) a phenomenon of disputed worth. Originally Freud and his colleagues viewed the analyst's emotional responses to his patients with deep suspicion, as Jung, Ferenczi, and other colleagues were drawn into quite suspect behaviour. This suspicion changed during the 1940s, and especially with the work of Paula Heimann (at the time one of Melanie Klein's group) and of Heinrich Racker in Argentina. Winnicott also wrote an early paper of his own on countertransference, recognising it as an important authentic aspect of the analyst at work.

Klein never accepted the change in view about countertransference and remained dubious, emphasising the unreliability of analysts' subjective experience. Nevertheless, her group did accept the new view and have accepted it as an important means of accessing the unconscious communications between patient and analyst.

A difference in the views of the Kleinian and Independent groups remains, with the Independents being more adventurous in following their countertransference feelings, while Kleinians may want to have more evidence of the validity of their feelings at any one time.

JA: Winnicott was one of the first analysts to develop the concept of countertransference when he presented "Hate in the

Countertransference" in 1947. In this paper, he differentiated between three types of countertransference, including one that was psychopathological and meant the analyst required more analysis. His clinical example in the paper highlights the way in which he used his countertransference in clinical work. The main argument was that "hate" when working with the psychotic patient has to be acknowledged by the analyst, otherwise the hate engendered will lead to serious acting out on the part of the clinician (analyst and/ or psychiatrist). Lobotomy and leucotomy were practices Winnicott saw as "acting out" the unacknowledged hate.

Creating the object

See THEORETICAL FIRST FEED.

Death instinct

RDH: For Klein the human infant has various inherited potentialities. Klein thought, however, that we inherit the potentiality for phantasies – and in particular phantasies of relations with objects. These phantasies may be unconscious, but whether conscious or unconscious they can be motivating, in the sense that philosophers mean when they talk of a propositional logic. However, instincts, for Klein, are not energy in the way Freud described, following Fechner's neurophysiology which derived from the discovery of the reflex arc and the flow of actual electrical energy from stimulus to response. This is one of the major and explicit disagreements between Winnicott and Klein.

Klein discovered that the infant had a sense of something evil that intends to cause harm to the self. She saw this as the polar opposite of love, and she tended to call it hate. She thought she saw children expressing in their play the struggle for love to overcome hate. Eventually she connected this polarity with Freud's dual-instinct theory.

It remains confusing whether Klein was therefore an instinct theorist like Freud and saw motivations as a biological form of energy. In fact, Klein did not describe instincts in the way Freud did, and it may be that she did not understand the radical difference she made to the concept. It is likely that it was Susan Isaacs (1948) who could formulate it more clearly. Isaacs described instincts as biologically endowed potentials for experiencing relations with others who are familiar. The innate is not an innate energy model. Instead, the capacity to find and love a good object that is securely embraced inside oneself enhances the capacity for benign experiences with the other – love in a sense breeds love (and, indeed, the same with hate). This is not an economic principle.

JA: Winnicott rejected both the Freudian and the Kleinian concepts of the death instinct. It was perhaps the one main disagreement he had with Sigmund Freud, which he referred to in his very late work (Winnicott, 1969a). In his last writings, Winnicott followed the Greek philosopher Empedocles who had proposed a love/strife force, like fire, that could be constructive or destructive (Winnicott, 1969a).

Depressive position

RDH: The depressive position is a key notion of Klein's. She thought that her children were continually showing in the narratives of their play the aggression that they then feared harmed and even killed their most loved objects. These narratives, Klein thought, were basic as phantasies in the minds of children from the earliest age, and all through life. She could link this with Freud's theory of melancholia (Freud 1917e), where the mourning for the loss of a loved one goes wrong due to excessive aggression. Her analyst and mentor, Karl Abraham, had worked closely with Freud on this. However, Klein thought that there were two developments to Freud's theory which emerged from her children's play.

The first was that the play emerged from the child's imagination as if the child was preoccupied with this *in his own mind*. It was, she thought, the *internal* loved one who would be lost as a result of the aggression. The idea of mourning a lost internal object was very perplexing at the time (the 1930s). Associated with this loss and mourning was a drive to repair, atone, and put things back to rights, a process known as "reparation". [see UNCONSCIOUS PHANTASY, INTERNAL OBJECT]

The second thing Klein pointed to in these phantasies was the importance of the recognition of the external world, and the real other people. Loved ones, however loving and needed they are, are never perfect, and they fail the child at times, leading to frustration and aggression, which might be excessive. That means that the depressive position is the crucial state of becoming aware of the reality of the people who love you, and of the reality of one's own feelings and the alarming aggressive potency that could ruin love and dependency.

Klein understood that this position of having to regret the harm one caused was the source of concern for others from an early age, all through life. It takes the form of guilt, and working through the depressive position successfully will see a transition from a punitive form of guilt to a reparative form [see GUILT].

For Winnicott's thoughts on the depressive position, see CONCERN.

Ego

RDH: This term is a neologism used by the English translators of Freud. Klein's original training was in German-speaking Budapest. In the German, Freud uses the more familiar term *"ich"*, meaning "I". There is therefore a much more personal and existential meaning to the term, and Klein tended to stay with that, even when she used "ego". But often in English her texts use "self" where others might use "ego". This emphasises Klein's lack of distinction between a technical perspective on a patient and a more personal perspective that starts with a person's experience.

JA: Winnicott distinguished between "ego" and "self". He defined the "ego" as a particular aspect of the self that organizes and integrates interpsychic experiences while forming the intrapsychic world of object relations. In his late work, Winnicott suggested that the ego starts before the self and depended on the mother's primary maternal preoccupation, which offers the infant "ego-coverage".

Environment

JA: Up until 1923, Freud's work focused on the topographical model of the mind, which did not take account of the subject's environment. Rather, it was psychosexuality in relation to the instincts that shaped the personality. In 1923, Freud introduced the "structural model" in *The Ego and the Id* (1923b), in which he revised his perspective on the environment, referring to the ego as having three masters: the id, the superego, and the external world – that is, the parents. In the early 1940s, Winnicott came to see that "there was no such thing as a baby" but a baby in relation to a crucial m/other. This observation led Winnicott to formulate a theory of the environment–individual set-up, his first major theoretical achievement (see chapter 2).

Envy

RDH: Late in her career, in 1957, three years before she died, Klein postulated a key role for envy, this worst of all vices. She thought it was an aberrant but common problem. In the paranoid-schizoid position, objects are misperceived as all good or all bad, and they are loved and hated accordingly [see PARANOID-SCHIZOID POSITION]. However, it began to seem likely that at times the good object could be hated precisely because it is good. The infant has a profound need for the good object in order to survive; such dependency – together with the independence of that object – makes it a very difficult situation to handle. While being an object that loves you is important, it actually shows you up as not in possession of the same kind of resources. The object is then hated precisely because its goodness is needed and it shows up the inadequacy of a self that cannot survive on its own. Need for and separation from the good object make its goodness a severe provocation. Klein thought that this was an exquisitely painful state and that there were specific ways in which we can defend against it.

JA: Winnicott concurred with Klein that unacknowledged envy caused deep problems that led to psychopathology. Envy that could be acknowledged, like hate and sadism, were affects that evolved in the individual in relation to the environment. Therefore, Winnicott would say that these affects are developmental achievements, and in health they would be integrated into the personality but in illness would lead to severe disturbance.

External object

RDH: In contrast to most other schools of psychoanalysis, and to Winnicott, Klein thought that the earliest ego had a sense of boundary and that there existed a world beyond itself. In this most primitive of stages, the outside world is experienced as an external object characterised by the state the baby feels itself to be in. If comfortable, the external object is felt to be "good"; if uncomfortable, it is felt to be "bad". Thus bodily states determine in a biological way how the external object is seen, until sensory perception can begin to give a truer picture – that brings in the depressive picture of objects that are felt to be both good and bad in parts.

JA: Winnicott's work, from 1945 onwards, develops the notion of the environment–individual set-up. The individual self, therefore, is inscribed with the earliest environment (see chapter 6). The parent–infant relationship plays a crucial role in shaping the internal world of each individual. In this sense, the external object plays a part in the development of the sense of self, but Winnicott's stress is on what the infant and growing child "makes" of his environment. The external object is "created" by each individual. The environment–individual set-up will be played out at unconscious levels in the analytic setting and affects the transference and countertransference.

Gratitude

RDH: Klein accepted Abraham's notion of whole-object love. While Abraham thought of this as a step to maturity, Klein thought of it as a very early emotional response. Not only is there a state of bodily satiation when the external object provides it – giving a feed for instance – but there is also a feeling of appreciation and gratitude that the object provides the satisfaction. It is felt not just to be satisfying, but to be benign and well-meaning. Another way of putting it is that the object wishes the baby to live, and gratitude is therefore the Kleinian version of the life instinct. The object supports the infant's wish to live. They happily (blissfully, it seems to the onlooker) work together.

JA: For Winnicott, gratitude is connected with the capacity for concern. As the baby is able to see his mother as a separate being, so he starts to realise all she has done for him. This leads to a sense of concern, related to a sense of guilt, for not having noticed before. In an optimal environment, this leads to a sense of gratitude and love.

Guilt

RDH: Klein eventually departed significantly from Freud when it came to conceptualising guilt. Instead of attributing it wholly to the introjected oedipal parents around the age of 3 years onwards, as Freud said, Klein could see that children tried to show in their play that they were troubled by their own impulses at an earlier age. Rather, they were reacting to an internal state of hating the loved one [see DEPRESSIVE POSITION]. They believed themselves to be responsible for the effects of their aggression and were troubled sometimes to the point of extreme terror by what they might do, or might have done.

Because this kind of self-assessment starts when the early paranoid-schizoid position is dominant, the experience for the infant is that its attitude towards its aggression is as violent as the aggression it feels towards its bad objects. Indeed, it has itself become a bad object. The experience is that the malignant bad object has been internalised (introjected) to give its malign colour to the inner world. It is this sense of something bad and self-attacking internally which is Klein's view of the origins of the superego.

That primitive superego could then be described as originating in what Klein eventually thought of — in her own terms — as the death instinct. It only later comes to take on the function of being the socialising and moral influence as the parents exert their encouraging and criticising influence.

Guilt therefore starts as the harshest of experiences, and only with the gradual experience of a more and more accurate perception of reality can the harshness be ameliorated, usually never completely. So this is a benign transformation from the earlier retaliatory self-punishment, when self-criticism is experienced as the persecution of the bad object that wishes the infant dead, and on towards a more reparative form of guilt that seeks to right the wrongs the ego believes it has done.

JA: Winnicott referred to the baby's sense of guilt related to his gradual perception that his mother was separate and different from himself. The baby is then able to look back and notice that he had been "ruthless" in relation to her when he could not tell the difference between what he needed from her and what that need may have done to her – that is, the damage he caused by his need. The "sense of guilt", therefore, is part and parcel of the capacity for concern. Winnicott's revisions of Klein's "depressive position", as noted above, places emphasis on a positive and healthy sense of guilt that leads to the capacity to develop insight that results in self-care and in care of other people in general.

Holding

JA: All the details of maternal care just before birth and immediately afterwards go towards making up the holding environment. This includes the mother's primary maternal preoccupation, which is at the heart of the holding environment and enables the mother to provide the infant with the necessary ego-support at the beginning of life. Physical holding is meaningless without an emotional sensitivity and care that will be internalised bodily and emotionally by the infant. Holding includes the mother's mirror-role in early development, which means she is able to mirror the infant's affects due to her deep identification with the infant's predicament of absolute dependence. Holding is often associated with containing, but it should not be confused with Bion's container-contained concept. The two concepts have similarities but emanate from their different theoretical paradigms – the container-contained is based on the Kleinian paradigm, in contrast to holding being a concept founded on Winnicott's paradigm.

Illusion (of omnipotence)

JA: The roots of imagination are initiated as a result of the baby feeling that he gets what he needs. The mother's capacity to tune in to his early needs that are both physical and emotional helps the baby feel he has created the world. The capacity to play is predicated on the success of the baby feeling as if he were God.

RDH: The nature of an illusion is at the root of imagination, symbolisation, and culture. It is the capacity to see one "thing" as if it were another. When this capacity is used for symbolisation, the symbol represents another as if it were equated, without losing the knowledge that they are different. We use words as if they were what the word means, while also knowing that words and what they mean are actually different. Klein would not have agreed with Winnicott that this capacity is acquired at birth (see SYMBOLISATION).

Inscription

JA: This is a term taken from French psychoanalysis (Roussillon, 2010). Through the early parent–infant relationship the infant's growing sense of self is inscribed by the parental psychic responses to every aspect of dependency and development (see chapter 2). Thus, every single person has the early environment inscribed in his or her sense of self, which could be said to be the psychic equivalent of genetic continuity.

Internal object

RDH: Following her work developing child analysis, Klein moved to an interest in the more severe mental disorders. From her child observations she observed that children's minds were made up of phantasies of relations with and narratives about others. This preoccupation with others therefore points to an emphasis on the experience of objects, including the objects in the mind which are externalised in the phantastical situations of play.

Internal objects are an artefact of representation. When we use our visual apparatus, we "see" a world of objects displaced in relation to each other in a world around us. But actually we know that seeing is the interaction of light on the retina at the back of the eye where it causes chemical and electrical events. We don't see those events, only as representations in terms of a visual field. Without putting it in such terms, Klein seemed to think that a baby underwent a similar process of converting sensory events into experience with the internal bodily receptors, the interoceptors. These sensations from the body are "experienced" as objects in relation to each other within the space of the body.

She understood, following Freud, that at the beginning there is not a proper distinction between mind and body. The mental experience of swallowing milk is no different for the infant from taking inside the mother who gives the milk (introjection). Indeed, Klein thought that a bodily state – for instance, hunger – is in fact the sensation of some nasty being actually inside the tummy that wants the infant to suffer the discomfort. And likewise, a feed that takes away that nasty being (the "bad" object) is actually mother getting inside (as a "good" object) to create the nice feeling of satiation. For the infant, as displayed in play, the inner world of the infant is a world of solid little beings with good or bad intentions towards the infant. These little inner beings are called internal objects.

JA: While Winnicott used the notion of the internal object, he disagreed that it was a given from the beginning of life. Rather, he saw that after a certain amount of needs being adapted to, the infant internalised the effects of the parent–infant relationship – that is, an internal object was formed through a process of internalisation rather than being an innate internal object.

Winnicott proposed the notion of a subjective object that was a product of the earliest parent–infant relationship when the mother was in a state of primary maternal preoccupation.

Interpretation

RDH: Conscious insight into unconscious conflicts and anxieties were, from Freud's earliest work, the core tool of psychoanalysis that distinguished it from suggestive and other therapies. Patients are frequently hesitant about accepting these painful pieces of knowledge about themselves, a reaction known as resistance. There is a wide range of views about why this is and what to do about it – from a fear of the pain of understanding and responsibility, to the enmity of a negative transference and the effects of envy on the analyst's abilities.

Klein thought that the most fruitful strategy is truth itself and to confront in as kindly a way as possible the hesitancy, fear, and aggression involved in resistance. In the more contemporary Kleinian approach, the "truth" is the meaning that patient and analyst can make together through the process of container-contained (introduced by Bion) – then the meaning comes from the analyst holding the painful experience in himself, if he can.

JA: While Winnicott saw interpretation as one of the principal elements of analytic practice, he laid stress on the analyst taking account of the patient's ability to receive the interpretation and capacity to play (i.e., free-associate). If the patient could not play, then the analyst had to facilitate understanding through interpretative comments. By his late work, Winnicott privileged the holding environment in any given analysis, which should provide the incremental steps towards the analyst's mutative interpretation. While this followed Strachey's argument concerning the therapeutic action of analysis, Winnicott emphasised the analyst's ability to facilitate the patient's discovery of self through the transitional and transferential elements at the heart of analytic practice.

Mother, environment/object

RDH: For both Klein and Winnicott, the mother (or primary carer) is seen as a vital element of an infant's world, even at first the whole of its world. This primary relationship colours all subsequent relationships and experiences. Klein thought of this as played out according to the anxieties and phantasies known as the depressive position and the paranoid-schizoid position, and the defences in those positions.

For Winnicott's notion of the environment, see ENVIRONMENT.

Object use

See SURVIVAL OF THE OBJECT.

Omnipotence

RDH: Possibly a Kleinian's view would be that Winnicott's observation of the necessary illusion of omnipotence would be one of the defences (see Part V Dialogue).

JA: Winnicott used the term "omnipotence" to refer to the infant feeling that he is God when his needs are met [see ILLUSION (OF OMNIPOTENCE)]. But this should be distinguished from the patient's omnipotent manic defence, which Winnicott would say has emanated from a deficiency of early illusion (of omnipotence). The latter experience is essential for the infant to feel he has created the object.

Paranoid-schizoid position

RDH: Melanie Klein's observations, made while using her method of child analysis, convinced her that children oscillate between seeing others (objects) as good or bad – that is to say, the objects have their own intentions (as attributed to the toys they play with) and play them out with other objects. This is a world of polarised "good" and "bad", and children see their world in this exaggerated way (as do adults at times). The objects may not be stable and can switch from good to bad or the reverse, and, as time goes on, this leads to the problems of the depressive position. What characterises the paranoid-schizoid position is the splitting of objects – their good side is seen as the whole of them, or their bad side is the whole of them. At first, a mixed object is seen as two objects, one good and one bad. This leads to intense experiences of rather pure feelings. In particular, the bad object with intentions to harm or kill the self arouses great terror, and children of some years may show this in what is called *pavor nocturnus*, or night terrors. Similarly, the good object, which has the intention that the infant survive and flourish, is experienced with great bliss.

This polarisation of objects into good and bad inevitably draws the child's attention to its own capacities for love and hate, and the child will see its own reactions at war with each other, the solution being a similar splitting of itself. As the child matures, splitting itself becomes a splitting-off of certain parts of itself. The parts of the self that are split off are those functions that give rise to experiences that are intolerable. Often that means the splitting-off of the capacity to perceive things realistically, especially for the child to see itself realistically. For example, commonly the capacity to feel guilt may be lost in order to lose the sense of guilt.

Guilt is a good example for demonstrating another important feature of the paranoid-schizoid position. When a person avoids a feeling of being guilty for something, and in effect splits off his conscience, he may then attribute the guilt to someone else. In more ordinary psychological language, that person makes a "counter-accusation" attributing guilt to some other object (sometimes the very object he may have hurt). This is a process called projective identification, which is now widely acknowledged by many psychoanalysts far beyond the Kleinian school.

JA: Winnicott thought that Klein's paranoid-schizoid position was a vivid description of a psychotic state of mind that was often mobilised in adult patients due to the analytic setting. However, he disagreed that this description could be transposed to the state of mind of the newborn infant, which led to his phrase "early is not deep". The newborn infant had not accumulated enough experience of the parent–infant relationship to be capable of this state of mind. Moreover, the infant who was fortunate enough to have a good-enough mother/environment would benefit from a very different environment from that described by the paranoid-schizoid position. For Winnicott, the paranoid-schizoid position was a good description of an infant who had suffered a deficient early environment.

Playing

JA: As shown in chapter 2, Winnicott was positively influenced by Klein's use of the small toys in working analytically with children. In his late work, however, he developed a theory of playing associated with symbolic thinking and free association. The quality of playing in the third area – transitional phenomena – is synonymous with creative living and constitutes the matrix of self-experience. In the context of the analytic experience, the ability to play is the ultimate achievement for the patient because, for Winnicott, it is only through playing that the self can be discovered and strengthened.

Play technique/child analysis

RDH: Klein learned the foundations of her particular approach from developing a form of psychoanalysis for treating children. She used free play, with toys she supplied, instead of the verbal free associations in adult analysis. She noted inhibitions in the play, where adults would show a resistance to associating. But she thought that fruitful intervention was the same as in an adult analysis; she made interpretations in which she put into words the narrative that she saw played out with the toys. In other words, insight into the unspoken phantasies of the unconscious was the key therapeutic factor in both child and adult analyses.

Primary maternal preoccupation

JA: This is a term that Winnicott used to describe the state of mind the mother normally goes into just before giving birth and for the early weeks of her infant's life. The infant's healthy development is contingent on the mother's ability to go into this state of mind in which she is completely identified with the infant's predicament of dependence.

Psychic creativity

JA: Winnicott refers to a creative drive, which I interpret as an extension of Freud's notion of the life instinct. It is the mother's ability to adapt to her infant's needs that facilitates the baby to feel he has created the object. This is the place from which the sense of self grows. Primary psychic creativity is associated with the female element in Winnicott's late work and is the basis for "creative living" and "feeling real".

Psychic pain (anxiety)

RDH: James Strachey's seminal paper on interpretation of 1934 refers to the focus as "the point of urgency" in the material. It directs attention to the affective moments of the session, at least as much as the thematic content of the associations. It seems likely that this was the influence of Melanie Klein at the time, who was interested in the point of anxiety.

Psychic transitionality

JA: A term I use to denote the emotional journey related to "creating the object" and "illusion". It refers to an evolving capacity to play and grow in the analysing situation.

Psychotic anxiety

RDH: Klein thought that her most important discovery about the mind was a layer of the unconscious beneath the oedipal neurotic level of conflict. The anxiety at these levels was about the very constituents of the mind or self. It could be felt as annihilation, as some people do when in states of schizophrenic psychosis. Losing one's mind is a saying in the vernacular language to indicate madness. It followed from Karl Abraham's work with severe mentally ill people, in which the processes of projection and introjection as well as splitting are destabilising of the self, but are also a means of managing the anxieties at these deeper levels. There were two specific anxieties: one of being annihilated in part or wholly, persecutory anxiety [see PARANOID-SCHIZOID POSITION]; and the second the destruction of the much-needed good objects inside the self, depressive anxiety [see DEPRESSIVE POSITION].

Reality principle

RDH: For Klein, the infant in the earliest stages must cope with the reality of a world populated with objects of an animate kind. Before a full command of the sense of distance perception, the infant makes full use of its capacity to phantasise in order to see its world as much to its convenience as possible.

For Klein this means addressing and managing both the objects/persons in the external world, and the affective inner psychic world of internal objects. From early in life, therefore, the simple experiences of need and satiation evoke affects and powerful experiences of a narrative kind, not necessarily one that an observer would see [see UNCONSCIOUS PHANTASY], and the infant has to ensure its affects do not harm and destroy those it needs in external or internal reality. This is particularly acute at the beginning of the depressive position when the experience of bodily needs may cause sufficient aggression to overwhelm the loved objects to which the infant feels gratitude [see AGGRESSION, ENVY, GUILT].

Response to interpretation

RDH: Melanie Klein found, through simply making interpretations of the unconscious, that it had an effect – very striking in some instances. The key observation was that children's play became less inhibited and also more imaginative. She took this to be the result of reduced anxiety when the child felt understood by the analyst. It was a repeated observation and gave her a strong argument that interpretation of the unconscious is as effective in children as in adults, if not more so. There were some conditions she insisted on: first, that interpretations were made in language the child understood – baby talk about body parts and functions; second, that she would not interpret psychoanalytic theory unless she was completely certain that she was being shown the specific narrative (of the Oedipus complex, for instance) in the child's play.

These principles she transferred to adults when her practice included adults, and when she became a training analyst (in 1930). Because her emphasis was on observation of play in the immediate moment, she naturally emphasised the importance of the relationship she saw being displayed in the immediate present (the here-and-now). As a result, her tendency was to stress less the early patterns of infant relationships, but those occurring now: the transference is alive in the session now, because this is the phantasy relationship active in the unconscious, right now. This emphasised the presently active phantasies, rather than the past traumas. The reasons are explained in the Strachey paper already mentioned. There, Strachey stressed the transference distortion of the analyst in accordance with the emotional expectations active in the present of the session. It is only now in the session that the patient has the possibility of reality-testing his (distorted) expectations of the analyst.

The upshot is that two specific features characterise the interpretations that Klein made. The first is that her emphasis on anxiety raises a debate about whether the interpretation is effective because it describes the anxiety, in words (often a new experience for the patient), or whether it addresses the defensive attitudes and behaviour – a much more familiar occurrence for the patient, who has received the exasperation and criticism of friends and relatives whom he has distorted. Klein implicitly focused on the anxiety, a process that came to be formulated theoretically by Bion as the container-contained process. The other feature of her interpretations is a tendency to regard transference as a distorting effect through the transfer from the active unconscious of the patient, rather than a transfer from the past.

Schizoid mechanisms/splitting

RDH: In the last decade and a half of her life, from 1946, Melanie Klein felt she had made profound discoveries of the deep layers of the unconscious, that domain where the process of splitting, projection, introjection, and projective identification occur. These are the schizoid mechanisms, and all rely on the misperception of objects and the self due to the fundamental distortion when self or object are seen as only perfect (idealisation) or, alternatively, as all bad. This Klein thought as the earliest, and still the basic, functioning all through life. She thought that we all revert to that kind of functioning. For instance, most people called up for military duty in wartime can become killers on the basis of perceiving an enemy as a bad object to be exterminated for his badness and threats.

Self

JA: Winnicott used the term "unit status" to define a formed self, which is distinct from the ego. The baby evolves "unit status" by the stage of relative dependence after the first three months of life. This stage of development relates to the developing capacity to perceive Me from Not-me. The terms Me and Not-me were created by Winnicott as words that have emotional meaning in a similar way to Freud using *das "ich"* instead of "ego" (see EGO).

Stage of concern

See CONCERN.

Survival of the object

JA: At the core of Winnicott's paper "The Use of an Object" is the notion of "survival of the object". This concept sets out an alternative concept to that of the "death instinct" for both Freud and Klein. The development and integration of the individual's innate benign aggression depends on "survival of the object".

Surviving and non-surviving objects

JA: "Surviving object" and "non-surviving object" are terms I have proposed to extend Winnicott's inference in his work on the "use of an object" and "survival of the object". I designated the "surviving object" as an intrapsychic subjective object that emanates from the object's interpsychic survival of the infant's ruthless needs. Conversely, the "non-surviving object" – also an intrapsychic subjective object – emanates from the object's non-survival in the early interpsychic relationship. The specifics of the interpsychic dynamic that take place in the early parent–infant relationship constitute the foundations of human development, which will be revivified in the transference–countertransference matrix of the analytic relationship (Abram, 2012a).

Symbolisation

RDH: Melanie Klein developed her method of child analysis over the period roughly from 1920 to 1932. But by 1930 she was already looking at what she would do next. This entailed also looking back and considering Abraham's work that he left unfinished when he died in 1925. In 1929 she treated a very disturbed 4-year-old boy, Dick, who had been psychiatrically diagnosed as a case of schizophrenia. He had a deficit in his intellectual development, rarely used words, and was only chaotically active. Klein believed she saw his deficit as arising from a lack of symbol-formation. Somewhat theoretically, she believed Dick was unusually frightened of an excessive propensity for anger towards his primary objects, mother and father. Whereas most children can turn to other objects (in the way Freud described that Little Hans did), Dick could not. As soon as he turned to someone who might substitute for mother, and start with a clean slate, as it were, his aggression followed almost immediately. Any substitute object therefore became impossible to relate to, as the inherent conflict was immediately aroused again.

Symbols, she thought, were formed on the basis of simple displacement, a view she took from Freud's discovery of dream symbols. One thing stands in for another. She failed to inform herself fully of the wide study of symbolisations in aesthetic and philosophical disciplines. And, in fact, she left the study of symbols to one of her most talented students, Hanna Segal, in the 1950s. Despite Klein's lack of sophistication here, she nevertheless had a good appreciation of literature and drama, derived from the interests of her older brother, who had written poetry.

Theoretical first feed

JA: This is a term Winnicott used to denote the very beginnings of symbolic thinking in the newborn infant. The "theoretical first feed" is a culmination of needs being met through the mother's "adaptation to need". It is associated with "creating the object" and "illusion".

Transitional phenomena and transitional objects

JA: This is one of Winnicott's well-known concepts and relates to an "intermediate dimension of living". Transitionality refers to the infant's psychological journey from being merged with the mother to developing the capacity to distinguish Me from Not-me. The transitional object refers to the infant's choice of an object that aids this journey – for example, a teddy bear.

Unconscious phantasy

RDH: With her play technique, Melanie Klein evolved a somewhat new method of entry into the unconscious mind, and, in particular, the mind of the young child, some as young as the third year of life. By observing and interpreting young children's play, Klein's notion of the mind therefore inevitably diverged somewhat from that of classical analysis, based, as Freud had done, on the physiological notions of Ernst Brücke and of Gustav Fechner. What Klein saw in front of her was a display of narrative in the play, rather than the discharge of energy. This narrative model of the mind is in some ways easier to recognise than a drive theory. It changed the emphasis from Freud, who saw instincts as having a source, an impulse, an aim, and an object. The change was to emphasise the object rather than the impulse – hence, object-relations theory.

Particularly when Klein was put on the spot to defend her theories and practice in the Controversial Discussions (1943–1944), she and her group struggled to formulate the difference. Eventually it was Susan Isaacs who came up with the formula that "instincts are mentally represented as phantasies" (Isaacs, 1948). The experience we have as sentient beings is in the form of persons engaging with each other in a narrative process. It is our mental representation of sensory inputs [see INTERNAL OBJECTS, SYMBOLISATION].

The emphasis in Klein is therefore on the narrative structure of the mind and not impulse satisfaction, and this made her aware of anxiety as well as satiation, recognising how much children (and adults) agonise over their impulses, and not just about getting them satisfied. As a result, the unconscious mind is a repository of narratives, pleasing and worrying.

JA: Winnicott did not subscribe to the proposal that unconscious phantasy was innate, because his view was that the infant's experience of the m/other was at the root of imagination and illusion and the ability to play and grow, in sharp distinction to delusion, the inability to play, and the lack of development.

Whole object

RDH: The term is somewhat ambiguous. More often it is used to convey how, in the paranoid-schizoid position, another person is seen only partially (a part-object) for his good features, or for the bad ones, thus idealising or denigrating the object. In either case, a part of the object is denied, and only a part is perceived – known as a part-object. Once the depressive position operates, a person is seen as a mixture and then becomes more approximated to the whole of his self, good and bad. This follows Karl Abraham's clinical descriptions, and his debate about the fetishist as reducing the individual to a single part – a "partial" object, as Abraham is translated.

In another sense, which neither Abraham nor Klein expressed clearly, the loved person is experienced in two ways: first of all, the object gives a feed and causes a state of satisfaction. This is loved, of course. But in addition, the satisfying object is felt to want to satisfy the infant, and is seen as having wishes as the infant does, and has motivations towards the infant as the infant does towards the object. This gives rise to a second level of love – the love that the object wants to satisfy. Similarly "bad" objects are hated, not only because they do not satisfy, but because they are believed to want to frustrate and cause the discomfort that needs satisfying.

For Abraham, this is the full expression of love, loving appreciation, as well as straightforward satisfaction. Abraham thought that it was possible for the second of these to disappear in a process in which the object is merely used, as a fetishist loves a particular body part as a thing to use, and not a whole person. Klein was less clear about this, though it is clearly implicit in her eventual late text on gratitude (as it relates to envy).

It is likely that Klein and Winnicott did not share views on this, though neither really expressed the state of affairs clearly. For Klein, the object is a motivated animate being – motivated for the good or for the bad. And the level of appreciation (for the goodness, and removal of appreciation for the bad) is there from the start. The infant sees the object in his own likeness as an animate and subjective sentient being.

Afterword

JAN ABRAM: Working with Bob has been a pleasure, and I have learnt a great deal. This was the value of dialoguing, which instigated new depths of understanding. Thus, the process of preparing this book has, for me, been an adventure in the best sense of the word. This is not to say there were no tensions, and, at times, it felt as if we were getting caught up with the unconscious dynamics that belonged to the controversies of decades ago. Through what felt like a mutual care and concern not to fall into that trap, we managed to find a way of navigating some of the inevitably intense feelings that arose.

Throughout our collegial work I have found Bob to be open, calm, and consistent in his responses as we tried to make sense of each other's presentations of our protagonists' thought. I feel very grateful to Bob, who has demonstrated how interesting and stimulating this kind of dialogue and comparison can be when two colleagues remain curious and open to each other's viewpoint. The hope is that the book will encourage further dialogues and comparisons that can only enrich our common aim to contribute to the psychoanalytic literature. And I look forward to the next venture – Winnicott and Bion.

R. D. HINSHELWOOD: This has been an unusual book to write. Having started as a public workshop discussion to compare our different schools of thought and their concepts and forms of psychoanalytic practice, we decided to continue the form of that debating exchange. The problem with most comparative work is that it involves two people from opposite camps giving position papers without a lot of credit for the other side's position. And that, in itself, engenders a sort of competitive spirit. In a workshop setting, both parties are understandably likely to assume that it is an opportunity to win the audience over to their own side, or as much of the audience as possible. And, in addition, in a public venue the tensions – again understandable – make it more difficult to listen in to another point of view; hence debate rises to a superficial level. In the end, the comparing is usually left to the audience, while the "experts" go away unaffected in their loyalties.

I am greatly admiring of Jan, as she seems not to have succumbed to such pitfalls and seems also to have avoided provoking me in those ways too. Nevertheless, there is necessarily a degree of risk and anxiety that one's confidence in one's own point of view will be shaken. It is particularly so in the field of psychoanalytic comparisons. One has all those internal objects acquired from teachers and colleagues, and one has to speak up for them as well as one can. And one may not give as good an account as they might require, so they become finger-wagging, and superego phantoms in our minds. There was, on my side at least, some comfort that the debate was in a sense a slow-motion one, conducted by emails at a pace comfortable to both Jan and myself. It provided space and time to consider and reflect on the task and the difficult questions, to keep an eye on the risks and tensions that could hinder calmer thoughts and responses, and to allow replies only once one had something not too impulsive.

I am grateful also to you, readers, who have struggled on through our various misunderstandings to reach this point. I hope you have found our meanderings and blind alleys informative as well as frustrating. If you have been left thoughtful about how this whole field could have been more clearly exposed, then you are now standing where I am. I have found it sufficiently stimulating that so many of the issues Jan and I hit upon have remained as curiosities or irritants that have needed continuing attention as, from time to time, the puzzles come back to me. I think that if we have achieved in your mind a state of informed uncertainty, rather than uninformed confidence, then we have truly conveyed what I believe we need. For the future of psychoanalysis to continue to be alive, we need to insist on differences being generative not oppositional, and to hold difference in view rather than collapse it into a slick equality with each other.

REFERENCES

Abraham, K. (1924). A short study of the development of the libido. In: *Selected Papers on Psychoanalysis*. London: Hogarth Press, 1927.

Abram, J. (1996). *The Language of Winnicott: A Dictionary of Winnicott's Use of Words*. London: Karnac.

Abram, J. (2005). L'objet qui survit [trans. D. Alcorn]. *Journal de la Psychanalyse de L'enfant, 36*: 139–174.

Abram, J. (2007a). *The Language of Winnicott: A Dictionary of Winnicott's Use of Words, Second Edition*. London: Karnac.

Abram, J. (2007b). L'objet qui ne survit pas. Quelques réflexions sur les racines de la terreur [trans. D. Houzel]. *Journal de la Psychanalyse de L'enfant, 39*: 247–270.

Abram, J. (2008). Donald Woods Winnicott: A brief introduction. *International Journal of Psychoanalysis, 89*: 1189–1217.

Abram, J. (2012a). D.W.W.'s notes for the Vienna Congress 1971: A consideration of Winnicott's theory of aggression and an interpretation of the clinical implications. In: *Donald Winnicott Today* (pp. 302–330). New Library of Psychoanalysis. Hove: Routledge, 2013.

Abram, J. (2012b). On Winnicott's clinical innovations in the analysis of adults. *International Journal of Psychoanalysis, 93*: 1461–1473.

Abram, J. (Ed.) (2013). *Donald Winnicott Today*. New Library of Psychoanalysis. Hove: Routledge.

Abram, J. (2015a). *Affects, Mediation and Countertransference: Some Reflections on the Contributions of Marjorie Brierley (1893–1984) and Their Relevance to Psychoanalysis Today*. Stockholm: European Psychoanalytical Federation.

Abram, J. (2015b). Further reflections on Winnicott's last major theoretical achievement: From "Relating through Identifications" to "The Use of an Object". In: G. Saragnano & C. Seulin (Eds.), *Playing and Reality Revisited: A New Look at Winnicott's Classic Work* (pp. 111–125). London: Karnac.

Abram, J. (Ed.) (2016a). *André Green at the Squiggle Foundation* (2nd edition). London: Karnac.

Abram, J. (2016b). Creating an object: Commentary on "The Arms of the Chimeras" by Béatrice Ithier. *International Journal of Psychoanalysis, 97*: 489–501.

Alexander, F. (1946). The principle of corrective emotional experience. In: F. Alexander & T. M. French (Eds.), *Psychoanalytic Therapy: Principles and Application*. New York: Ronald Press.

Balint, A., & Balint, M. (1939). On transference and counter-transference. *International Journal of Psychoanalysis, 20*: 223–230.

Bick, E. (1964). Notes on infant observation in psycho-analytic training. *International Journal of Psychoanalysis, 45*: 558–566.

Bion, W. R. (1959). Attacks on linking. In: *Second Thoughts* (pp. 93–109). London: Karnac, 1984.

Bion, W. R. (1962a). *Learning from Experience*. London: Heinemann.

Bion, W. R. (1962b). A theory of thinking. In: *Second Thoughts* (pp. 110–119). London: Karnac, 1984.

Bowlby, J. (1940). The influence of early environment in the development of neurosis and neurotic character. *International Journal of Psychoanalysis, 21*: 154–178.

Brenman Pick, I. (1985). Working through in the countertransference. *International Journal of Psychoanalysis, 66*: 157–166. Reprinted in E. Spillius (Ed.), *Melanie Klein Today, Vol. 2: Mainly Practice* (pp. 34–47). London: Tavistock, 1988.

Brierley, M. (1937). Affects in theory and practice. *International Journal of Psychoanalysis, 18*: 256–268.

Ezriel, H. (1956). Experimentation within the psychoanalytic session. *British Journal for the Philosophy of Science, 7*: 29–48.

Freud, A. (1926). *Four Lectures on Child Analysis*. London: Hogarth Press, 1948.

Freud, A. (1936). *The Ego and the Mechanisms of Defence*. London: Hogarth Press.

Freud, S. (1895d) (with Breuer, J.). *Studies on Hysteria. Standard Edition*, 2.

Freud, S. (1901b). *The Psychopathology of Everyday Life. Standard Edition*, 6: 1–279.

Freud, S. (1909b). Analysis of a phobia in a five-year-old boy. *Standard Edition, 10*: 3–149.

Freud, S. (1911b). Formulations on the two principles of mental functioning. *Standard Edition, 12*: 218–226.

Freud, S. (1911c). Psycho-analytic notes on an autobiographical account of a case of paranoia (Dementia paranoides). *Standard Edition, 22*: 3–82.

Freud, S. (1912e). Recommendations to physicians practising psychoanalysis. *Standard Edition, 12*: 109–120.

Freud, S. (1917e). Mourning and melancholia. *Standard Edition, 14*: 239–258.

Freud, S. (1918b). From the history of an infantile neurosis. *Standard Edition, 17*: 3–122.

Freud, S. (1920g). *Beyond the Pleasure Principle. Standard Edition, 18*: 7–64.

Freud, S. (1923b). *The Ego and the Id. Standard Edition, 19*: 3–68.

Freud, S. (1925h). Negation. *Standard Edition, 19*: 235–239.

Freud, S. (1930a). *Civilization and Its Discontents. Standard Edition, 21*.

Freud, S. (1933a). *New Introductory Lectures on Psycho-Analysis. Standard Edition, 22*: 7–182.

Glover, E. (1945). Examination of the Klein system of child psychology. *Psychoanalytic Study of the Child, 1*: 75–118.

Goldman, D. (2012). Vital sparks and the form of things unknown. In: J. Abram (Ed.), *Donald Winnicott Today* (pp. 331–357). New Library of Psychoanalysis. Hove: Routledge.

Green, A. (1975). Potential space in psychoanalysis: The object in the setting. In: *On Private Madness*. London: Hogarth Press, 1986. Also in: J. Abram (Ed.), *Donald Winnicott Today* (pp. 183–204). New Library of Psychoanalysis. Hove: Routledge, 2013.

Green, A. (1977). Conceptions of affect. *International Journal of Psychoanalysis, 58*: 129–156.

Green, A. (1991). On thirdness. In: *André Green at the Squiggle Foundation* (pp. 39–68). London: Karnac.

Heimann, P. (1950). On counter-transference. *International Journal of Psychoanalysis, 31*: 81–84. Reprinted in: *About Children and Children-No-Longer* (pp. 73–79). London: Routledge, 1989.

Heimann, P. (1960). Counter-transference. *British Journal of Medical Psychology, 33*: 9–15. Reprinted in: *About Children and Children-No-Longer* (pp. 151–160). London: Routledge, 1989.

Hinshelwood, R. D. (1989). *A Dictionary of Kleinian Thought*. London: Free Association Books.

Hinshelwood, R. D. (1991). *A Dictionary of Kleinian Thought, Second Edition*. London: Free Association Books.

Hinshelwood, R. D. (1994). *Clinical Klein*. London: Free Association Books.

Hinshelwood, R. D. (2006). Melanie Klein and repression: An examination of some unpublished notes of 1934. *Psychoanalysis and History, 8*: 5–42.

Hinshelwood, R. D. (2008). Melanie Klein and countertransference: A historical note. *Psychoanalysis and History, 10*: 95–113.

Hinshelwood, R. D. (2013). *Research on the Couch: Subjectivity, Single Case Studies and Psychoanalytic Knowledge*. London: Routledge

Hinshelwood, R. D. (2016). *Countertransference and Alive Moments: Help or Hindrance*. London: Process Press.

Isaacs, S. (1939). Criteria for interpretation *International Journal of Psychoanalysis, 20*: 148–160.

Isaacs, S. (1943). The nature and function of phantasy. In P. King & R. Steiner (Eds.), *The Freud–Klein Controversies 1941–45* (pp. 264–321). London: Routledge, 1991.

Isaacs, S. (1948). The nature and function of phantasy. *International Journal of Psychoanalysis, 29*: 73–97. Reprinted in: M. Klein, P. Heimann, S. Isaacs, & J. Riviere, *Contributions to Psychoanalysis* (pp. 67–121). London: Hogarth Press, 1952.

Jones, E. (1935). Early female sexuality. *International Journal of Psychoanalysis, 16*: 263–273.

Jones, E. (1955). *The Life and Work of Sigmund Freud, Vol. 2*. London: Hogarth Press.

Joseph, B. (1975). The patient who is difficult to reach. In: P. L. Giovacchini (Ed.), *Tactics and Techniques in Psycho-Analytic Therapy, Vol. 2: Counter-Transference*. New York: Jason Aronson. Reprinted in: B. Joseph, *Psychic Equilibrium and Psychic Change*. London: Routledge, 1989.

Joseph, B. (1989). *Psychic Equilibrium and Psychic Change*. London: Routledge.

King, P. (1972). Tribute to Donald Winnicott. Commemorative Meeting for Dr. Donald Winnicott, January 19th 1972. *Scientific Bulletin of the British Psychoanalytical Society, 57*: 26–28.

King, P., & Steiner, R. (Eds.) (1991). *The Freud–Klein Controversies 1941–45*. London: Routledge.

Klein, M. (1921). The development of a child. In: *The Writings of Melanie Klein, Vol. 1* (pp. 1–53). London: Hogarth Press, 1975.

Klein, M. (1923). The role of the school in the libidinal development of the child. In: *The Writings of Melanie Klein, Vol. 1* (pp. 59–76). London: Hogarth Press, 1975.

Klein, M. (1932). *The Psychoanalysis of Children. The Writings of Melanie Klein, Vol. 2*. London: Hogarth Press, 1975.

Klein, M. (1935). A contribution to the psychogenesis of manic-depressive states. In: *The Writings of Melanie Klein, Vol. 1* (pp. 262–289). London: Hogarth Press, 1975.

Klein, M. (1936). Weaning. In: *The Writings of Melanie Klein, Vol. 1* (pp. 290–305). London: Hogarth Press, 1975.

Klein, M. (1945). The Oedipus complex in the light of early anxieties. In: *The Writings of Melanie Klein, Vol. 1* (pp. 370–419). London: Hogarth Press, 1975.

Klein, M. (1946). Notes on some schizoid mechanisms. In: *The Writings of Melanie Klein, Vol. 3* (pp. 1–24). London: Hogarth Press, 1975.

Klein, M. (1957). Envy and gratitude. In: *The Writings of Melanie Klein, Vol. 3* (pp. 176–235). London: Hogarth Press, 1975.

Klein, M. (1959). *Autobiographical Notes*. Wellcome Library Archive: Shelfmark PP/RMK/E.6/3:Box 11. Available at: www.melanie-klein-trust.org.uk/domains/melanie-klein-trust.org.uk/local/media/downloads/_MK_full_autobiography.pdf

Kuhn, T. (1962). *The Structure of Scientific Revolutions*. Chicago, IL: Chicago University Press.

Laplanche, J., & Pontalis, J.-B. (1973). *The Language of Psychoanalysis*. London: Hogarth Press.

Loparic, Z. (2010). From Freud to Winnicott: Aspects of a paradigm change. In: *Donald Winnicott Today* (pp. 113–156). New Library of Psychoanalysis. Hove: Routledge, 2013.

Mahler, M., Pine, F., & Bergman, A. (1975). *The Psychological Birth of the Human Infant*. London: Hutchinson.

Money-Kyrle, R. (1956). Normal counter-transference and some of its deviations. *International Journal of Psychoanalysis, 37*: 360–366. Reprinted in: *The Collected Papers of Roger Money-Kyrle*. Perthshire: Clunie Press, 1978. Also in: E. Spillius (Ed.), *Melanie Klein Today, Vol. 2*. London: Routledge, 1988.

Money-Kyrle, R. (1964). Politics from the point of view of psychoanalysis. In: *The Collected Papers of Roger Money-Kyrle*. Perthshire: Clunie Press, 1978.

Riviere, J. (1927). Symposium on child analysis. In: A. Hughes.(Ed.), *The Inner World and Joan Riviere: Collected Papers 1920–1958* (pp. 80–88). London: Karnac, 1991.

Rodman, F. R. (Ed.) (1987). *The Spontaneous Gesture. Selected Letters of D. W. Winnicott*. Cambridge, MA: Harvard University Press.

Rosenfeld, H. (1947). Analysis of a schizophrenic state with depersonalization. *International Journal of Psychoanalysis, 28*: 130–139. Reprinted in: *Psychotic States*. London: Hogarth Press, 1965.

Roussillon, R. (2010). Winnicott's deconstruction of primary narcissism. In: J. Abram (Ed.), *Donald Winnicott Today* (pp. 270–290). New Library of Psychoanalysis. Hove: Routledge, 2013.

Rycroft, C. (1968). *Critical Dictionary of Psychoanalysis*. London: Penguin.

Sandler, J., Sandler, A.-M., & Davies, R. (Eds.) (2000). *Clinical and Observational Psychoanalytic Research: Roots of a Controversy*. London: Karnac.

Saussure, F. de (1916). *Course in General Linguistics*. New York: Philosophical Library, 1959.

Segal, H. (1950). Some aspects of the analysis of a schizophrenic. *International Journal of Psychoanalysis, 31*: 268–278.

Segal, H. (1957). Notes on symbol formation. *International Journal of Psychoanalysis, 38*: 391–397. Reprinted in: *The Work of Hanna Segal*. London: Free Association Books, 1981. Also in: E. Spillius (Ed.), *Melanie Klein Today, Vol. 1*. London: Routledge, 1988.

Spillius, E. (1992). Clinical experiences of projective identification. In: R. Anderson (Ed.), *Clinical Lectures on Klein and Bion*. London: Routledge.

Spillius, E. (2007). *Encounters with Melanie Klein: Selected Papers of Elizabeth Spillius*. New Library of Psychoanalysis. Hove: Routledge.

Spillius, E., Milton, J., Garvey, P., Couve, C., & Steiner, D. (Eds.) (2011). *The New Dictionary of Kleinian Thought*. Hove: Routledge.

Stern, D. N. (1985). *The Interpersonal World of the Infant*. New York: Basic Books.

Strachey, J. (1934). The nature of the therapeutic action of psychoanalysis. *International Journal of Psychoanalysis, 15*: 127–159; *50* (1969): 275–192.

Thompson, N. (2012). Winnicott and American analysts. In: J. Abram (Ed.), *Donald Winnicott Today* (pp. 386–417). New Library of Psychoanalysis. Hove: Routledge, 2013.

Waddington, C. H. (1942). *Science and Ethics*. London: George Allen & Unwin.

Wallerstein, R. S. (1988). One psychoanalysis or many? *International Journal of Psychoanalysis, 69*: 5–21.

Wilde, O. (1898). *The Ballad of Reading Gaol*. London: Weidenfeld & Nicolson, 1995.

Winnicott, D. W. (1931). *Clinical Notes on Disorders of Childhood*. London: Heinemann.

Winnicott, D. W. (1945a). Primitive emotional development. In: *Collected Papers: Through Paediatrics to Psychoanalysis* (pp. 145–156). London: Tavistock Publications, 1958.

Winnicott, D. W. (1945b). Towards an objective study of human nature. In: *Thinking about Children* (pp. 3–12). London: Karnac, 1996.

Winnicott, D. W. (1949). Hate in the countertransference. In: *Collected Papers: Through Paediatrics to Psychoanalysis* (pp. 194–203). London: Tavistock Publications, 1958.

Winnicott, D. W. (1951). Transitional objects and transitional phenomena: A study of the first not-me possession. In: *Collected Papers: Through Paediatrics to Psychoanalysis* (pp. 229–242). London: Tavistock Publications, 1958.

Winnicott, D. W. (1952a). Anxiety associated with insecurity. In: *Collected Papers: Through Paediatrics to Psychoanalysis* (pp. 97–100). London: Tavistock Publications, 1958.

Winnicott, D. W. (1952b). Psychoses and child care. In: *Collected Papers: Through Paediatrics to Psychoanalysis* (pp. 219–228). London: Tavistock Publications, 1958.

Winnicott, D. W. (1955). Metapsychological and clinical aspects of regression within the psycho-analytical set-up. In: *Collected Papers: Through Paediatrics to Psychoanalysis* (pp. 278–294). London: Tavistock Publications, 1958.

Winnicott, D. W. (1956). Primary maternal preoccupation. In: *Collected Papers: Through Paediatrics to Psychoanalysis* (pp. 300–305). London: Tavistock Publications, 1958.

Winnicott, D. W. (1957a). *The Child and the Family: First Relationships.* London: Tavistock.

Winnicott, D. W. (1957b). *The Child and the Outside World: Studies in Developing Relationships.* London: Tavistock.

Winnicott, D. W. (1958). *Collected Papers: Through Paediatrics to Psychoanalysis.* London: Tavistock Publications.

Winnicott, D. W. (1960). Ego distortion in terms of true and false self. In: *The Maturational Processes and the Facilitating Environment* (pp. 140–152). London: Hogarth Press, 1965.

Winnicott, D. W. (1962a). The aims of psycho-analytical treatment. In: *The Maturational Processes and the Facilitating Environment* (pp. 166–170). London: Hogarth Press, 1965.

Winnicott, D. W. (1962b). A personal view of the Kleinian contribution. In: *The Maturational Processes and the Facilitating Environment* (pp. 171–178). London: Hogarth Press, 1965. Reprinted in J. Abram (Ed.), *Donald Winnicott Today* (pp. 159–167). New Library of Psychoanalysis. Hove: Routledge

Winnicott, D. W. (1962c). Providing for the child. In: *The Maturational Processes and the Facilitating Environment* (pp. 64–72). London: Hogarth Press, 1965.

Winnicott, D. W. (1963a). Dependence in infant-care, in child-care, and in the psycho-analytic setting. In: *The Maturational Processes and the Facilitating Environment* (pp. 249–260). London: Hogarth Press, 1965.

Winnicott, D. W. (1963b). The development of the capacity for concern. In: *The Maturational Processes and the Facilitating Environment* (pp. 73–82). London: Hogarth Press, 1965.

Winnicott, D. W. (1963c). Morals and education. In: *The Maturational Processes and the Facilitating Environment* (pp. 93–105). London: Hogarth Press, 1965.

Winnicott, D. W. (1964). *The Child, the Family and the Outside World.* London: Penguin.

Winnicott, D. W. (1965). *The Family and Individual Development.* London: Tavistock Publications.

Winnicott, D. W. (1966). Ordinary devoted mothers. In: *Babies & Their*

Mothers (pp. 3–14), ed. C. Winnicott, R. Shepherd, & M. Davis. London: Free Association Books, 1987.

Winnicott, D. W. (1967a). The location of cultural experience. In: *Playing and Reality* (pp. 95–103). London: Tavistock Publications.

Winnicott, D. W. (1967b). Mirror-role of mother and family in child development. In: *Playing and Reality*. London: Tavistock Publications.

Winnicott, D. W. (1967c). Postscript: D.W.W. on D.W.W. In: *Psycho-Analytic Explorations* (pp. 569–582). London: Karnac, 1989.

Winnicott, D. W. (1968). Communication between infant and mother, and mother and infant, compared and contrasted. In: *Babies and Their Mothers*, ed. C. Winnicott, R. Shepherd, & M. Davis. London: Free Association Books, 1987.

Winnicott, D. W. (1969a). The use of an object. *International Journal of Psychoanalysis*, 50: 711–716.

Winnicott, D. W. (1969b). The use of an object in the context of *Moses and Monotheism*. In: *Psycho-Analytic Explorations* (pp. 240–246). London: Karnac, 1989. Also in: J. Abram (Ed.), *Donald Winnicott Today* (pp. 293–301). New Library of Psychoanalysis. Hove: Routledge, 2013.

Winnicott, D. W. (1970). Living creatively. In: *Home Is Where We Start From* (pp. 39–54), ed. C. Winnicott, R. Shepherd, & M. Davis. London: Penguin, 1986.

Winnicott, D. W. (1971a). Creativity and its origins. In: *Playing and Reality* (pp. 65–85). London: Tavistock Publications.

Winnicott, D. W. (1971b). *Playing and Reality*. London: Tavistock Publications.

Winnicott, D. W. (1971c). *Therapeutic Consultations in Child Psychiatry*. London: Hogarth Press.

Winnicott, D. W. (1971d). The use of an object and relating through identifications. In: *Playing and Reality* (pp. 86–94). London: Tavistock Publications.

Winnicott, D. W. (1977). *The Piggle: An Account of the Psychoanalytic Treatment of a Little Girl*. London: Hogarth Press.

Winnicott, D. W. (1986). *Holding and Interpretation: Fragment of an Analysis*. London: Hogarth Press.

Winnicott, D. W. (1988). *Human Nature*. London: Tavistock Publications.

Zetzel, E. R. (1956). An approach to the relation between concept and content in psychoanalytic theory (with special reference to the Work of Melanie Klein and her followers). *Psychoanalytic Study of the Child, 11*: 99–121.

Zilkha, N. (2013). Au fil du transfert, jouer. *Revue Française de Psychanalyse, 77* (3): 659–670.

INDEX

Abraham, K., xxiii, xxiv, 2, 12, 14, 15, 34, 69, 100, 138, 178, 187, 190, 199, 202, 205
Abram, J., *The Language of Winnicott*, xv, xviii, 182
acting out, 116, 117, 131, 168, 171, 186
   of dream, 146
active self, 41
actualisations, 117, 148
Adler, A., 12, 34, 60
agency:
   vs. responsibility, 57, 75, 110, 114, 120, 126
   sense of, 110, 120, 126
aggression:
   benign, 20, 27, 106, 183, 202
   concept of:
      Klein's, 179, 182
      Winnicott's, 104–107, 183
   phantasies of, in children, 138
   primary, 102, 183
agony, primitive, 3, 104
Alexander, F., 168
alone, capacity to be, 76
altruism, 73
ambivalence, 4, 59, 83, 109, 139

analysis, therapeutic action of, 172, 195
analyst, theoretical orientation of, 142
analytic relationship, transference–countertransference matrix of, 202
analytic technique:
   transitional and transferential elements of, 195
   use of, with children, 12
annihilation, 16, 70, 71, 84, 199
   fear of, 86, 101
   paranoid-schizoid fear of, 138
antisocial act, 116
antisocial tendency, 104, 105, 116
   concept of, Winnicott's, 183
anxiety(ies):
   castration, 183
   children's, 31
      observing, 97–98
   defences against, 137
   depressive, 56, 69, 73, 86, 108, 199
   in depressive position, 99–102
   existential, 150
   experience of, 17, 26, 27, 31, 183
   about identity, 70

anxiety(ies) (*continued*):
    internal:
        in baby, 39
        innate, 38
    Klein, 97–103
    Kleinian concept of, 4, 136–138
    maximum, point of, 5, 15, 135–138
    newborn's, 3
    oedipal, 37, 183
    in paranoid-schizoid position, 69, 99–102
    persecutory, 73, 97, 100, 101, 199
    and phantasy, Klein's focus on, 69–75, 137
    primitive, 70, 183
    psychotic, xxv, 72, 150, 199
    subjective experience of, 183
    unthinkable, 3, 24, 52, 104, 153, 183
après coup, 163, 172
Armistice Letter, 47
attachment theory, 126

baby(ies):
    active, 44–45
    ego of, 30
    internal anxiety in, 39
    Kleinian, 3, 41–45, 174
    "no such thing as", 4, 22, 33, 34, 48, 153, 181, 189
    observation of, 42
    Winnicottian, 3, 46–50
Balint, A., xxii, 149, 150
Balint, M., xxii, 149, 150
Bergman, A., 30
Bick, E., 42
binary narratives, 41
biological drives, 53, 62, 106
biology and mammals, 126
Bion, W. R., 17, 88, 150, 153, 154, 158, 159, 161, 184, 185, 192, 195, 201
bodily functions, imaginative elaboration of, 126
body–mind dissociation, 108
borderline patients, 91, 117, 127, 174
Bowlby, J., xxii, 42, 88, 91, 126, 150
breakdown:
    fear of, 104
    mental, 97, 101
Brenman Pick, I., 158
Brierley, M., 47, 48, 62, 152, 160

British Psychoanalytical Society, 2, 6, 11, 21, 47, 77, 88, 89, 141, 142, 154, 155, 160, 161, 177
Brücke, E., 204

cancer, 100
castration, threat of, 74
castration anxiety, 183
child(ren):
    analysis for, method of, 12
    anxieties of, 31
        observing, 97–98
    clinical disorders of, 21
    existence of transference in, 12
    localisation of fantasy, related to bodily functions, 23, 26, 27, 102, 126
    phantasies of aggression in, 138
    play of, as narratives, 137
    psychic pain of, 102
    stage of dependence, extreme, 104
    stage of dependence-independence mixtures, 105
    stage of independence, 105
    stage of independence–dependence, 105
    stage of social sense, 105
    use of analytic technique with, 12
child analysis, xxiv, 2, 11, 20, 21, 29, 45, 47, 183, 193, 196, 198, 202
    development of, 12–14
    Klein's invention of, 17, 26, 27
clinical approach, Klein's, 16–18
clinical infant, 33, 42, 144
clinical paradigm, 184
    Freud's, 1
Coleridge, S. T., 129
combined parent figure, 98, 103
compliance, 46, 145
concern:
    affective state of mind of, 184
    capacity for, 28, 58, 99, 114, 117, 127, 184, 191
    and sense of guilt, 192
    stage of, 23, 24, 58, 87, 88, 92, 104, 108, 114, 130, 202
container–contained, 17, 88, 153, 184, 185, 192, 195, 201
containing, 72, 150, 154, 161, 185, 192
    Klein's use of term, 184

Contemporary Freudian school, 142, 154
continuity of being, 53, 150, 153
   sense of, loss of, 99
Controversial Discussions, xvii, xxi, xxii, 24, 47, 62, 124, 155, 160, 180, 204
corrective emotional experience, 6, 157, 158, 164–170, 181
countertransference:
   concept of, Winnicott's, 5, 185
   hate in, 46
   misuse of, 112
   negative, 116, 118, 151
   use of, 5, 117, 152, 156
   Winnicott's three types of, 6, 186
creative act, vs. creative living, 125
creative drive, 115, 125, 198
creative process, 129
creativity, 54, 104, 127, 129, 179
   concept of, Winnicott's, 183
   non-reparative form of, 130
   primary, 5, 115, 125, 130, 141
   psychic, primary, 125, 173, 198
   theory of:
      Klein's, 130
      Winnicott's, 6
cultural experience, location of, 77

Darwin, C., 143
Davies, R., 34, 42
day-dreams, 13
death instinct:
   concept of, definition, 186–187
   disagreement between Klein and Winnicott on, 2, 24, 27, 53, 54, 58, 63, 182
   Freud's concept of, 32, 138, 187
   Winnicott's disagreement with, 43
   innate, 3, 32, 49, 107, 128
   and innate evil, 105
   Klein's theory of, 37, 50, 60, 102, 105, 116, 138, 191
   survival of object as alternative to, 202
deeper levels/layers of unconscious, 4, 11, 15–16, 18, 26, 27, 69–71, 75, 99, 137, 180, 199
deep interpretations, 5

defence(s), 15, 16, 31, 75, 83, 137, 182, 195
   against anxiety, 137
   manic, 23, 26, 28, 100, 103, 108, 196
   mechanisms of, 69, 99
   primitive mechanisms of, 69
   psychotic, 183
   splitting, 71
deferred action, 117
delusion, 114, 204
   and illusion, 125, 129, 170, 173
delusional transference, 117, 125
denigration, 100
dependence:
   absolute, 38, 53, 77, 192
   child's stage of, 104
   infant's, on mother, 79
   relative, 77, 202
   total, 109, 110, 121
dependence-independence:
   child's stage of, 105
   phase of, 110
   six points of, 109
dependency:
   and regression, 145–147
   stages of, 104, 115
depersonalisation, 127
depression and guilt, 70
depressive anxiety, 56, 69, 73, 86, 108, 199
depressive position:
   anxieties in, 99–102
   concept of, Klein's, 24, 184, 187
   psychic pain of, 100, 103
   working through, 188
destructiveness, 54, 55, 97, 98, 100, 179
   primary, 102
development:
   emotional, 19, 32, 76, 144, 153, 154, 181
   primitive, 46
   sequence of, 64
disintegration, 16, 38, 72, 101, 103
dissociation, 167
   body–mind, 108
dream(s):
   acting out of, 146
   phantasies in, 137
dream symbols, 203

drive(s), 14, 102
    biological, 53, 62, 106
    libidinal and aggressive, 107
    life instinct as, 115
dual-instinct theory, 186

early development, differences between Klein and Winnicott, 51–53
economic depression, xxi
economic model, 12, 178
economic theory, 21, 22, 32, 116
    chronology of, 29, 30
ego:
    baby's, 29, 30
    concept of:
        Klein's, 188
        Winnicott's, 188
    disintegration of, 16, 99
    formation or disintegration of, 16
    parts of, split off, 71
    and self:
        concepts of, 3
        Winnicott's distinction between, 188
    splitting of, 37, 75, 99, 101
ego boundary, 18, 26, 27, 29, 30, 44, 52, 71, 178
    at birth, Klein's concept of, 3
ego-support, 144, 192
emotional development, 19, 32, 76, 144, 153, 154, 181
    primitive, 46
emotional sensitivity, 192
empathy, 159
Empedocles, 187
enactments, 117, 148
    phantasies in, 137
energy theories, 60
environment:
    and death instinct, major divergences between Klein and Winnicott, 2
    deficient, 53, 153, 154
    failure of, 49, 64, 116, 125
    holding, 38, 46, 63, 83, 144, 146, 192, 195
        as crucial, 5
    psychic, 49, 80, 106, 108, 178, 181
    Winnicott's use of term, 48

environmental deficiency, early, 82
environmental failure, 104, 105
    early, 81, 146
environmental neglect, 101
environment–individual set-up, 4, 20, 48, 49, 141, 142, 153, 189, 190
    Winnicott, 76–82
environment mother, 58, 87, 90, 92, 108, 178
envy, 3, 71, 75, 91, 92, 99, 182, 200, 205
    effects of, on analyst's abilities, 195
    Kleinian, 73
    primary, xxv
    role of, Klein's concept of, 189
ethics, natural, 121, 127
evil:
    innate, 115, 128
    Klein's use of term, 115, 124
Exchange Lectures, 21
existential anxiety, 150
existential terror, 99
experience versus observation, 51
experimental infant, 42
external object, 17, 53, 79, 84, 86, 90, 91, 93, 128, 165, 166, 175, 178, 181, 190
    Klein's use of term, 62
    relationship with, 75
    role of, 67
        summary of differences between Klein and Winnicott, 83
    Winnicott's use of term, 62
extreme dependence, child's stage of, 104
Ezriel, H., 17

facilitating environment, 3, 19, 51, 76
    Winnicott's use of term, 115
Fairbairn, W. R. D., xxii, 62
false self, 37, 59, 64, 168, 170
    and true self, concept of, Winnicott's, 183
Fechner, G., 186, 204
Ferenczi, S., xxiii, 11, 149, 180, 185
fetishist, 205
fixation points, 69, 79, 81–82, 180
formlessness, 130, 147, 171
free association, 14, 195, 197
    Freudian concept of, 6
    Freud's "fundamental rule" of, 24

free-floating attention, 145
free play, 12
　as free association, 198
Freud, A., xxiv, 16, 60, 62
　Controversial Discussions, 47–50
　criticism of Klein, xxiv, 60, 138
　and Klein, controversy between, 47–50
Freud, S. (*passim*):
　Anna O, 36, 137
　clinical paradigms, foundational, 1
　dream symbols, 203
　dual-instinct theory, 186
　instinct, use of term, 12
　Little Hans, 11, 203
　negation, 72
　paradigm change from, to Winnicott, 184
　on psychosexuality, 4
　reality principle, 16
　topographical model of the mind, 188
　transference neurosis, 17
　unconscious-to-unconscious communication, 14, 122
　and Winnicott, disagreement re death instinct, 187
　Wolf Man, 14, 37
Fromm-Reichmann, F., xxii
frustration, Winnicott's use of term, 56
fusion, concept of, 107

gastro-colic reflex, 44
gender identity, 175
genetic continuity, 14, 17, 26, 27, 36, 41, 193
genital layers, 18, 26, 28
"gentlemen's agreement", over Controversial Discussions, 47, 160
Gillespie, W., 160
Glover, E., 69, 123, 124, 128, 160
Goldman, D., 167
good-enough environment, 38, 49, 52, 126, 183
good-enough holding, 46, 127, 153, 171
good-enough mother(ing), 3, 23, 49, 59, 77, 78, 108, 197
　Winnicott's concept of, 88, 183

good object, separation from, 189
gratitude, 56, 90, 190, 191, 200, 205
Green, A., xxvi, 34, 36, 42, 144, 146, 152
gross impingement, 46
group dynamics, unconscious, 154
guilt, 54, 57, 73–75, 86, 98, 101, 179, 184, 188, 200
　capacity to feel, 197
　concept of, Klein's, 191
　and depression, 70
　reparative form of, 191
　sense of, 23, 26, 28, 115, 130, 191, 192, 197

hate, 3, 50, 55, 74, 99, 108, 121, 129, 148, 186–189
　in countertransference, 46
　destructive, 54, 58
　as developmental achievement, Winnicott's concept of, 3, 49, 54, 58
　disavowed, 57
　and love, 59, 102, 103, 182, 196
　split-off, 57
Heimann, P., 112–113, 149, 152, 155–156, 159–160, 185
helplessness, infant's state of, 78
here-and-now interpretation, 137
Hinshelwood, R. D., *A Dictionary of Kleinian Thought*, xviii, 63, 182
holding, 3, 38, 49, 63, 83, 108, 126, 148, 150, 152–154, 161, 165, 192, 195
　good-enough, 46, 127, 153, 171
　mother's capacity for, 144
　physical, 144
　psychic, 144
　Winnicott's concept of, 141–147, 153, 185
holding environment, 38, 63, 83, 144, 146, 192, 195
　as crucial, 5
　good-enough, 46
human nature, 19, 21, 38, 126, 141
　Winnicott's triple statement on, 77–78
Hungarian Psychoanalytical Society, xxi, xxiii, 11

identification, forms of, 16
identity problem, 168, 170

illusion(s):
    and delusion, 125, 129, 170, 173
    and imagination, 127–131
    of omnipotence: see omnipotence, illusion of
    related to early mother–infant merger, Winnicott's concept of, 130
    symbols as, 130
    term:
        meaning of, 174
        Winnicott's use of, 6, 125
imagination, and illusion, 127–131
imaginative elaboration of bodily functions, 126
impulse satisfaction, 204
incest, 13
incorporation, 15, 178
independence, child's stage of, 105
independence–dependence, child's stage of, 105
Independent school, 61, 142, 154–155, 160–161, 177, 185
infant:
    clinical, 33, 42, 144
    experimental, 42
    inherited tendencies of, 115
    internal world of, 5
    psychic pain of, 107
    relating, 43–44
infant development, Klein's model of, 180
infantile responsibility, 4
infantile states of mind, regression to, 126
infant observation, 118
inherited tendencies, of infant, 115
innate evil, 128
innateness, 43, 55, 113
    biological, 120
    problem of, 110
    psychic, 120, 126–127
innate self-preservative instincts, 106
inscription, 22, 49, 76, 143, 190, 193
instinct(s), 2, 22, 27, 29, 32, 38, 53, 60, 102, 125, 186–187, 189, 204
    concept of, 15, 30
    Freudian, 107
    or relationships, 14–15
    self-preservative, innate, 106

term:
    Freud's use of, 178
    Klein's use of, 12, 60, 63, 178
instinct theory, 21, 30, 37, 63, 144
    Freudian, 2, 22, 32, 49, 53, 62
    misperceptions about, 178
instinctual energy, 15
Institute of Psychoanalysis, xiv, xvii, xxiv, 19, 46
integration, primary, 38
intermediate area of experiencing, 77, 78
intermediate dimension of living, transitional phenomena and objects as, 203
internal anxiety:
    in baby, 39
    innate, 38
    Klein, 97–103
    and psychic pain, 4
internalisation, process of, 194
internal object(s), 108, 159, 166, 178, 187, 193–194, 200, 204, 208
    Klein's concept of, 89
internal parents, intercourse between, unconscious phantasy of, 131
internal world, 5, 77, 83, 89, 90–93, 163, 174, 176, 190
    formation of, 39–65
interoceptors, 194
interpretation(s):
    analyst's, 117, 173
    deep, 5
    here-and-now, 137
    mutative, 5, 25, 135, 161–162, 195
        Winnicott, 141–147
    persecuting, 179
    response to, 5, 135
    timing of, 150, 152, 154, 156, 158
    transference, 36
    in transference, 142
    of unconscious, effect of, 200
    Winnicott's view of, 195
introjection, 16, 23, 29, 44, 45, 164, 194, 201
    oral, 178
    processes of, 199
    and projection, 71, 72, 101
Isaacs, S., 35–36, 41, 120, 137, 186–187, 204

Jesus College, Cambridge, xxiii
Jones, E., 12, 89, 91, 155
Joseph, B., 151, 152, 157, 163
Jung, C. G., 12, 34, 60, 149, 184, 185

Keats, J., 129
King, P., 21, 47, 81, 143
Klein, A., xxiii
Klein, E., xxiii
Klein, H., xxiii, 11, 203
Klein, M. (*passim*):
    and Anna Freud, controversy between, 47–50
    Armistice Letter, 47
    biography and chronology, xxi–xxiii
    case of Ruth, 5, 139–140, 146
    clinical approach, 16–18, 24–25
    Controversial Discussions, 47–50
    on development of baby, 41–45
    internal anxiety, 97–103
    terminology, 12
    and Winnicott:
        disagreement between, 186
        early development, differences between, 51–53
        introduction to, 20–24
        major divergences between on environment and death instinct, 2
        points of agreement and disagreement between, 27–28
    work with children, xxii
Kleinian school, 154
Kuhn, T., 184
Kuhnian scientific revolutions, 1

Lacanian psychoanalysis, 131
Laplanche, J., 32
learning, pain of, 97
leucotomy, 186
libido, phases of, 29
libido theory, Freudian, 178
life instinct, 41, 43, 53, 63, 106, 125, 179, 183, 190, 198
    as drive, 115
Little Hans, 11, 203
lobotomy, 186
Loparic, Z., 184
love and hate, 59, 102, 103, 182, 196

Magritte, R., 122, 127, 174
Mahler, M., 30, 34, 42
Main, R., xiv
manic defence(s), 23, 26, 28, 100, 103, 108, 196
manic-depressives, 15
maturational processes, 19, 28, 92
maximum anxiety, point of, 5, 15, 135–138
    Klein's focus on, 137
Me and Not-me, 33, 35, 51, 52, 53, 58, 59, 61, 63, 64, 77, 117, 203
    Winnicott's use of term, 202
melancholia, Freud's theory of, 187
mental breakdown, 97, 101
metapsychology, 6, 136, 141
micro-process, 136, 156, 157, 163
Middle Group, Glover's use of term, 160
mind, narrative structure of, 204
mirror-role of mother, 104, 192
Money-Kyrle, R., xx, 6, 112, 113, 116–118, 122, 123, 127, 157, 163, 165–169, 171–173, 175
mother:
    environment, 58, 87, 90, 92, 108, 178
    mirror-role of, 104, 192
    object, 53, 58, 87, 88, 90, 92, 108, 178, 184
    primary relationship with, 195
mothering, good-enough, 23, 183
mourning, and melancholia, Freud's work on, 23
murder, 13, 54, 55, 57, 85, 138
mutative interpretation, 5, 25, 135, 161–162, 195
    Winnicott, 141–147

Nachträglichkeit, 117, 163
narcissism, 41, 72
    primary, Freudian concept of, 2, 22, 29, 32, 33, 143
narrative(s):
    children's play as, 137
    of experience in unconscious phantasy, 42–43
    pre-symbolic, 148
    primitive, 55, 61, 87
narrative structure of mind, 204
natural ethics, 121, 127

Nazism, xxi
negative transference, 139, 156, 179, 195
newborn:
　anxiety of, 3
　gastro-colic reflex of, 44
　merger of object and subject in the, 3
night terrors, 196
non-surviving object, 202
　revivification of, 118
normality and pathology, 4
"no such thing as a baby", 4, 22, 33–34, 48, 153, 181, 189

object(s):
　creating, 172–173, 186, 199, 203
　non-surviving, 118, 202
　splitting of, 196
　survival of, 53, 85, 104, 107, 141, 195, 202
　surviving, 202
　use of, 19–20, 33, 64, 104–107, 141, 202
　　Winnicott's concept of, 183
objectivity, 3
object mother, 53, 58, 87–88, 90, 92, 108, 178, 184
object relations/relating, 11, 15, 26–27, 29, 49, 51, 62, 91, 106, 107, 188
　innate, 43
　sequence of, 106
object-relations theory, 131, 204
object theory, 62
object use, 107
observation versus experience, 51
oceanic feeling, 130
oedipal anxieties, 37, 183
oedipal competition, 71
oedipal conflict(s), 16, 99, 103
oedipal theories, Freud's, 138
Oedipus complex, 13, 18, 21, 51, 60, 99, 200
　dating of, 12
　early stages of, 37, 38
　Freudian, 4, 20, 23, 28, 87, 108
　pain of, 103
　resolution of, 106
　theory of, 98

omnipotence, 4, 6, 34, 35, 171, 196
　baby's perception of, 110
　defensive, 108
　illusion of, 6, 33, 52–54, 58, 63–64, 76, 79, 83, 87, 100, 108, 114, 119–121, 123–125, 157–158, 168, 170, 192
　early, deficiency of, 196
　Winnicott's concept of, 4
　Klein's use of term, 114
　normal, 170–172
　pathological, 4, 170–172
　primary, 29, 33, 168
　Winnicott's use of term, 4, 6, 114, 170, 196
omnipotent manic defence, 196
omnipotent phantasies, 101
oral introjection, 178
ordinary devotion, 19, 78, 124

Paddington Green Children's Hospital, xxiii, xxvi
paediatrics, xxiii, 19
paradigm, 1, 142, 149, 166, 192
　clinical, Kleinian vs. Winnicottian, 1, 184
paradox, 61, 76
paranoia, 63, 126
paranoid mechanisms, 112, 116
paranoid-schizoid anxiety, 69
paranoid-schizoid functioning, primitive, 128
paranoid-schizoid position, xxv, 3, 4, 11, 16, 18, 22, 23, 42, 53, 56, 57, 63, 71–74, 83–85, 88, 91, 123, 128, 153, 183–184, 189, 191, 195–197, 199, 205
　anxieties in, 99–102
parental failure, 105
parent figure, combined, 98, 103
parent–infant relationship, 2, 3, 20, 22, 38, 48, 49, 59, 143, 152, 153, 181, 190, 197
　earliest, 144, 194
　early, 127, 193, 202
part-object, 18, 205
pathological omnipotence, 4, 171
pathological states of mind, 123
pathology and normality, 4
patient feeling like God, 168, 170–171

INDEX 227

patient's experiences, priority of, 136
pavor nocturnus, 196
Payne, S., 47, 62
penis envy, 80–81, 92, 162
perception, Klein's concept of, 6
persecution, 63, 86, 191
persecutory anxiety, 73, 97, 100–101, 199
personalisation, 126
personality, basic split in, 46, 49
phantasy(ies):
    of aggression in children, 138
    and anxiety, Klein, 69–75
    mental representations of instincts, 204
    omnipotent, 101
    unconscious: see unconscious phantasy(ies)
    of unconscious, unspoken, 198
Pine, F., 30
Plato, xviii
play:
    ability to, 27, 114, 198, 204
    capacity to, 127, 130, 192, 195, 199
    children's, as narratives, 137
    as communication, 137
    communication through, 14
    creative expressiveness of, 130
    inability to, 204
    inhibition in, as resistance, 12, 13, 198
    narrative in, 204
    observation of, 200
playing, 6, 22, 24, 35, 61, 104, 130, 139, 167, 175, 198
    as creative, 131
    and symbolic thinking and free association, 197
    with toys, 17, 26
play technique, 14, 34–35, 102, 130, 183, 198, 204
pleasure principle, 72, 74, 79, 90
point of maximum anxiety, Klein's focus on, 137
Pontalis, J.-B., 32
potential space, 77, 79
pregenital layers, 18, 26, 28
pre-symbolic narrative, 148
primal scene, 28, 37
primary aggression, 183

primary creativity, 5, 115, 125, 130, 141
primary destructiveness, 102
primary envy, xxv
primary integration, 38
primary maternal preoccupation, 38, 52, 58, 76, 78–81, 92, 115, 188, 192, 194, 198
primary narcissism, 22, 29, 32–33, 143
    Freudian concept of, 2
primary omnipotence, 29, 33, 168
primary unintegration, 37–38, 77
primitive agony(ies), 3, 52, 83, 104, 153
primitive anxieties, 183
primitive defence mechanisms, 16
primitive emotional development, 46
primitive mechanisms, 16, 69, 71–72, 180
primitive narrative, 55, 61
primitive superego, 191
primitive unconscious phantasies, 75
projection(s), 16, 29, 63, 71–72, 101, 164, 171, 201
    capacity for, 23
    from child's psychic reality, 22
    processes of, 199
projective identification(s), xxv, 100, 111, 151, 185, 197, 201
    analysts' use of term, 101
    Klein's discovery of, 184
propositional logic, 186
provenance, 150, 152, 154, 159–161
psyche and soma, 58, 60
psyche-indwelling-in-the-soma, 108, 126
psychic creativity, primary, 125, 173, 198
psychic energy, 31, 51, 178
    economics of, 12, 17, 26–27
psychic environment:
    early, deficiencies of, 108
    quality of, relevance of, 106
psychic holding, 144
psychic pain, 104–108, 111, 112, 182, 183, 199
    of children, 102, 107
    and internal anxiety, 4
    interpersonal vicissitudes of, 113
    psychoanalytic concept of, 4, 95–103
    summary of differences between Klein and Winnicott, 108

psychic transitionality, 20, 199
psychic trauma, 105
psychoanalysis:
    as science, 143
    therapeutic action of, 5, 141
psychoanalytic practice, key issues in, summary of differences between Klein and Winnicott, 148
psychoanalytic treatment, aims of, 143–145
psychopathology, 64, 114–115, 126, 141, 148, 154, 189
psychosexuality, 4, 32, 38, 189
    Freud's, 33, 37
psychosis(es), 150, 153, 199
psychosomatic collusion, 126
psychotic anxiety, xxv, 72, 150, 199
psychotic defences, 183
psychotic patient(s), 126–127, 150, 186
psychotics, 151

Queen's Hospital for Children, Hackney, xxiii

Racker, H., 185
Rank, O., 34, 60
reaction formation, 16
reality principle, 16, 41, 71–72, 79, 83, 88–90, 121, 135, 150, 199
    disrupted, 153–155
reality-testing, 201
    therapeutic benefit of, 17
reflex arc, 186
regressed patient, 145, 146
regression, 5, 69, 75–76, 81–82, 92, 152, 164–166, 181
    and dependency, 145–147
    Freud's theory of, 180
Reizes, M., xxiii
relating, patterns of, 46, 105
relating infant, 43–44
relationships, or instincts, 14–15
reparation, 54, 75, 86, 100, 125, 129–130
    creative, 57
    Klein's concept of, 187
repression, 13, 16, 37, 49, 99, 125
repression mechanisms, early, 99
resistance, 194

resistance analysis, 12
response to interpretations, 5
responsibility:
    vs. agency, 120
    baby's sense of, 110
resting place, 77
Riviere, J., xxiv, 46, 47
Rodman, F. R., 143
Rosenfeld, H., 150
Roussillon, R., 22, 33, 193
Rycroft, C., 62

sadism, 3, 63, 189
Sandler, A.-M., 34, 42
Sandler, J., 34, 42
Saussure, F. de, 131
schizoid mechanisms, xxv, 37, 70, 101, 112, 116, 149, 151, 201
schizoid patients, 15
schizoid processes, 99
schizophrenia, 104, 203
schizophrenic patient(s), 15, 111, 116, 118, 199
schizophrenic psychosis, 199
Schmideberg, M., xxiii, 160
Searles, H., xxii
Segal, H., 5, 122, 125, 129, 130, 150, 152, 203
self:
    and ego:
        concepts of, 3
        Winnicott's distinction between, 188
    existential problems of, 37
    existential sense of, 97
    fragmentation and loss of, Winnicott's use of term, 99
    sense of, 19, 99
self-destructiveness, 138
self-preservative instinct(s), 20, 24
    innate, 106
semiotics, 131
Sharpe, E., 143
signifier and signified, 131
social sense, child's stage of, 105
Socratic method, xix
soma and psyche, 58, 60
Spillius, E., xviii, 112
split, basic, in personality, 46, 49

INDEX

splitting, 16, 49, 71, 97, 197, 199, 201
   concept of, xvii
   of ego, 37, 75, 99, 101
   of object, into good and bad, 22
   of objects, 196
splitting defences, 71
splitting-off, of parts of self, 197
squiggle game, 19, 22
standard analysis, 143–144, 165
Steiner, R., 21, 47, 81
Stekel, W., 12, 34
Stern, D. N., 30, 34, 42
Strachey, J., 20, 46, 62, 117, 161–163, 166, 171, 172, 195, 199–201
   paper on therapeutic action of psychoanalysis, 5, 17, 25, 97, 135, 141, 163, 168, 199
structural model of the mind, Freud's introduction of, 189
subjectivity, 3
superego, 60, 74–75, 83, 189
   analyst's, 156, 158
   ego-destructive, 57
   harsh, 83, 112, 121
   origins of, 12, 191
   primitive, 191
survival of object, 53, 85, 104, 107, 141, 195, 202
surviving object, 202
symbol(s) as illusions, 130
symbol-formation, 150, 203
symbolic thinking, 78, 79, 83, 197
   newborn infant's, 203
symbolisation, 129, 193, 202, 204
symbolism, 129, 174

talion dread, 22
terminology, Klein, 12
theoretical first feed, 79, 127, 186, 203
theory, points of view on, 109, 110
third area of mind, 77, 125, 197
Thompson, N., 48
topographical model of the mind, 188
total dependence, stage of, 110
transference(s):
   in children, existence of, 12
   concept of:
      Freudian, 6
      Klein's and Winnicott's, 7

delusional, 117, 125, 173
   interpretation in, 142
   maternal and paternal, 164
   negative, 139, 156, 179, 195
   paternal, 173
   playing in, 167, 171
   positive, 111, 139, 180
   power of, 33, 147
   reality in, 170, 172–173
transference–countertransference frame/matrix, 6, 34, 146, 172–173, 175, 202
transference illusion, 169–170, 173–176
transference interpretation, 36
transference matrix, 155
transference neurosis, 17
transference repetition, 35
transitionality, 203
   psychic, 20, 199
transitional object(s), 30, 33, 76–77, 155, 159, 203–204
transitional phenomena, 19–20, 76–78, 141, 197, 203
   Winnicott's concept of, 183
Trevarthen, C., 42
true self, 37, 53
   and false self, Winnicott's concept of, 183

unconscious, the:
   concept of, 135
   deeper (psychotic) layers of, 26
   dynamic anxiety-defence structure of, 136
   processes in, 69
unconscious phantasy(ies), 6, 11, 17, 26, 44, 53, 100, 120, 137, 159, 180, 187, 200, 204
   children's, 138
      Klein accessing, 14, 41
   constantly active, 69, 180
   deep, 69
   deep innate, 82
   Freud's concept of, 13, 42
   innate, 81, 128
   of intercourse between internal parents, 131
   Isaacs' concept of, 35
   Kleinian concept of, 4, 127, 174

unconscious phantasy(ies) (*continued*):
　narratives of experience in, 42–43
　primitive, 75
　real effects of, 71
　regression and fixation points, 81–82
unconscious-to-unconscious communication, 14, 122
undoing, 16
unintegration, 46
　ego's state of, 37
　primary, 37–38, 77
　Winnicott's use of term, 38
unit status:
　of self, 52, 53, 59, 201
　Winnicott's use of term, 201
unthinkable anxiety(ies), 3, 24, 52, 104, 153, 183
urgency, point of, 97, 199
use of object, 19–20, 33, 64, 104–107, 141, 183, 202

Waddington, C. H., 121, 127
Wallerstein, R., 136, 141
war neuroses, xxi
whole object, 205
whole-object love, 190
Wilde, O., 56
Winnicott, D. W. (*passim*):
　aggression, concept of, 104–107
　on babies, 46–50
　biography and chronology, xxi–xxiii
　clinical innovations, 142–147
　environment, effect of, on formation of intrapsychic world, xxii
　environment–individual set-up, 4, 20, 48–49, 76–82, 141–142, 153, 189–190
　and Freud, 184
　disagreement re death instinct, 187
　holding, 141–147
　and Klein:
　　disagreements with, 186
　　early development, differences, 51–53
　　introduction to, 20–24
　　major divergences between on environment and death instinct, 2
　　points of agreement and disagreement between, 27–28
　language, use of, 4
　medical experience with children's development, xxii
　mutative interpretation, 141–147
　"no such thing as a baby", 4, 22, 33–34, 48, 153, 181, 189
　object, use of, xxvi, 20, 33, 52, 64, 77, 105, 106
　Phase 1: environment–individual set-up, 20, 48
　Phase 2: transitional phenomena, 20, 76
　Phase 3: use of object, 20, 130
　primary maternal preoccupation, 38, 52, 58, 76, 78, 79, 92, 115, 188, 192, 194, 198
　theoretical matrix, 19–20
　transitional phenomena, 19–20, 76–78, 141, 183, 197
　and transitional objects, 203–204

Zetzel, E. R., 124, 128
Zilkha, N., 167